HEIHO
Martial Arts
Concepts & Strategy

by

Dr. J.L. Aiello
Hanshi

A Warrior Broadcasting Network® Publication, 1997

WARNING

This book has been written as a means of presenting a unique perspective and a history of the Martial Arts and Karate. Neither the Warrior Broadcasting Network, Inc., the author nor anyone involved in the editing and production of this book makes any representation, warranty or guarantee that the techniques described or illustrated in this book are safe or effective in any self–defense situation or otherwise. Nothing described or illustrated in this book should be undertaken without personal, expert instruction and it is essential that a physician be consulted before beginning any exercise or physical fitness program. Please consult Federal, state and local law to determine the applicable self–defense responses in any particular situation or circumstance.

ISBN 1-883702-12-7

The Warrior Broadcasting Network™ Inc.
P.O. Box 1412
Berkley, Michigan 48072
Printed by McNaughten & Gunn
Saline, Michigan
USA

About the Cover

The cover and renditions of the great Masters of the Martial Arts that are seen throughout this book are the work of Martin Brill, student of Shito Kan Karate Do and dedicated artist. The picture on the previous page and on the cover is a reproduction of an original drawing presented to Master Harold Long and Dr. Aiello in March of 1997. Master Long accepted this gift enthusiastically as representative of the Shimabuku/Long/Aiello heritage of Isshin Ryu.

As the story goes, one night atop the town water tank and under the influence of tea and meditation Master Tatsuo Shimabuku dreamt of a goddess. The vision of Master Shimabuku included an intruder who demanded that he fight. Shimabuku responded by stating that Karate was for training the mind, not for fighting. The intruder then indicated that he would burn Shimabuku and the water town to the ground and proceeded to light the wooden water tank on fire. Being atop so much water, it was simple for Shimabuku to save himself and the water tank. The following day in the Okinawan city of Naha, Shimabuku noticed a picture of a Shinto god in the window of a small store. Upon inquiry, Shimabuku found that the name of the god was Go Shu Jin Sama, "the goddess that protects."

Tatsuo Shimabuku was so struck by the dream and by seeing the picture of the Go Shu Jin Sama the following day that he told the story of his "goddess of protection," the Mizu Gami-water goddess, the water tank and raging fire to his top student Eiko Kaneshi. The oval patch that is seen prevalently in Isshin Ryu practice today the Mizu (water) Gami (goddess) stands hip deep in troubled waters, the trouble of mankind. Behind her is the dragon, ascending to the heavens, rising above the limits and problems of humanity. Tatsuo means "Dragon Boy," Shimabuku's chosen name and it is thought that it is he that the dragon represents. Dragons were thought to be good luck. A serpent tail slashes the water around the Mizu Gami representing the complexity of the human condition and the duality of nature. The orange or red surrounding the goddess was the fire set by the intruder and the stance the Mizu Gami has taken, the peace-war stance with one hand clenched and one open, shows her unwillingness to resort to violence even when provoked but ability to defend as a last resort. The grey sky of the background stands for the calmness shown in the face of adversity, the turbulent water.

The events leading to the creating of the icon of Isshin Ryu marked the consolidation of a lifetime of work into the official Martial Art of Isshin Ryu Karate Do. It was at this point in time that Tatsuo Shimabuku broke away from Shorin Ryu (Chan Migwa Te) and formed his own system of Isshin Ryu. The version of the Mizu Gami on the cover of *Heiho: Martial Arts Concepts and Strategy* by Martin Brill depicts the historical evolution and lineage of the Master Tatsuo Shimabuku -Master Harold Long heritage of Isshin Ryu as passed on to Dr. J. L. Aiello.

Seen in the foreground, left Master Harold Long, right Dr. J. L. Aiello, center Master Tatsuo Shimabuku, top Mizu Gami-the goddess of Master Shimabuku's' dream.

Dedication

The true Warrior Masters and philosophers of the past whose hard work, wisdom and perseverance was so necessary for the making of the Martial Artists of today must be recognized for not only passing on their knowledge, but also their love of the Martial Arts. The heritage and destiny of Budo, the Martial Way or Warrior Way will be determined by these Masters of old, the Masters in the making we see around us today and those to come in the next century, just a few short years away. May this book be one more building block in the foundation of the Budo of the future.

In memory of:

Bushi-*Warriors*

Sokon Matsumura *Shuri-te*, Kanryo Higaonna *Naha-te*, Kanbun Uechi *Pwangai Noon Ryu*, Yasutsune Itosu *Shorin Ryu*, Shinko Matayoshi *Matayoshi Ryu Kobudo*, Chinen Sanda *Yomani Ryu*, Sokaku Takeda *Daito Ryu*, Kosaku Matsumora *Tomari-te*, Chotoku Kyan *Shobayashi Shorin Ryu*, Juhatsu Kiyoda *Toon Ryu*, Kenwa Mabuni *Shito Ryu*, Morihei Ueshiba *Aikido*, Jigoro Kano *Judo*, Gichin Funakoshi *Shoto Kan*, Choki Motobu *Shorin Ryu*, Chojun Miyagi *Goju Ryu*, Chosin Chibana *Kobayashi Shorin Ryu*, Moden Yabiku *Ryukyu Kobudo*, Shinken Taira *Ryukyu Kobudo*, Hiranori Otsuka *Wado Ryu*, Masatoshi Nakayama *Japan Karate Association Shotokan*, Gogen Yamaguchi *Japanese Goju Ryu*, Yashahiro Konishi *Ryobukan*, Chomo Hanashiro *Okinawan Te*, Gozo Shioda *Yoshinkan Aikido*, Yabu Kentsu *Shorin Ryu, Itosu Chief Assistant*, Tatsuo Shimabuku *Isshin Ryu*, Shigoru Igami *Shoto Kai*, Rysho Sakagami *Ittosu Kai Shito Ryu*, Shimpo Matayoshi *Matayoshi Ryu Kobudo*, Kanei Uechi *Uechi Ryu*, Taganouchi Hisamori *Kogushuku Father of Jujutsu*, Iso Mataemon *Tenshin ShinYo Ryu Jujutsu*.

Kengo - *Skilled Swordsmen*

Miyamoto Musashi *Niten Ichi Ryu-Musashi Ryu from legend*, Yamoaka Tesshu *Itto Shoden Muto Ryu*, Yagu Munenori *Yagu Shinkage Ryu*, Tsukahara Bokuden *Hitotsu Tachi - The One Strike Kill*, It Ittosai Kagehisa *Itto Ryu*, Kaniiyumi Nobutsuna *Yagu Ryu Progenitor*, Hasegawa Eishin *Muso Jikiden Ryu-19th Master*.

Hakase No Heiho-*Doctoral Degree Holders, the Philosophy of Strategy*

Napoleon Hill, *Personal Success;* Matsuo Munefusa, *Basho-Haiku Poetry;* B. J. Palmer, *Chiropractic Philosophy;* Ayn Rand, *Objectivist Philosophy;* D.T. Suzuki, *Zen Buddhism;* Takuan, *Zen Philosophy;* Jin Yutang, *Eastern Philosophy*.

Preface

Heiho: Martial Arts Concepts & Strategy was written with the intent of clarifying the nature of Ko Ryu, Martial Classical Traditions. According to dictionary definition *classical* is that which conforms to certain established standards of form and style and is of enduring interest and value. When looking at something from the standpoint of classicism it is implied that aesthetic principles combined with technical perfection and simplicity are at its heart.

It is not the intention of the author to imply that this is the ultimate definitive text on Karate Do and Kobudo for Okinawa and Japan. It is only my desire to contribute to the insight of anyone who is serious about following the traditions of the classical art of Karate from Okinawa, specifically Isshin Ryu and the modern art of Shito Kan Karate Do.

By doing what the masters of Karate have done in the past we can learn what they knew. Once the preparation has been made, by reading, studying and learning all there is to know, then the opportunities will arise for insight into the training of our minds and techniques as we develop the perspective of Heiho, Martial strategy.

The book of *Heiho* was written to continue the vision of Tatsuo Shimabuku of Isshin Ryu Karate and Budo practice into the third generation and with the coming of the turn of the century, into the next millennia. This book is a tribute to the exquisite art of Isshin Ryu and to the late Grandmaster Tatsuo Shimabuku himself as well as to Master Harold Long. Throughout the book the component parts of strategy and the concepts of Shu Ha Ri will be interwoven as we study the Karate code laid down by most major Masters or Soke of Martial Arts systems. Included are the concepts of Dojo Kun, the Four Aspects of Karate Do and the Twelve Key Points of Isshin Ryu from Master Tatsuo Shimabuku.

This book of *Heiho* tells the story of why a Martial Arts practitioner should be interested in strategy from a personal viewpoint, that of self defense, but more importantly that he should continually contemplate his place and purpose in the making of Martial Arts history and tradition. It is only through the strategy of certain individuals that we have the knowledge of Martial Ways and Forms today. Without strategy we are dead ends in our practice and shortsighted in our training regimen. How could one truly understand the beauty of Karate and not wish to see it passed on to future generations of Karate Ka (students) to learn and enjoy? The answer is that if one delves deeply into the soul of Karate he finds himself. The strategy of seeing this ultimate form of self discovery and improvement propagated is the desire of every person who wishes to see the world and their lives become more fulfilled and peaceful.

Forward

Forward by Sensei Sally Eaton, Yondan
Clawson, Shito Kan Hombu Dojo

Strategy in itself is an art and a science. Karate Do is also an art and a science. We would be obtuse in our thinking if we did not realize and accept this fact from the beginning.

The art of strategy is devising a plan toward a goal, any goal, in every aspect of life. Devising the plan and then implementing it takes an inexhaustible amount of energy, fortitude and knowledge. On a Martial level, without strategy (the plan), a person has only luck to rely on. Luck is not a formidable weapon. Skill, knowledge, common sense, fate and destiny all play important roles in putting the plan into motion. The tools necessary for survival are there. The goal is now attainable.

The science of strategy is an adaptation of the plan that serves in achieving evolutionary success. If one does not strive for excellence, his mind will become stagnant and his spirit will become dormant. The body will have no purpose to continue to function.

There is a stratum of society who are content to live their lives in that fashion, to merely exist. Living their lives by accident rather than by design. That layer of society will not achieve evolutionary success because they lack strategy.

There are many facets of strategy contained within the pages of *Heiho: Martial Arts Concepts and Strategy*. The art and science of Karate Do is being presented to you. Seek the knowledge and use the tools provided for you to forge the mind, body and spirit, for it is truly a matter of survival.

Zensho!

Sally Eaton

Forward by Sensei Lynn Ross, Yondan
Clinton Township, Shito Kan Shibu Dojo

The majority of people in society today look outward for the answers to their problems. Not only do they look outside of their own wherewithal to resolve conflict and pain, but the remedy must be quick, simple and have the stamp of approval from the masses. The expectation is for great things to occur with little or no effort on their part. Psychological counseling, medicinal addiction, alcoholism, obesity, welfare programs and the lack of ethics, morals and productivity are not only alive and well, but flourishing.

There is no doubt that the stress, anxiety, depression and misfortune experienced by many individuals is real. Life is full of challenges, and the only constant in life is change. Dealing with change on a daily basis requires personal conviction, for the challenges are diverse and there is no standard operating procedure that will apply to all situations. People must arm themselves with a strategy to succeed and have the heart, perseverance and patience to see it through.

Strategies for personal success may be somewhat of an enigma. The word "strategy" has a different connotation to most people, thinking of it primarily in relation to business or war. In *Heiho*, Dr. Aiello speaks of *Martial Arts* concepts and strategy, which may also trigger thoughts of self defense and aggression in people's minds. In actuality, if one understands the true meaning of Karate Do, or the empty handed way, it is clear that the physical victories experienced through Karate training are easily assimilated into one's mind and spirit if directed properly by an experienced and knowledgeable Sensei (teacher). As the student progresses through their training, the concept becomes more lucid with little separation between the way the student behaves and thinks in the Dojo (training hall) and outside of the Dojo. This reinforces the fact that Karate Do is a way of life.

What is required in either case is a strategy, or a plan to win. Setting goals and having a vision of exactly where you want to be and how you will succeed in getting there, is absolutely necessary. The training enables the student to develop the physical, emotional, and intellectual skills that will be utilized to face challenges with confidence and fortitude, enjoying one success after another. Individuals will begin to look inward for the answers as they realize a greater sense of well–being.

These were the ideals set by the ancient Masters of Karate Do. It is a timeless concept based upon their vision, recorded for our benefit many years later. *Heiho: Martial Arts Concepts and Strategy* continues the legacy of these great Masters in the austere fashion they had envisioned.

Lynn J. Ross

Forward by Sensei Dina Baganz, Yondan
Clawson, Shito Kan Hombu Dojo

It is safe to say the it is the rare person who trains in the Martial Arts and is not forever affected by it in a positive manner. Even those who only dabble or have trained for short periods of time, regardless of style or system, can be assured of having a change in their lives for the better. The longer one trains, the more it becomes evident that there are endless things to be gained through training in such a thing as Karate Do. As we better ourselves we find more areas to improve. This is due partly to the heightened self–awareness gained through Karate training. It is more likely due to the tenets of perseverance and quest for personal excellence that are stressed in most Martial Arts.

Today it may seem archaic and old fashioned to hold traditional values in high esteem. The advent of sport Karate and the diluting of so many systems and styles with other activities such as aerobics and boxing, has changed the face of the Martial Arts as it has changed the intent and result. The ancient ways of training fostered independence, confidence and stressed strength of character. These things were acquired not by talking about them, but through austere, physical training. The movements done by Martial Artists were not happenstance, nor were they solely for the purpose of self defense. Through Martial training one gains the insight into one's strengths or overzealousness and weaknesses or faults. This is done in a way that affects not only the body, but also the mind at a deep level of consciousness. One can not only see the problem clearly, but the answer and the path to correct the problem.

It is because of the awesome potential that lies within Martial Arts training that each and every student who is sincere will come to understand the concept of Giri–debt of obligation. This is not a monetary debt, nor a debt of guilt, but one that is felt out of gratitude for the wisdom that is made available by those who traveled the path before. Our Giri to the coming generations of Martial Artists takes shape in not only the physical training we do but also the words we say and the material things we leave behind. It is good *heiho,* strategy, to pass on what one has been taught–especially if it is correct. *Heiho: Martial Arts Concepts & Strategy* fulfills the Giri of Shito Kan Karate Do by laying down the teachings of Grandmaster Tatsuo Shimabuku, and then expanding on their brilliance.

Table of Contents

Introduction   19
Section I: The Concepts   25

Chapter 1: The Book of Heiho 27
Chapter 2: The Four Aspects of Karate 45
Chapter 3: The Twelve Key Points of Isshin Ryu Karate Do 65
Chapter 4: The Code of Karate 73
Chapter 5: The Strategy of Mastery & Destiny 85

Section II: The Basics   95

Chapter 1: Kihon & Reigisaho 97
Chapter 2: Isshin Ryu Chart One 125
Chapter 3: Isshin Ryu Chart Two 155
Chapter 4: Shito Kan Chart Three 181

Section III: The Kata   237

Chapter 1: Bushi No Kata 239
Chapter 2: Bushi No Kata–A Pictoral View 243

Section IV: Addendum   271

Addendum: Interview with a Master 273
Bibliography: 331

Introduction

Defining the Essence of Karate Do

Karate Do is a modern discipline of empty handed self defense. It evolved from Martial survival techniques indigenous to Okinawa, Japan. The combative Warriors of the arts of Naha–Te, Shuri–Te and Tomari–Te laid the foundation for Karate Do during the eighteenth century. Along with the practice of the art of defense we have received insight into the minds and lives of those who have traveled the path of ancient Warriorship right into the present day ideals of Budo, the Martial or Warrior Way.

The Warrior Way or path included methods of forging the spirit. Throughout history, the Warrior Arts have been interwoven with strict codes of conduct. When training austerely and in the traditional manner, thought and action are affected in the realm of social conduct as well as in the techniques themselves. These ideals of training practice and life style brought to us by the Martial Arts of Okinawa and Japan have left the legacy of a Warrior's method of physical, emotional and spiritual conduct. Today we call this Way of the Warrior Karate Do and its sister art is Kobudo, ancient Okinawan weapons. Any in depth study of the Martial Arts of Okinawan Karate Do and Kobudo will lead to an Asian journey through not only 18th and 19th century Japan, Okinawa and China but also through out 20th century American culture.

History and Purpose of Isshin Ryu Karate Do

Tatsuo Shimabuku was born on September 9, 1908 in Chun Village, Okinawa. His first Kobayashi Shorin Ryu instructor was his uncle, Irshu Matsumora, aka Kamasu Chan. Later on Shimabuku began studying Kobayashi Shorin Ryu under Master Gajoko Chioyu. Master Chioyu, realizing Shimabuku's potential introduced him to Chotoku Kyan (1870–1945), who was a very famous instructor. Chotoku Kyan, of course, is known as the founder of Shobayashi Shorin Ryu. Master Kyan, also called Chan Migwa, studied under Kosaku Matsumura and Yasutsune Itosu. Master Kyan instructed Shimabuku in many kata such as Seisan, Naihanchi, Wansu, Chinto and Kushanku. He also worked with Shimabuku on what is called Chinkuchi, which is the Okinawan term for Ki or intrinsic energy. Some Okinawan weapons were also taught to him at this point. Tatsuo Shimabuku spent many years with Chotoku Kyan and studying with him was his brother Eizo Shimabukuro who was to become the Menkyo Kaiden of Shobayashi Shorin Ryu at the very young age of 35. Shinkuchi was Tatsuo Shimabuku's original first name prior to his changing it to Tatsuo, meaning "dragon boy," which was his nickname.

Tatsuo Shimabuku also studied with Chojun Miyagi (1888–1953) who was the founder of Goju Ryu, the hard/soft system of Karate. Chojun Miyagi studied under Kanyro Higashionna, well known for teaching many of the most famous Karate masters. Master Higashionna studied in Fukien, China and is recognized as the father of Naha Te Karate. Chojun Miyagi taught Tatsuo Shimabuku for approximately two years, teaching him in Sanchin and Seiuchin Kata. The third of Tatsuo Shimabuku's main instructors was Choki Motubu (1871–1944) who was known as one of the most powerful fighters on the island of Okinawa. He also taught a number of the fighters. It is thought that Choki Motobu taught or influenced Tatsuo Shimabuku's Naihanchi Kata because the Naihanchi used in Isshin Ryu is very unusual. One other instructor that would later play a role in Shimabuku's training life was Shinken Taira (1902–1970), the developer of many Kobudo Kata. Shimabuku also trained with Shinken Taira's Karate teacher, Yabiku Moden either indirectly with him or through Shinken Taira when he learned several of his weapons kata. The weapons Kata were not used by Shimabuku for testing or grading as is the case today in some of the Isshin Ryu organizations. There are eight empty hand kata used by Shimabuku for Isshin Ryu Karate. These Kata are Seisan, Seiuchin, Wansu, Sanchin, Naihanchi, Chinto, Kushanku and Sunsu. The Kobudo or weapons Kata, of which there are six, are sometimes used as extra curricular training. The Kobudo Kata that are included in Isshin Ryu are Tokomini No Kon, Urashi Bo, Shi Shi No Kon No Dai Bo Kata, Kushanku Sai

Kata and Chatanyara No Sai Kata. There is also thought to be Chifa Tonfa Kata by some Isshin Ryu practitioners. It has been said Shimabaku knew other weapons and I am sure that he not only knew other weapons but had learned many other empty handed kata. He practiced the series of eight empty hand kata and the series of six or seven weapons Kata. Some dispute the Tonfa kata, some actually even go as far as to say there was the hidden, secret Nunchuku kata. There is also thought to be a short Sai Kata. Sensei William Duessel, ninth degree black belt in Isshin Ryu Karate teaches this Kata, as he has film footage of it to verify that Shimabuku did do a short Sai Kata.

On January 15, 1954 Isshin Ryu was officially born. One night, after teaching, Tatsuo Shimabuku had a dream that would change the direction of his Karate career forever. Of course, this was the beginning of the Mizu Gami or Go Shu Jin Sama, the spirit of Isshin Ryu. On the Monsho, the Isshin Ryu patch, there are usually seen three stars at the top implying his teachers. One of his head students, Eiko Kaneshi, brought the name Isshin Ryu into being. Isshin Ryu means one heart or one mind method indicating a commitment to act with a single sense of devotion towards correct action.

The Isshin Ryu system utilizes an eight–point Code and a Dojo Kun, a set of rules for the Dojo. Tatsuo Shimabuku, instead of utilizing only Kata to teach techniques developed what he called the chart system. They covered the Kihon Waza, basics, as well as the kicking techniques. In some Martial Arts systems today such as Shito Kan Karate Do, because of the extensive knowledge of fitness, anatomy and physiology, a separate set of warm up exercises is utilized along with the fifteen hand techniques and the nine kicks. In addition to the eight–point Isshin Ryu Code, the Dojo Kun, the four aspects of Karate, Chart I and, II, of course, he would develop the vertical hand punching technique, the blocking with the back of the arm, the muscular portion of the arm, and developing it into a speed punching and, speed kicking system, where retraction was faster than other systems creating the snap or whip like action to his techniques. There were many other aspects to this including close–in fighting and the use of multipurpose techniques. There were twelve key points to Isshin Ryu that were devised.

Around 1955 Tatsuo Shimabuku began teaching some American GIs Karate in Chun Village, Okinawa. Two of these GIs were to become famous, Don Nagle and Harold Long. For all three, this would turn out to be a great and very important time in history. For Harold Long and for Don Nagle because they were to become two of the three U.S.A. representatives for Shimabuku. The third representative was Steve Armstrong and although he was an ambassador of Isshin Ryu in the United States and a great pioneer here, he became ill and unable to continue in that position. The fourth and last of the most recognized Masters to come out of the early days with Shimabuku, was Harold Mitchum. Harold Mitchum, Steve Armstrong, Don Nagle and Harold Long all would become eighth degree black belts under Shimabuku and representatives of Isshin Ryu in the United States. Harold Mitchum eventually retired, leaving Don Nagle and Harold Long who have now both gone into semi–retirement. They do however, continue to teach their personal students.

In 1964 Master Shimabuku made his first trip to the United States to Pennsylvania. This was not a good trip for Shimabuku, it was a disturbing trip for him. He did not adapt well to the United States. He was brought by a fellow who had not trained, at that time, in Isshin Ryu and by another fellow named Harry Smith who had. The fellow that did not train was named James Morabeto. This was, however, would prove to be an historical time because William Duessel achieved his Shodan at that time. William Duessel trains with the son of Grandmaster Tatsuo Shimabuku, Master Kichiro Shimabuku who is the current Okinawan Soke of Isshin Ryu. Sensei Duessel is Kichiro Shimabuku's number one student in Okinawa and the United States and he is ninth Dan. In 1966 Master Shimabuku returned where he spent several weeks with each of his top students: Harold Long, Don Nagle and Steve Armstrong. He awarded them all eighth degree black belts, unbeknownst to each of them that this would occur. This essentially put them in charge of the United States, giving each of them a portion or the authority to oversee the whole country together. It was never made perfectly clear which it would be. In 1974, Kichiro Shimabuku formed the Isshin Ryu World Karate

Association. Also, in 1974 Master Harold Long returned to Okinawa for a month to discuss the formation of his new Karate organization with Master Shimabuku. This was the beginning of the I.I.K.A., the International Isshin Ryu Karate Association. On May 30, 1975 Master Tatsuo Shimabuku passed away.

Today Master Kichiro Shimabuku is recognized as the defacto heir of Isshin Ryu in Okinawa and we have Master Harold Long, the current patriarch of the Master Tatsuo Shimabuku/Harold Long lineage of Isshin Ryu in the United States. The remaining, peripheral lineage is under Don Nagle who has appointed Nick Adler, ninth Dan, as his successor. Master Harold Long appointed three major successors to Isshin Ryu. Jointly Master Harold Long and Don Nagle appointed Toby Cooling and J.C. Burris ninth degree black belts. In March of 1997, Master Harold Long promoted Dr. Aiello to Hanshi. Hanshi is the highest certified instructor level in the Martial Arts, reserved for ninth and tenth degree black belts. This indicates that Dr. Aiello would be Menkyo Kaiden and successor to carry on a direct lineage of Master Tatsuo Shimabuku and Harold Long. At that time in March of 1997 an extensive recording session took place which included over 72 hours of personal conversation. This constitutes the most extensive personal interview ever done with a major Soke of a Karate system in the history of the Martial Arts. Some of the recorded material has been included here in the addendum of this book. Much of what was spoken of between Dr. Aiello and Master Long is invaluable to the Martial Arts community as it reflects many of the nuances in a master's conversation that is left out in edited books or in the spoken word to students or lay people.

History and Purpose of Shito Kan Karate Do

The Shito Kan Karate Do system was founded by Dr. Jerry L. Aiello in 1974. Dr. Aiello combined the **kicking skills** of Tang Soo Do, some structured technique of Japanese **Koei Kan,** the **fighting skills** found in American Karate (Shito Ryu), the speed of **Isshin Ryu** and ancient Okinawan weapons or **Kobudo.** The style includes five Kata or forms developed by Dr. Aiello, taught after Shodan, 1st degree black belt. These Kata can be found in other of the Warrior Training Manuals such as *Zensho* and *Warrior Legacy.* In the study of Shito Kan Karate Do one finds equal emphasis on the following aspects of martial training:

Taiso	**-health exercises**
Kihon Waza	**-basic techniques**
Makiwara training	**-traditional Okinawan striking post**
Traditional Kata	**-forms**
Nage	**-throwing or take down techniques**
Jiyu Kumite	**-free fighting**
Kobudo	**-ancient Okinawan weapons**
Gyaku Te	**-joint reversal techniques**
Buki Waza	**-weapon defense**
Suwari Waza	**-Seiza techniques (sitting)**

One of the most important aspects that is stressed in the Shito Kan system is the philosophy of the ancient masters. Some of what is taught includes etiquette, history and tradition. Focus is on the essence of the art rather than solely on the physical forms and defense. This is not to say that the physical aspects of the training are not important, for they play a vital role in the development of character and skill. In Shito Kan training such activities as Shugyo, austere training, Mukuso, meditation and Kokyuho, breathing techniques are practiced regularly. Each student is taught the value of training with full intensity and sincerity for their own health, personal development and inner strength. Shito Kan Karate Do training employs a standardized teaching/training curriculum that pairs physical fitness with self defense competence and academic skills. The concept of *Bun Bu Ichi,* "be as well versed in the pen as the sword" plays a major role in Shito Kan Karate. Reading and writing skills are honed as are drilling punches and kicks.

Shito Kan Karate Do Comes of Age

Heiho: Martial Arts Concepts & Strategy is a book focused on the fundamental technical principles of Karate Jutsu and Budo. This is in contrast to current trends in the Martial Arts toward sport and Olympic competition and commercialism as well as crude displays of gladiator style theatrics and entertainment using the "Warrior" words and superficial ideas. It is written from the perspective of one who has watched as many styles of Martial Art have grown and died away and few remained to flourish. It is from the viewpoint of someone who has developed and nurtured a system with hopes of it lasting through the turbulence that has been the ultimate demise of many fine Arts.

The book of *Heiho* is focused upon the ideal of Ensho, the Zen circle. The Zen circle is the epitome of the concept "what goes around comes around" and "the long way around is the shortest way home." The meaning of the Zen circle is that sooner or later we find that the well worn methods and ideas handed down from the masters from one generation of Martial student to the next hold all the elements necessary to fulfill those seeking the answers to life's most troubling mysteries. These thoughts are passed from the teacher to the student via what the Japanese call Isshin Denshin or direct transmission. It is not entirely through verbalization that learning takes place, but through a complex and dynamic set of circumstances set up by the master such that the student is exposed to physical, intellectual and emotional experiences in a pattern that allows him to learn. Only the path of Budo has this kind of systemized learning method and only Budo can boast of the results.

In the text and pictorial sections of *Heiho* you will find the Chart System created by Grandmaster Tatsuo Shimabuku. These ingenious segments of his teaching ideology give one a glimpse of the magnitude of a complete Martial Arts system. It is also clear that the Charts create the ability of this once isolated martial art of Karate jutsu and Budo practice to be passed down to selected students. Only certain students would receive all of the information and knowledge necessary to promote the vision of the "One Heart/Mind Method" of Isshin Ryu as a system of Budo. Many students are taught Karate technique, very few are ever brought into the inner sanctum of a Budo system and shown the true meaning of the "Martial" or "Warrior Way."

It is truly the gifted student, such as Tatsuo Shimabuku himself, who can take all that is given them by their teachers and expound upon it in such a way as to make it better and more accessible. Dr. Aiello has done this with the creation of Shito Kan Karate Do as did many of the most famous Karate and Martial Arts masters of all time. Gichin Funakoshi, Eizo Onishi, Kenwa Mabuni, Tatsuo Shimabuku, Juhatsu Kiyoda, Kanken Toyama the list goes on and on. For every great teacher there was the potential for a student to not only learn what his teachers knew, but to build upon that knowledge.

Section I

The Concepts

HEIHO

Chapter 1

The Book of Heiho

Strategy & the Super Human Master

The book of Heiho is a book of Martial Arts strategy of different levels and can be distinguished from a book about tactics. Strategy is the art or science of planning and directing military operations or campaigns. Different books have been written about military tactics and strategy. The book **Heiho Kadensho**, written by Master Takuana and **Go Rin No Sho** by Miyamoto Musashi both discuss aspects of strategy and tactical combat applications at an individual and group level.

The ideas in *this* book of strategy, *Heiho: Martial Arts Concepts & Strategy,* are directed toward skillful planning applicable in business, politics, social relations, personal defense and life in general. Strategy is developing a plan to achieve specific goals, whereas tactics are the plan of action, or a device used to achieve the goals. Combat tactics would indicate there had been planning and maneuvering involved with a tactical position for war or actual fighting.

Books that lend insight into the strategy of the Warrior are the **Book of the Samurai Hagakure** by Yamamoto Tsunetomo and **The Code of Bushido**, written by Nitobe on the code of the Samurai. Both books give insight into the thought process, philosophy and strategy of the Warrior, but are more linked to the codes of ethics, life-styles and philosophies the Warriors lived by. **Heiho Kadensho** deals with the concept of *Shu Ha Ri,* which is becoming well known in this country amongst Martial Artists as beginning, intermediate and advanced stages of training. It is the growth stages one progresses through as they conceptualize their training and proceed along the Path of the Way.

Strategy, when used in Karate training such as Shito Kan includes elements on a technical level, similar to the concepts found in Musashi's **Go Rin No Sho**. These are well known within the Martial Arts and any classically trained Martial Artist will be familiar with these aspects of Heiho.

The physical principles of action are the elements of Martial Arts that are familiar to any classical practitioner involved with a structured art such as Karate. They are Riai (timing), Maai (distancing), Kime (focus), Kokyu Ho (proper breathing techniques). Also, the In-Yo Kokyu Ho, uniting the Kiai to focus the internal rage into the ultimate goal of delivering Ikken Hissattsu (one blow, one kill). There are four stages to be traversed with the eventual goal reaching the level of Sen Nin, super human Master. This term is reserved for what we call the Meijin Master. Each traditional system of Martial Arts has a Meijin Master.

1. *Go No Te*: Block and counter, two moves done separately. This is demonstrated in Kihon Waza (basic techniques), in Chart I of Isshin Ryu Karate and Chart III of Shito Kan Karate.

2. *Go No Sen:* Block and counter, two moves done simultaneously.

3. *Sen No Te:* Deflective block and counter, one move creating two actions.

4. *Sen Sen No Te:* Reading the Ki (intrinsic energy) or the Metsuke (gaze) of an opponent, one or two moves done preemptively. The premise is that in Sen Sen No Te, we perceive the intent of the individual and preempt a situation by using a move defensively.

5. *Sen Sen No Sen:* This is the level of Sen Nin. One who has achieved Sen Nin can win with his Metsuke or Kiai (spirit letting yell). One can win with a stare or a sound, the vibrations of the Kiai uniting the spirit within the human being. No physical technique is used. At this level, the avoidance of conflict is considered to be the ultimate. There is no loss if you can avoid a conflict and the Sen Nin will go to any length to avoid a physical confrontation.

The *ultimate* goal of the Sen Nin is not combative or to develop the Ikken Hissattsu. That is the outcome when confronted with a life or death struggle and in the cause of justice. Sen Nin is a state of mind or consciousness typical only to a Meijin Master. The Meijin Master strives to live the daily spirit of Budo, to grasp the concept on the philosophical level, to transcend the physical applications of the Martial Arts, to leave the physical discipline behind and to train daily for the sake of training. He strives daily for the perfection of what he is doing and to forge his spirit, to control his temper or bolster his flagging enthusiasm, whichever the case may be. He seeks to maintain the skills, yet continue to remain in the **Shoshin**, or the beginner's mind.

Striving for Sen Nin means the perfection of the physical skills, perception, consciousness. It also requires the forging and controlling of the spirit and temper of that raging ferociousness that exists within every Warrior, thereby enabling him to apply all that he does in a focused, constructive manner for the benefit of himself and humanity.

Training Procedure

Each training center and Martial Arts system has its own Dojo Kun, however, there are several Dojo Kun recognized universally within Martial Arts literature. Grandmaster Tatsuo Shimabuku's was a seven point Dojo Kun. Literally translated:

1. We will train our hearts and bodies for a firm, unshaken Spirit.

2. We will pursue the true meaning of the Martial Way so that in time, our senses may be alert.

3. With true vigor and energy, we will seek to cultivate the true spirit of Budo.

4. We will observe the rules of courtesy, respect our superiors and refrain from violence.

5. We will pay homage to our creator and strive to follow the path of humility.

6. We look upwards to wisdom and strength, not seeking other desires.

7. All our lives, through the discipline of Karate, we will seek to fulfill the true meaning of the Way.

In Dr. Peter Urban's book, **The Karate Dojo**, he has a five step Dojo Kun called the Karate Virtues:

1. We are proud to study the spirit of Goju.

2. We shall always practice courtesy.

3. We should be quick to seize opportunity.

4. We shall always practice patience.

5. We shall always keep the fighting spirit of Karate.

These are recited in unison at the conclusion of formal training as the guiding principles of the style of Goju Ryu. Along with the Dojo Kun in Master Urban's book, he has the Precepts of Karate. He said, "A Karate man in training is *in* Karate." The Precepts are:

Strength comes from health.
Speed comes from effort.
Technique comes from experience.
Willpower comes from faith.
Serenity comes from old knowledge.
Progress comes from new knowledge.

The Dojo Kun of Uechi Ryu, also known as Pang Gai Noon Ryu as taken from **The Secrets of Uechi Ryu Karate Do**, by Allen Dollar are:

1. We will embody the principles of familial piety and make efforts to be upright citizens.

2. We will deepen our understanding of everyday life and pursue the hard working, humble and frugal life–style.

3. We emphasize physical exercise and bodily health.

4. We will cultivate moral behavior and increase our appreciation of others.

5. We will promote social spirit and contribute to the public well being.

The well known "founder" of modern day Karate, father of Shoto Kan Karate and author of **Karate Do, My Way of Life**, Gichin Funakoshi, had these five Dojo Kun:

1. Work to perfect your character.

2. Have fidelity in seeking the true way.

3. Cultivate a spirit of endeavor and perseverance.

4. Always act with good manners.

5. Refrain from violent and uncontrolled behavior.

If we examine Martial Arts in this country, we do not often see these Dojo Kun in actual application. We seem to have a tremendous split in the Martial Arts. The traditionalists are seeking a philosophical and ethical approach to their training while the sports–minded practitioners are endeavoring to bolster the ego through competition and placing the value solely on the physical aspects of training. All practitioners that have roots in traditional systems have the Dojo Kun, yet even here the inconsistencies of the application are astounding.

Hopefully, as we seek a solution to the great divide in the Martial Arts, we will come to realize that what separates Martial Art from the sport of boxing or grappling, or the "no-holds-barred" contest is a philosophy. If this is recognized, then as Martial Artists age and are no longer capable of performing at the physically athletic levels they did as youngsters, they will continue to have value and recognition for their wisdom. Moreover, they will continue to have reason to train.

The consistent ideal within all Dojo Kun is the perfection of character. Not the physical applications of power, strength, speed, or youthful athletic ability. This translates into working toward self improvement and personal excellence in all activities; to apply the skills and dexterity, physical and mental focus in the work place, social life and personal life, thereby enhancing productivity and creativity. It is the utilization of the finely tuned human body and mind, working together synergistically.

Persevering to be Loyal

There is also a focus on fidelity while seeking the true Way in the Martial Arts. This means not digressing off the path and recreating the art for personal benefit or recognition alone. Although there seem to be many paths to the top of the mountain, one still must climb the mountain. In the case of the Martial Arts Master, there is only one correct path that leads to becoming a "superhuman," Sen Nin. Training in an Art for the purpose of self-perfection, being loyal to the tried and true methods will create a different value system and totally different benefits from that of playing a game of soccer or racquetball for sport and fun.

Cultivating a spirit of perseverance is stressed throughout all of the different Dojo Kun. The discipline to practice the Kun and the classical training to synchronize the mind and body must be fostered and grown. It certainly does not happen by accident.

There are many people who are unwilling to stay involved in a traditional Martial Art long enough to reap the benefits. Everyone wants the benefits of the training and the end result, yet so many do not want to put a Gi (uniform) on, get in the class, bow, sweat, Soji (clean) and pay Giri (debt of obligation). The people who lack fidelity to their Art and who have not cultivated the spirit of perseverance take the easy way out. They cannot conquer *themselves* long enough to get proficient. They simply quit or alter the training to suit their whim.

These individuals who lack the discipline to follow through are also those who lack good manners, politeness and Reigisaho (etiquette). Acting with good manners creates good citizens and good citizens avoid conflict, which reflects Budo. "To stop the iron spear" is the common translation of Budo. What it means to Martial Artists is to stop conflict, within one's self and between others. Without politeness and reigisaho it is almost impossible to achieve Budo. Often times someone will slight us, insult us, or short us in some way and our initial reaction is immediate repayment with harsh directness. This could be avoided by having the perception to avoid those individuals to begin with and not overreacting to the situation.

Martial Arts are one of the most effective ways to achieve total physical conditioning integrated with a strong, healthy, disciplined mind and a clear reality based thought process. This results in an individual who is capable of outperforming, out-creating and out-producing the average person in society. It is a way of maximizing the natural gifts that one is born with.

Budo was first formulated as a way of life, or the Path, as it is called in Martial Arts. In ancient Japan and Okinawa it was a discipline which replaced Bujitsu, the actual combat skills. Unfortunately, the misconception is prevalent today in that we still see people view the Martial Arts as aggressive, violent behavior. This is due to the Martial Arts not being identified as Budo but as Bujitsu.

The one important aspect of Martial Arts as Budo is that they are designed to stop conflict by helping an individual be confident and respect themselves. This then helps them to have the ability to respect others and to be confident in their actions and behavior. Although it may appear as a paradox, the Budo Arts actually have the ability to help someone with their values, their ethics and their morals through prolonged years of training.

Shu, the Beginner

The concept of *Shu Ha Ri* involves the levels of development an individual goes through in Budo training. The beginner's stage is where one joins a traditional Ryu Ha (a style) to begin learning. In this stage, limitations and parameters in training are set forth. The student is put through regimented classes so that they can grow and learn up to a particular level. There is a clearly defined curriculum, format and methodology to learning. This is the stage that most individuals never get through. Before they are able to get a fundamental grasp of the basics skills many drop out of training. The most disturbing part of this is that most of the individuals who leave the training during this stage have a great misconception about their abilities. They do not know that they are only in the *first* stage of *three* and they are unable to grasp the magnitude of their inadequacies.

If one considers this application throughout society, in all aspects, whether in the work force, socially, or in the educational systems, we realize there are a lot of people who have learned a little bit, think they know it all and retard their learning at that point. They become stagnant, spreading their lack of discipline to the individuals they are allowed to be exposed to. Then there are those who do not quit, but remain in the training without moving up or gaining any ground. Many people are very content to stay in the Shu, or beginning stage, because it is comfortable and there are no challenges beyond the initial "entrance jitters." Training is defined and clear cut. This is not the Way of the Warrior nor the way to mastery of the self and one's life. The Way of the Warrior is a constant progression forward, striving to expand beyond the comfort level. For those who stick it out and remain, great things are in store. During the beginner's stage of training every new technique learned and every level belt rank achieved is a major event.

Ha, the Martial Arts Apprentice

The intermediate stage, *Ha*, generally occurs between Shodan, the first black belt rank and Sandan, the third. The individual becomes generally less rank conscious and there is a foundation of basic skills which are well developed. Although progress on a day to day basis is not as noted, regular training is essential to maintain and grow further. The health benefits are evident, as they were in the *Shu* stage, improved muscle tone, flexibility, lowered blood pressure and cardiovascular fitness while keeping the mind sharp and staying on the cutting edge competitively at work. The big picture of things begins to reveal itself to a Shodan in the early years and they are entering their truly serious level of training.

At this intermediate stage the responsibilities start to mount. The individual will be required to start student teaching at this point. Often at this level the individual does not yet have a comprehensive grasp of what their own system is about. They feel they have a certain amount of mastery with the skills they have, yet do not seem to understand or grasp the mystery of training in a Budo Art. There is a tendency in the initial black belts levels for experimentation. Unfortunately, this is where many Martial Artists break away from their instruction and attempt to "make it" on their own. They frequently are interested in testing their mettle, or trying out their skills and believe that they do not need the guidance of their Sensei any longer. How tragic, for they soon find out that they can only achieve success to their own level of incompetence. Without the support and teaching of a master the lone black belt soon finds out just how little he knows.

Ri, Mastery

The third stage in this journey of *Shu Ha Ri* is the *Ri* stage. This is where everyone wants to be, but few are willing to do the work and spend the time required to achieve this coveted stage. Generally, the Ri stage starts to occur at about fourth, fifth, or sixth degree black belt. This is the point where the training is done totally for the sake of training, the external desires for ornamentation and egotistical soothing have been overcome. It is the stage where technical mastery has been achieved. Individualized appearance in techniques and teaching styles are prevalent without these being a threat to system.

It is also the stage that considerable responsibility is taken on and also a certain amount of earned status through rank and real mastery. It is at this stage that many individuals do not continue to adhere to the discipline of earlier training and fall behind.

Many Martial Artists reach this level and immediately claim to be Masters. Self proclamation of mastery does not make it so. When someone truly reaches the Ri stage they exhibit wisdom and insight into the whys and wherefores of Budo. The crises and the moving out of one's comfort zone which is so traumatic throughout the Shu and Ha stages are becoming less frequent but actually sought after. When it does occur, whether physical, mental or spiritual there is the benefit of having the experience in going through many crises, knowing that a crisis is also an opportunity for tremendous growth.

This the stage of no mind, the form of no form. The "sword of no sword," as Yamaoka Tesshu speaks of in his book, **Sword of No Sword**. This is the aspect of mastery whereby the practitioner, without intellectualizing technique, is able to perform the technique flawlessly. The motion of the body has become a reflexive action, part of the neurological system just as breathing. Performance of the Kata that have been studied for ten years or so is done without concentrating on the movements, moving into that Zen state of mind, or "no mind." The Kata is where the focus of time and skill levels is centered to develop a higher ability to perform with perfection, learning to live the form rather than merely memorize and perform it.

In this final stage, the Ri stage, adapting to new schedules and overcoming crises that occur require the implementation of more personalized regimen of training. There is a certain amount of flexibility in the training because the skills are inherent in the nervous system due to the tens of thousands of repetitions. Concentrating on creating new vehicles for self expression, finding new methods to challenges and seeking breakthroughs for creativity are priorities. It no longer feels like a discipline to be forced upon oneself, but a pleasure, an expression of life. This is the stage at which many Masters begin to truly grasp Zensho, to live completely and die without regret. For the Martial Artist who has Budo is in his blood, to live a life without training would be harsher punishment than any other.

At the Ri stage most aspects of the physical training are second nature. It is no challenge to adhere to all of the codes, the Dojo Kun and the ethics of traditional Martial Arts practice. However, the road to mastery never ends, it is a skill that is earned every day with hard work and contribution to the Art by sharing and teaching.

Teaching becomes a higher priority to the Master apprentice and the full fledged Master. For anyone else to follow the Path, they must have guidance. There are sidetracks to all paths. If one trains on his own, as we are seeing now with the videotape Martial Arts society where students are training in their homes and are never with a Sensei, they have no way to know if they are on the wrong path until it is too late.

The History of Mastery

We are continuously reminded of the uncommon ground between the traditional, classical systems of Karate, Judo, Jujutsu, Aikido and the sport element and those who are just interested in the self defense or combative aspects of martial training. It becomes more and more apparent that those who take a serious study of what they do and pursue the Martial Arts as the Path of a lifetime, or Budo, view their Art totally differently from those who are involved in the sport or mechanical portions alone.

Martial Arts systems that advocate only one aspect of the training— sports, fitness, meditative or self defense, for example—only reveal themselves as commercial and solely for the purpose of exploitation of the Arts. This is nowhere more evident than in the "ultimate combat" matches seen on pay–per–view television. They will come and they will go, like any other fad. Unfortunately, the media continues to exploit the Martial Arts for profit, creating a distorted view of the Budo Arts. The true aficionados and their philosophy, those seeking the Path of Budo such as Gichin Funakoshi, Morihei Ueshiba, Jigoro Kano, Yamaoka Tesshu and Grandmaster Tatsuo Shimabuku have stayed year after year. The Budo Masters of today are insuring that there is continuous growth worldwide despite all of the negative and opposing viewpoints.

Surprisingly, there is a claim that Budo has a sport component from a most unlikely source. The Dai Nippon Butoku Kai, the Great Japan Martial Virtues Association established in April of 1895, requires that there be a competitive component for it to accredit any Martial Art. This governmental organization originally was designed to license masters and be the recognizing accreditation body in Japan by setting controls, regulations and standards. The organization set up a committee to set standards for the issuance of rank. It utilized the *Dan–Kyu* system ranking below and above black belt levels of training. The Mudansha are those below black belt, Yudansha are black belt level and Kodansha are considered advanced black belt level. They utilized Professor Jigoro Kano's method of ranking, ten Kyu under black belt, ten Dan in black belt. The Dai Nippon Butoku Kai at that time, did not particularly want the Martial Arts to be thought of as a sport. They stressed aspects of compassion, respect and etiquette. They wished to establish and standardize Arts that would demand the respect and esteem of the Emperor.

Along with the Dai Nippon Butoku Kai the Budo Simon Dai Gakku, or the Martial Arts Technical College was established. These organizations were sponsored and sanctioned by the Japanese government and funded by the Emperor's family. They wanted to establish Budo training in the educational system to forge the Martial or Warrior spirit. The code of Bushido, the Samurai or Warrior code, would be the standard with which this martial attitude would be fostered. It was an indoctrination process and it was intended to create a more productive, martial-like individual with intense national pride.

Between 1901 and 1907, Judo, Kendo and Karate Do were assimilated into the elementary and middle schools of Japan and Okinawa. The Dai Nippon Butoku Kai created the distinguished titles of Renshi, Kyoshi and Hanshi as teaching certifications. The Shihan level ranking systems were also established at this time. These titles were honorary and were given to the individuals who had excelled considerably in the promotion, teaching and contributions to their Art. The ranking system is, generally speaking, an evaluation of physical skill and knowledge, while these teaching degrees recognized the attainment of personal excellence through the practice of Martial Arts. Since the inception of the Dai Nippon Butoku Kai, ranking has never been based solely on physical techniques of Bujitsu. It has always been considered to encompass the mind, the body and the spirit. Rank should be considered on the basis of Budo, not just physical skills.

Shidoin is a certified instructor, Renshi the low-level master, Kyoshi the master teacher and Hanshi, teacher by example, or professor. Hanshi is the highest level that can be achieved in the Martial Arts and is considered equivalent to a 9th or 10th degree black belt.

Today the credentials of Shidoin, Renshi, Kyoshi and Hanshi are very distinguished titles and are not all that common. Many Martial Artists are not even aware of what they mean or that they exist. There are actually some who claim to be Soke of an organization or a Grandmaster who are unaware of these titles.

There are two methods of being granted the titles of Shidoin, Renshi, Kyoshi and Hanshi, as well as Shihan, which is a certification given at fifth Dan, simply meaning Master. They are granted to individuals via their membership in a national or international association based on their contributions and achievements, participation in the organization and their teaching and promoting the Art. The second and more prestigious way is to be given a direct lineage certificate by the senior most Sensei, the Soke (founder or head) of the Ryu (style).

Shidoin occurs at 2nd or 3rd degree black belt, indicating a Sensei level, or teacher. This differentiates those black belts who merely train from those who teach. Shidoin level Sensei are knowledgeable of the curriculum and are able to teach students below black belt, or Kyu level students. Renshi is a 4th, 5th, or 6th degree black belt and have achieved low level master status. Gichin Funakoshi was awarded Renshi in 1922 when he went from Okinawa to Japan. This indicated that he was a Master instructor and equated to 5th degree black belt. Kyoshi, Master teacher certification, is generally awarded to those making an outstanding contribution to the Art, having stayed with the Art and progressed through the Shu Ha Ri process. Exhibiting loyalty, discipline and character, they are presented the Kyoshi teaching certificate title at 7th and 8th degree black belt.

Hanshi is teacher by example, or professor level certification. The title of Hanshi is presented by the individual's own teacher. Generally, Hanshi is reserved for those few who have shown exceptional insight, enthusiasm and ability. Not only do they have the physical ability but also the mental dexterity to persevere above and beyond what thousands of others have not. They have gone through countless difficulties, overcome all obstacles, risen to the top in their profession and are respected by their peers. Those who achieve the Hanshi level in the Martial Arts have made great contributions that are unique to their Art. They support and promote their Sensei, the Art as a whole and their organization.

Hanshi Sei is the Soke or Grandmaster of the organization. When he presents his top student with Hanshi, this generally means the Art, the Ryu or style, will eventually be passed on to this individual upon the death of the Hanshi Sei. This is an incredible honor which carries with it tremendous responsibility. Of course, the expectations are high that are placed upon anyone receiving the certificate of

Hanshi. These direct descendant Hanshi certificates are rare in the world, with perhaps only twelve to fifteen existing worldwide.

The following are the Shito Kan Karate Do Dojo Kun:

1. Look at life and act with a positive attitude and direction, seeking self improvement and personal excellence.

2. Maintain consistency of thoughts, words and actions.

3. Be aware of the law of cause and effect and utilize it by always preparing for opportunity.

4. Actions speak louder than words. Show who you are through your actions. Reflect a constructive and productive attitude and image.

5. Walk softly, carry a big stick. Only use the Martial skills in the defense of life and in the cause of justice. Never brag or boast about skills attained through Karate training. This leaves one open to assault. Then one becomes the instigator, not a defender of justice.

6. Share the message of Budo and Shito Kan Karate Do by setting an example and teaching. It is through teaching of others that we learn ourselves. It is impossible to learn the higher levels of Budo without teaching, sharing and testing our knowledge to see if what we *think* we know we really do know.

7. Karate is much more than kicking, punching and blocking. The spirit of each individual that emanates from within, the Warrior Spirit, is the nuclear power of the human being. It is from this that one derives the strength and the willpower to continue on in the face of adversity. Martial Arts are the vehicle for transformation between the physical, intellectual and spiritual.

8. Every class, every workout and every challenge is a new opportunity for personal growth and development, for personal excellence. Concentrate on using all of the senses and be sure to apply 100% effort. Remember that worthwhile things take time. Every day that training takes place puts time in on the side of the Martial Artist. In order to master anything, one must master time. Anything worth learning is worth taking the time to learn well.

9. Although training is done for self improvement, we must also work with our fellow students. To understand ourselves better, seek to understand others and their viewpoints as well. This is where the saying, 'Kill the ego before the ego kills you' rings true. Seek personal

saying, 'Kill the ego before the ego kills you' rings true. Seek personal discipline over self aggrandizement and brash displays.

   10. Seek the Way (Do), or path of Budo. This is not just an esoteric path. This is a path of doing the right things for the right purpose, adhering to the laws of nature, following the principles of the universe and maintaining the rules of politeness and etiquette at all times. This is the Way of the Warrior.

On a day–to–day basis, as we work toward our goals, our focus should be on the process, or path, not only on the end result. Many goals tend to be too short term, such as a green belt, a brown belt, or a black belt. We should be concerned with the development of the end product which is ourselves, not just the measurement of it.

Keeping the thought processes clear is vital and requires that one check his basic premises. The Way of the Warrior is found not through being narrow minded, or by allowing others to easily influence the thinking. What we know to be true must be kept firmly and foremost in our minds. That which we are unsure of we must research and seek advice on from true Masters of their trade.

We must realize to become a Renshi, Kyoshi, or Hanshi in the Martial Arts, to become a Master of Shito Kan, one must master one's self. Enlightenment comes from within, it does not come from outside sources. It is not inherent in a physical technique, however, it is apparent when one uses the physical techniques of the Martial Arts to forge the spirit, temper the mind and prepare the self for the opportunity of seeing realistically.

Shito Kan Karate Do, like other Budo Arts, is the study of life. It is the study of survival through the practice of Do, a way of life. Working within the parameters of the universal laws, man's search for understanding of existence takes many paths. But for those who identify themselves as Warriors, there is only one: the quest for personal excellence through Martial Arts training. Man's work justifies his existence. To produce is the next step beyond survival. This is a higher level of existence we call the Way. Leaders, or Sensei, identify this and share it in their teachings, thus contributing to the Art.

The Heart of Strategy: Ten Percent of Life

Heiho means strategy. The importance of strategy in the Martial Arts is seen in the physical element as well as the scholastic portion. Most Martial Artists do not realize that there is a part of their training beyond the technique, the science and philosophy of Martial Arts. For example, many people who study Karate, do some training and then pack up their Keikogi (uniform) and go home. The uniform stays in the car because it was not sweaty and they get it out for the next class later on in the week. Another scenario is that they train, work up a good sweat and have a challenging exercise class in a Dojo where they join on a membership for a black belt or on a contract for belt ranks. What these people are doing is going to a place with "Karate" on the sign, where a person wearing a Karate uniform and Karate belt and who has a certificate on the wall does some type of physical exercise that involves kicks and punches. That is not Karate Do, Budo or anything close to Martial Arts with Heiho. Many people who would like to become Martial Artists stagnate because of this lack on the part of the instructors. These instructors have failed to progress in a traditional paradigm of Martial Arts practice and therefore, their students will be destined to fail as well.

We know the approximate amount of time per day required to become a Master: ten percent. That amounts to approximately 2.5 hours a day. That leaves 21.5 hours of the day for other activities.

In Karate Do, ten percent means a mixture of:

Taiso-calisthenic exercises
Kihon Waza-basic drilling techniques
Kata-the essence of Karate
Makiwara and bag work
Jumbi Undo-conditioning exercises
Study & Meditation

Watching tapes, reading books and generally garnering as much education about the Art as possible is essential to becoming a Master. A structured, analytical process, whether it is found by accident, by use, stumbled across in the process of training, or discovered as the result of a Sensei, is essential. Without it, the end result or the Sensei will be incomplete. The individual may not know why they are incomplete, or even worse, they may not know that they are incomplete.

Either the Martial Artist is training and learning or they are not. There is no gray area. As the Samurai well knew, death is not a gray area. The true Martial Arts Master has faced death and knows more than how to physically overcome adversity. The Master also is well versed in the philosophical and historical aspects of his trade such that he knows the meaning and essence of his Art. The facts are, either one is at the Dojo or not. The ten percent is either put in or it is not. Ten percent is the turning point. If there is not that much invested the outcome will be less than a Master level Martial Artist. The different levels of student and Master move at different rates, however. For the first ten or twenty years it is *critical* that fundamental skills are established in the body. The ten percent is so essential during these developmental years of a Martial Arts Master.

The most effective approach to Mastery is found by having a scientific formula for training and teaching. It must be measurable and reproducible. The problem arises when there is a lack of scientific evaluation by the Sensei in the Dojo, it does not matter if the Sensei is world famous. If there is no reproducible, systematic formula for people to learn, there will be failure.

There must be a conscious effort to search beyond the physical application of technique and get to the root, the essence of the Martial Arts. It is not enough to come to the Dojo and spend ten percent of the time kicking and punching. The underlying metaphysics of training must be analyzed. If one does not connect with the metaphysical principles that govern the Arts, failure will be the final outcome.

No one can afford to spend ten percent of their time on something as limited as kicking and punching. That view is based on fear and paranoia that victimization is inevitable. If someone is paranoid they should get a gun, take a shooting and safety course and stay away from people. If fear governs our lives, then we should live in an isolated little world where we would not be affected by others. There is much more to the saying "self–fulfilling prophecy" than meets the eye. When someone concentrates on fear and the possibility of being a victim it is attracted. Within months of being enrolled in a traditional Karate training program students are able to adequately defend themselves in most assault situations. Does one need to spend his entire existence for ten to thirty years on learning self defense? That would be a waste of time. The Martial Artist who has gone beyond the physical and delves into the more esoteric aspects of the training soon realizes that there is so much more to be had in training than just some self defense moves.

The Symbols Game

Karate is a thing of action. Martial Artists are people of action versus the people who shop, Dojo hop and never become anything. The Dojo "hoppers" are people will never reach Mastery in the Martial Arts.

They put up barriers to their own progress and success with their indecision. They need to talk to a spouse, finish school, or change work schedules and when they finish it all and the cow jumps over the moon, then they will start or dedicate themselves to Martial Arts training. These are the unfortunate people who are misled by the media into thinking that Martial Arts training is something like tennis or volleyball. They do not know that there is a philosophical path laid down by Masters and proven by thousands of Martial Artists each century. They do not know that it is a life path and a way of thinking and acting that is different than any other type of activity.

These unfortunates walk into Martial Arts stores looking to buy Mastery and walk out wearing peace signs, Yin/Yang shields and Kung Fu emblems. They display all of the symbols of Christianity, Budo, Shintoism and Taoism, they wear them, but few understand them. Perhaps two percent of Martial Artists worldwide understand the depth of the symbolism used by their system. Even less of the non–Martial Artists have a clue as to what these things stand for. The privilege of wearing one of these symbols should be earned, not purchased at the local Martial Arts emporium. In this way they foster fantasy and incorrect thinking about the Martial Arts.

Symbolism, emblems and logos are very important. The Shito Kan Karate Do logo stands for Personal Excellence. The Kanji (Japanese characters) reflect the names of two of the greatest Sensei in history: Yasutsune Itosu and Kanryo Higashionna. Isshin Ryu, founded by Grandmaster Tatsuo Shimabuku, was named in 1954 by Eiko Kanaeshi, one of Shimabuku Sensei's top students. It represents one heart, one mind, one spirit. He did not say just the body, or the mind, or the spirit but indicated all three: the One Heart, One Mind, One Spirit method of Martial Arts training. They reflect the meanings of what the Sensei understood their Art to be. However, many people believe that the symbolism grants them the expertise and knowledge without having done the work.

The following scenario is an example of the progression of events in a traditional system that follows a Budo path in doing things:

Grandmaster Tatsuo Shimabuku, the founder of Isshin Ryu Karate Do, delegated official activity of the system somewhere between 1972 and 1974 to his son, Kichiro Shimabuku, making him Soke of the System. In this country, he appointed four main Shihan or Hanshi. Don Nagle brought Isshin Ryu to the United States. Master Harold Long was the second pioneer in this country followed by Steve Armstrong and Harold Mitchum. There were four American Grandmasters in the United States and one hereditary Soke in Okinawa. This practice is not uncommon in many systems today in an attempt to keep their technical ability and their philosophy of training alive. Although Isshin Ryu may not have come to terms with this situation, in reality there is a hereditary Soke at the head of the system symbolically and yet there are other Grandmasters who are more proficient. This has occurred because the American Grandmasters are senior in experience and training and have more years in Isshin Ryu than the son. This is not an insult. It is not acceptable for someone with less experience and less rank to become senior to their instructor who has superior experience, knowledge and technique. Because it has occurred indicates there are those incomplete in their training and unable to recognize this.

Juniors cannot go above seniors, unless something unique occurs along the way, such as death of the senior. Ranking after fifth degree black belt is not based on physical skill alone. Around fifth degree black belt a peak is reached physically. After that point, what matters is contribution to the Art, creativity, number of students taught and organizational activities. When a Sensei falls out, in most organizations they do not have their black belt taken away, however, they are given a certificate and a belt and they willingly retire.

Another example of misusing Martial Arts symbolism such as rank is found when individuals drop out of training. It is not unusual for someone to come back after years of not training, especially if they have achieved a high degree of black belt and expect to be recognized as having remained at that rank. There is an instance where a sixth degree black belt literally stopped training for twenty years, came back and put his sixth degree black belt on as if he had been training all along. Again, this is not reality. This person does not know that they do not know. They are fooling themselves thinking that the proficiency that they had years before has not faded or completely disappeared. The ego of these types of individuals did not become tempered to the point where they were aware that after a twenty year break in training, they could not possibly be as good as a even a new Shodan who is training regularly to hone his skills and perfect his character.

In Asia, the great tradition in the Martial Arts is that many of the Sensei were also the village healers. This tradition was passed on through the family. Such a situation is impossible in this country. One cannot grow up apprenticing under someone to be a healer. One cannot match the education in an institution of higher learning or at a university. One cannot teach such skills from the Dojo. If one does not have a license as a doctor, he cannot practice those things.

Often, a local Martial Artist will have a kit of acupuncture needles. The person may have studied tapes and attended a seminar learning from books how to do needles and call it acupuncture. They get what appears to be good enough to do this on people, but if a Master were to look at their work or ask them questions, they could not answer them. What they are doing is fraudulent and unethical. Acupuncture is an entire philosophy and life–style. It is an art, with as much depth as the Martial Arts. One cannot dabble and become a Master.

Part of being a Martial Arts Master is becoming a philosopher. It is not enough to be a physical practitioner. Without these other elements in the education of a student, there will be gaps in the thinking and therefore gaps in the practices and actions. Knowing basic tenets of Keizu (background history and tradition) is not philosophy. Knowing the underlying essence, theory, laws and principles is where philosophy comes from. The core source of knowledge is the essence, not coming to class two times a week and going through aerobics with a Karate Gi on. It is not acceptable for the Martial Arts Master or student to accept what *any* leader says, just because they are "great" and have something to say. It also has to be true. But the truth of any statement must be judged by each individual. Symbolism has been used to help in the acceptance of fraudulent Martial Arts leaders. Those who are unwilling to check the validity of what these people say will fall for their falsehoods.

The law of cause and effect remains intact even in the Martial Arts. How Martial Arts practice is defined is the choice of those who participate. The words cannot alter the law of causality and the reality of what is done on a daily basis. If one does 100 Yoko Geri (side kick) with perfecting the technique in mind, they will become better. If none are done, they are not going to get better. Train on the Makiwara (striking post) and the technique is going to be different than by punching the air or a heavy bag or piece of paper of x–ray film. Martial Arts students who do not train on the Makiwara have no sense of reality with their techniques when compared to those who do. It is physical reality of the technique. Is a paper the same as a Makiwara when hit? NO! Is there anybody that cannot figure that out? It is ridiculous to assume that hitting a piece of paper and hitting a six–inch piece of pine or oak with hemp on it is the same. Where is the reality? An incomplete person who calls himself a Sensei is teaching that one can punch a piece of paper and have the same effect as a Makiwara. We can reproduce this experiment repeatedly. Hit the paper, then hit the rope and see if it is different. It does not take a rocket scientist to have the scientific theory to invalidate inappropriate statements that are based on mysticism. What is learned in training will determine the outcome in the Martial Arts, just like anywhere else. Easy training will not have the same result as hard training. That is the Makiwara story, however, the same principle applies to Kumite (sparring) and Bunkai (practical application of Kata).

The Fear Factor, the Fat Factor

Fear, greed, anger, pettiness; these all occur. These are all used in an attempt to manipulate others. True Martial Artists Masters cannot be manipulated by mysticism and distorted reality. What is known is a certainty because it is proven each time in the Dojo and it is scientifically reproducible.

What would it be worth if Martial Arts groups called themselves a psychological counseling subspecialty focusing on phobias? Fear is one of the major areas that Martial Arts training, when done correctly, deals with very directly. Through traditional methods of psychology or psychiatry it often will take years to get someone over the fear of something, or the fear of fear. What would it be worth for these people to overcome fear in a short period of time? It would be worth thousands or tens of thousands of dollars to most people. Why are people going to these clinics, when all they have to do is put on a Gi, tie on a white belt, get in the back row and confront their fears for $50 or $75 a month rather than the same or double per hour? The reason they do not get in the back row is their fear. The only problem with a person who is fearful is they are scared to get well because they will not have a crutch. Were it not for their fear they would have no excuse not to be productive and successful. In the Martial Arts they would have to be a person of action.

Teachers of the Martial Arts have the ability to help a human being overcome fear within weeks. Why are so many focused solely on self defense? Why are so many training centers advertising antirape courses? Because they lack the understanding of Heiho. They have not learned that there is a strategy and a philosophy to any complete Martial Art. What a small thing self defense is compared to the total value of what Martial Arts has to offer. The resolution of fear is one microscopic area of the training. Yes, Martial Arts is valuable as an antirape tool. It is good for self defense. It is great cardiovascular conditioning. There are so many advantages, but the greatest is the ability to make the mind healthy.

Look at another example; medical clinics that do nothing but specialize in blood pressure. For the last thirty years, research on cholesterol is still inconclusive. No doctor will put it in writing that if cholesterol ratios are proper and a person is on a low fat diet, the likelihood of having a heart attack or getting heart disease is slim, because they cannot. The Martial Artists can give conclusive evidence. Wouldn't every medical doctor like a sure way to lower blood pressure? All research on hard, intense, sweaty, prolonged exercise indicates that it lowers blood pressure. Millions of dollars are spent each year for research on heart disease, high blood pressure and stroke. How have they failed to uncover the fact that in a little Karate Dojo in Clawson, Michigan, for the last five years *blood pressure has gone down in the students*! Is this by accident? Cholesterol ratios improve when one does traditional Karate, hearts strengthen and fat percentages go down.

How many people go to fat farms every year and pay thousands of dollars? How many Martial Arts facilities advertise that they are better than the local fat farm? What a gift and what a tool Martial Artists have. Why are so many Martial Arts centers focused on the tournament circuit or the latest spandex fad? They are helplessly caught in their own *snafu*. They have not trained long enough and learned enough about the essence of what they *call* the Martial Arts to know that it is so much more than just a weight loss or health and fitness craze. It is nothing unless the essence of Heiho is grasped. The Martial Arts are not unexplainable chaos when there is a strategy at the core of the training.

Choosing what to do in life is the ultimate human experience. There are no limits in the Martial Arts once this concept is understood. The Heiho of Martial Arts is the stylizing of physics and the application of philosophy of Budo to life. In the training we see the Bunkai of physics, the practical application of force, mass and energy. In the world of Martial Arts, style or Ryu means a grouping of material or techniques organized into a system of application. By research and development, we have come to where we are today. That does not mean we have to stay where we are ten years from now. The greatest Sensei to come has not yet arrived. The greatest Sensei that ever was may not even be born yet and he will be the Sensei who has taught the most students. Perhaps that person is training somewhere today as a white belt. There is nothing stopping anyone from becoming the greatest Martial Artist, except excuses and barriers put in the way accidentally on purpose by not following the correct path. All of the tools to make this achievement a reality in the Martial Arts training are available. Unfortunately, most people are too busy with their milk route to realize this.

The Art in Martial Arts

Are Martial Arts really art? Absolutely, they are artistic and an art form. Art means there is an human and interpretive component. Each of us is an individual and each of us has our strengths and weaknesses. If we analyze cause and effect with what we do in the Dojo, we will stay consistent, even though physically we are not all the same. Some of us are 6'2" and some of us are 5'2." Some of us are 220 pounds and some of us are 120 pounds. The expression of the style varies, this is the Art, while the purpose and result remains the same, this is the Martial portion or the science.

If we function by the principles of cause and effect, we use it to keep the training based on reality. Good sailors are not made on smooth seas. Excellent sailors are made on tough seas. Commodore Baganz sailed the Great Lakes for fifty–two years. He told me tales of head winds and gusts and of bows of huge freighters going up and down while being pushed onto rocks. These are tales of a Warrior. He left his mark because of his greatness. He overcame his fear by mastering the elements as much as humanly possible. He knew there were laws and principles. He knew when his ship was in trouble he would have to do certain things to correct it. He knew he was responsible and he could not run away and quit. He could not jump off his ship because things got bad. That is what losers do. They jump off. What is worse is that they jump off when they have it in their grasp. They betray themselves, they betray the Masters and they betray their Sensei. There are incomplete teachers in the Martial Arts because they understand it, grasp it and do not realize that what they have grasped is incomplete. Martial Artists who are truly artists must have the concepts of the universe integrated into what they do.

One of the Codes of Isshin Ryu Karate reads: "A person's heart is the same as heaven and earth." This is from an Okinawan who never ventured off the island to the outside world until 1964. Yet, Grandmaster Tatsuo Shimabuku had the microcosm in his Dojo and those principles are evident in his work. This is why it is imperative that one have a teacher who has experience and has learned to pass along the knowledge and supply the missing links in this material.

Systems are a product of consciousness and are works of art. The Art is more than putting together physical skills. If the philosophy is not understood, then there is no Art. If one is not following Grandmaster Tatsuo Shimabuku's One Heart, One Mind Method by putting the heart and the mind together in the technique, then it is not Isshin Ryu. If one is not working on personal excellence, then it is not Shito Kan. The philosophy is essential to the Art. Otherwise it is merely an aerobic form of exercise or another self defense course. Bizarre Martial Arts characters are products of that. They were allowed to skip the laws and principles of metaphysics. They were allowed to have divergent thinking and major flaws and still given rank because they could kick and punch well. But none checked their premises and saw that they were not philosophically where they should be at a given rank. The physical will come sooner or later if one trains long enough, but the mind will not develop with it unless one works on it constantly.

Many Martial Artists have not consciously analyzed the purpose for which they practice or teach the Art. Many Martial Artists are locked in an adolescent state of existence. They have not gone past eighteen or nineteen years old. They are worried about fighting and beating someone up. The day will come when the physical skills will be competent to handle somebody on the street, whether that is the goal or not. No matter how tough one is or how high ranking, there is no guarantee that someone will not take him out on the street.

Part of the beauty of the Budo life is that once we transcend the physical and egotism we then can see and appreciate the fragility of being human. We can then recognize that we are *just* human beings with all of our particular strengths and weaknesses. That it is a constant process of self mastery becomes apparent. No one is the *consummate* Martial Artist. No one is a *complete* Master. As Master Harold Long reminds us, "I have a lot more to learn, Dr. Aiello. There is a lot more to go. Just because I am a tenth Dan does not mean I do not learn from everybody." He demonstrated that a tenth Dan is not immortal. They are just further down the Path, still working, still growing.

M. BRILL '96

Chapter 2

The Four Aspects of Karate

In any Martial Art that uses Heiho in their training regimen the uniqueness of each style or system is exhibited in the result: the students. In the practice of traditional Arts like Shito Kan Karate Do or Isshin Ryu Karate Do the basis for practice is practical, applicable and can integrated in to one's life.

In many systems all that is spoken of is side kicks, Kata and Bunkai (practical applications). Rarely are the deeper concepts of Budo brought up. Master Shimabuku left behind his theory and philosophy of Karate Do in a few areas. He left the Code of Isshin Ryu Karate; the Dojo Kun; the twelve differentiating factors of Isshin Ryu, or the twelve key points that separate Isshin Ryu from other styles; and the Isshin Ryu aspects, of which there are four.

In the **History and Evolution of the One Heart Way** by David Euseeff and Millage Murphey, who are Isshin Ryu black belts on the East Coast, the four aspects attributed to Grandmaster Tatsuo Shimabuku are as follows:

1. To develop the mind, the body and the spirit to its fullest extent.

2. To develop self–confidence and gain control of your life.

3. To develop self–discipline, along with self–respect.

4. To develop a way of defending yourself and your loved ones.

Apparently these authors felt it important enough to put these concepts in their book. Most people would read them, think about them for a minute or so and be done with them. One word might catch the attention, however, they apparently were not thought highly enough of to expand upon even in the text that quotes them. They were only listed as four basic concepts, or aspects. If one is to carry on a legacy, one must understand the work from the historical and traditional perspective of what was passed down and of what occurred during and prior to the time it was handed down. Vision into the future, the vision of destiny to determine where to go with a legacy is so important and often forgotten when analyzing the written word. If material is not understood at its very essence it will be of no help in continuing the legacy or keeping the style alive. I have spent many hours, discussing in detail, technique, history and philosophy with many contemporary Masters so that I may better understand where these Martial Arts came from. I have literally spent thousands of hours researching books and texts. I can say that much of what is written, taught and dispensed is off track and it is not accurate. It is deceptive, either by choice or by accident. The people, no matter how high ranking they are and what level master they say they are, somewhere along the line did not grasp it at the core level.

Every great Master that I have read about has had a very similar experience to what I have had. They lock themselves away with their training for years at a time, put blinders on and study the mechanics, the physics, the theory and the application of every technique in their Art. Once it is owned at the level of its essence, then Mastery results. Anything and everything there to learn is within the field and scope of practice for the Martial Arts Master. All of this is then under the aegis to teach once mastery of it is had. The mind is the totality of functions associated with or involving the brain and related nerve cells that deal with the conscious and unconscious process of thought, perception, memory, imagination, will and reason. It is a repository of cognition. This is the scope of practice. The scope of practice for the Martial Arts Master is the universe.

The people who say it takes thirty or forty years to become a master do so because it may have taken them that long. That is their experience, however the Martial Arts are full of people who have grasped the brilliance and essence of the Art in greater or lesser amount of time. Becoming a master is not having technical and physical competence alone and many people claim to be a master with just that. They are part of the group who are off track. Without the philosophy and theory, it is not an Art, it is not a Do or Way for them, it is just a sport or a business. If the practice of the Martial Arts remains in the physical, it is a sport, self defense or it is an exercise regimen and there is nothing wrong with that. However, those who do those things can never become great *Martial Arts* Masters. One could call himself a sport champion of a tournament or an exercise guru, but not a Grand Master carrying on a legacy like Tatsuo Shimabuku and Harold Long. The true separation between the paper tigers and someone like Master Long is the fact that he dedicated his entire forty plus years in the Martial Arts to the One Heart Way of Master Shimabuku. His total dedication was to understanding that man, everything that he was taught by him and not veering off the path.

As Master Long and I have had these extended conversations, Master Long feels that I have been able to grasp the exact same essence he has. We concur on the issues of what Master Shimabuku's work was and what it was not. For much of the material, we have concurrence from other Masters. They do not know the Isshin Ryu system or the Shito Kan system, but they agree with the concepts, the theories, the precepts, the Code and the Kun, for those do not change from style to style.

When the Masters spoke of the Martial Arts, that is what they spoke of. There is plenty of time, in other situations, to talk about a side kick, a front kick, or a punch; how one defend one's self; or is this or that Kata right or wrong. To speak of it in terms of philosophy, concepts and theories creates a greater understanding of what exactly Martial Artists do and why.

The people that stay and become great are the ones that grasp it at this level. Physically and intellectually, it is not worth the time and effort to do if it is not done in this way. It is not worth the time spent to compete in Karate tournaments on the weekends for a lifetime, the body cannot keep up over the years. It is not worth the time to work on self–defense this many hours a week. How paranoid can one become? When it is grasped that the essence of Martial Arts and Karate is a way of life, then what philosophers have tried to understand since the beginning of time becomes clear; the meaning of life. The fundamental function and coexistence of all things can be understood through training in the Martial Arts.

This takes a critical analysis of the training being done by each individual. Master Shimabuku's Isshin Ryu Karate Do did not leave simply a regimen for transforming oneself into a strong Karate Ka. It also left a method for transforming one into a morally strong person as well. This is a quote out of the book by Euseeff and Murphey. "He left this message, as well as the means to accomplish this goal through a number of axioms, codes and rules of conduct." Yet, we have rarely heard these discussed by anyone in Isshin Ryu.

Unfortunately for all the Karate Ka (practitioners of Karate) these axioms, codes and rules of conduct are a side note even in the books written about Martial Arts. Euseeff and Murphey further state that these codes, axioms and rules are not universally implemented by Karate Dojo practicing Isshin Ryu. Yet, if they are ignored and only the physical is focused on, then the major part of the Art and Grandmaster Shimabuku's vision and legacy are lost. This means that they are only doing part of Isshin Ryu. One cannot say that they are doing Isshin Ryu if they just do one of the Kata, or Chart One or Chart Two. They are doing the physical part of Isshin Ryu, but not all of Isshin Ryu. They are not practicing the legacy of Isshin Ryu, the heritage of Master Tatsuo Shimabuku.

Tatsuo Shimabuku's son, Kichiro Shimabuku, the current Okinawan Grandmaster of Isshin Ryu and Master Angi Uezu have agreed that very few Americans have grasped the essence of the One Heart One Mind Method. Isshin Ryu is the One Heart One Mind Method. It does not say One Fist. It does not say the Ikken Hissattsu (one blow, one kill) Method. It says "The One Heart One Mind Method," yet those aspects are rarely discussed.

A Critical Analysis of the Aspects of Isshin Ryu

Aspect #1: To Develop the Mind, Body and Spirit: The intent here will be to explore the concepts while analyzing them from the perspective of purposeful integration. These four aspects do no good unless they can be integrated into life activities.

The first of the four aspects of personal development is: *To develop the mind, body and spirit to its fullest extent.* The term "develop" is used in all four of these aspects. To develop the mind, to develop self–confidence, to develop self–discipline and to develop a way of defense.

> Definition #1. To bring into existence or into activity.
> Definition #2. To change something or someone gradually through successive stages or periods.
> Definition #3. To bring to a more advanced state and cause to grow or expand.
> Definition #4. To bring into activity.

How many people bring thoughts of their *mind, body and spirit* into existence or into activity in their daily lives? How many people are changing something or someone gradually through the successive stages of training? One of the definitions, *to bring to a more advanced state*, causes one to question the goals of those who today are practicing Isshin Ryu Karate and the Martial Arts in general. Have we seen advancement in the Art of the One Heart, One Mind Method in this country? Ask any ten Masters, most will say that Martial Arts and Isshin Ryu in particular is extremely stagnant and not understood by most of the people who participate. Therefore, they fail to grasp the second word in the four aspects and should not have gone on beyond this point. How can one be a Master of Isshin Ryu if the basic aspects written by the founder are not known, understood and practiced?

To bring it into activity, does that mean to train regularly? Yes it does. That is an activity. It could also mean to go to a tournament, that is an activity. It could also mean to teach and that is an activity. What is really meant is to live it. We can see by the definition that the word 'develop' would translate well for constructive purposes as well as for other purposes. It applies to these four aspects of Isshin Ryu when specifically paired with the second part of the aspect, the thing to be developed.

To develop the mind, body and spirit to its fullest extent is the first aspect. That is powerful and much more profound than just several simple words would indicate. "Fullest extent" means personal excellence. This implies much more than just one or two days of training on a physical activity per week. If one could only commit to two days a week, the "fullest extent" achieved is going to be the meager. That would be more likely, only developing the body alone. The aspect states, *mind, body and spirit.* What was Tatsuo Shimabuku referring to when he said "mind?" This man, on the island of Okinawa, who had never been off the island and trained with these other Masters who had never been off the island either except to China. What was the mind according to Tatsuo Shimabuku? Was he referring the physical brain? We know there is a physical brain, it can be dissected. What Grandmaster Shimabuku was referring to was the motive force behind the body. He was speaking about character, thoughts and intentions.

Of course, we assume that these were Grandmaster Shimabuku's precepts to personal development. These were important enough to him to make sure that somebody wrote these down and understood that this was what he wanted to pass on as part of his legacy, his heritage and his understanding of Budo. If they were important to him, they should be important to us because we cannot go beyond him until we understand everything that he did. When I go back to understand a great Master like Tatsuo Shimabuku, Sokon Matsumura, Yasutsune Itosu, Kanryo Higashionna, or even masters of Chiropractic like B.J. Palmer,

D.D. Palmer, Clay Thompson and Russell Erhardt, I study and contemplate every word they wrote. Then I apply the techniques over and over. What did he mean by that? How could that work? Why? What was he thinking? I think about it. I dream about it. I visualize it. I try it. I analyze it until I grasp the essence.

When someone writes something, there is a Isshin Denshin, direct transmission put on the paper. One can grasp their direct transmission just like the Kanji written by these Masters. Words exude Ki, or energy, with their meaning. To master what is said by those who have gone before, the Sensei, one must understand and define the words clearly and specifically. They must be analyzed and applied and cross examined. The trashy articles that appear in some journals, the "Enquirers" of the Martial Arts world, lack this type of understanding of the words and their meanings. The authors are expounding upon superficial levels of understanding and they are not credible sources or masters, regardless of their rank. They are merely physical experts, aerobic wizards, fitness gurus, or partial practitioners of the Martial Arts.

The higher level the Master, the more polite they are and the more active their mind is. Those who claim to be Masters have gaps in their reigisaho (etiquette) and have a much narrower scope of thought.

In this first aspect of Grandmaster Tatsuo Shimabuku we see the conventional *mind–body–spirit* triad. Is this meant as a separation of mind, body and spirit? Many Martial Artists discuss the concepts of mind, body and spirit. Why do they speak of these things as if they are separable within the human being? Would not development of one's self to the fullest extent be satisfactory?

Certainly, incorporating the concept of spirit reaches into the potential realm of mysticism. We constantly have people claim that as Martial Artists we are mystics. Spirit is defined in mystical or religious terms as that part of man, believed to be immortal, which enters at birth (or conception, depending upon the philosophy) and separates from the body at death. The non–mystical definition would be that spirit is the animating, fundamental, or vital principle of man; the breath of life. The Japanese call this Ki, intrinsic energy. The concepts of the mind, body and spirit have the potential to open many subjective and emotional doors with many hallways and rooms filled with mysticism. This need not be the case. One need to go back to the beginning of the first conscious thought; the memory. Analyze how the thoughts have matured to where they are today. Who influenced one and what was their foundation of thinking? Thoughts that are not based on a solid foundation need to be evaluated and if they are not true, they need to be disposed of.

For the Martial Arts to be understood and for it to grow it must be analyzed on the basis of objective, rational metaphysics. This is where the physical meets the philosophical. Where the gap is bridged between the intellect and the body and where the concept of *mind, body and spirit* are put back together. There are mystics, gurus and shaman teaching Martial Arts. They continue to wallow in subjectivity and the practitioners of these "arts" will be farther from understanding themselves and the universe with each step they take. We cannot condemn an entire worldwide phenomenon, the Martial Arts that are based on objective premises because a few do not approach it from that aspect. We must focus our energy, effort and time on that which we know exists. We cannot live our lives on hearsay and innuendo, or emotional, irrational and mystical thought processes about our Art.

Unfortunately, many who have read Tatsuo Shimabuku's translated words may have mistook them for the mysticism so prevalent today. The Masters of old pointed out in so many ways and so many times that the foundation of learning and understanding is based upon correct thinking and action. There is not enough time on this planet to spend on erroneous concepts. We must focus our work on concepts that can be shown to be demonstrable and reproducible. Otherwise, it can be trickery, mysticism and deception. That is the direction of the art, science and philosophy of the Martial Arts, correcting one's thoughts and behavior. Not what one sees the Arts portrayed as by those who have *failed* to grasp the essence and have flaunted themselves as Masters only for personal gain. We utilize the concept of the Shito Kan Warrior Spirit to differentiate it from mystical theologies and religions. The concept of Warrior Spirit links the mind and the metaphysical to the physical. The Warrior Spirit cannot be defined as mysticism or cultism. It is the phenomenon of human energy generated from the mind and exhibited in physiological function. The realm of mystical spirituality is a remnant of tribal, pagan occultism. Most educated persons of the twentieth century recognize this primitive approach to explaining certain phenomenon as unacceptable. In the light of modern day physical science, biology and organic chemistry, mysticism is unacceptable to the rational mind.

Objective thinking individuals can easily conclude through a series of deductive evaluations that life is primarily a physical phenomenon and that the function of the mind, the thought process, is bioelectrical and chemical. This does concede the presence of an electromotive force, as Dr. Yang states, within the body. This presents the question of the source of the electromotive force, or Ki, in Japanese. This is the force that pulls all things together in an organized manner.

A Master must assess these concepts as a scientist with the laboratory of the body and of the training experience. If one seeks greatness, he must have an analytical mind. It is necessary to be a philosopher like Aristotle or Ayn Rand. They used their minds. They knew they existed and they acknowledged that there was a mental activity. Most people go through their lives and never think, "I have a mind." It is amazing that a person can come and go on this planet and not think about their mind, the electromotive force within the brain, about Ki and how to direct it properly. It is sad, because we all have relatives, friends and ancestors who came from dust and returned to dust and never thought about their mind.

The evident misrepresentation or misunderstanding of the first aspect of Grandmaster Shimabuku is apparent in the condition of Isshin Ryu today. There is very little personal excellence practiced and even less focus on the development of Warrior Spirit. The physical is all that seems to be accentuated. This form of dissection from the mind and body is not acceptable as a philosophical paradigm in the future for those wishing to become Masters. Moreover, I believe that it is not what Grandmaster Shimabuku intended with his four aspects. It is not appropriate to say "mind, body and spirit" unless it is used in the proper context.

Many people want to go further in their mysticism. There are people going off to Indonesia, India, China and to the South Pacific studying pagan mysticism and confusing it with Martial Arts. They want mysticism. They want to believe that someone can instill a power in them that is supernatural and that there is going to be something that Grandmaster Shimabuku, Master Long and Master Nagle, along with other great Masters in this country, have not discovered in their forty or fifty years of study and effort.

Ryu Ryu Ko, of the Fukein Province in China is no longer alive. The Masters that Chojun Miyagi, Kanryo Higashionna and Sokon Matsumura studied under are dead. They cannot be asked about these things directly. We cannot go in search of their knowledge by asking them. It came to this country with the people who are the current leaders. They not only have the knowledge that was passed on to them, they also have the thirty to fifty years they worked on the Art. Know the past and the tradition, but also see the future, where it needs to go and then build on it scientifically, not through mysticism.

We must conclude that the mind, body and spirit must be developed as a unit concurrently. Even though we have mind, body and spirit, they cannot be separated and remain human life. They have to function together as a unit. If they function together as a unit, one should be able to develop them as a unit and they will stay in balance. We can conclude that the physical training will strengthen the body, alter the chemistry, stimulate the reflexes and neurology, catalyze chemical biochemistry and increase blood flow, resulting in stimulation of brain gray matter activity. The increased brain activity may result in greater intelligence of the individual if he is able to harness the capacity.

This can all occur, however, it is the Master who harnesses it and creates a legacy in the Martial Arts so that others can learn to do the same. Think all the great thoughts in the world. If nothing is done they are not worth a dime. They only exist beyond the thinker's lifetime if something constructive and positive is done with them. They are a figment of the imagination until they make physical and tangible impressions upon the world; until action is put behind them. The individual has to harness the capacity of thought through a process of focus.

This is why Makiwara (striking post) is so critical to Martial Artist. Only a small percentage of Martial Artists include Makiwara in their training. It is the greatest tool for focus that exists in the Dojo. Can someone who does not include Makiwara in their training accomplish the focus that is needed to harness the internal energy force and nuclear power of the body to the fullest extent of the mind, body and spirit? No. That is why all the great Karate Masters did Makiwara.

It is the same premise for a Shinai (bamboo practice sword). It is used worldwide to create greater consciousness at the right time with the right intention. A Shinai will help maintain focus if used properly. Just as with the Makiwara board, if it is misused, it can cause damage. Turning thoughts into action requires great focus. This is the proper equation for constructive activity. Action without correct thought is a concept with dire results.

This means that one cannot be a victim of one's thoughts. By not following the aspects, such as laid down by Grandmaster Tatsuo Shimabuku one could easily achieve a victimized thought process. One can train and choose to use the mind destructively, or one can train and choose to use the mind constructively. Karate and Martial Arts training cannot make the determination for the student. Martial Arts are inanimate and controlled by the practitioner. Some people think, "I will train and *it* will answer all my questions." *It* will not answer any questions. Martial Arts training has the potential to increase the capacity to think through an issue and arrive at proper conclusions, even to arrive at the correct questions to ask. It will not arrive at a conclusion or answer questions, that still remains for the thinker to achieve. This, as anything worthwhile, will take time and effort on the part of the seeker. Master Shimabuku stated, "If one wants to know something in a short period of time, one will know nothing good."

The Second Aspect of Isshin Ryu: Self Confidence and Control

The second aspect of Karate is *to develop self–confidence and gain control of your life.* Confidence means a firm trust or reliance in oneself and having feelings of excessive self assurance or boldness. There is no doubt about one's ability or worth. Confidence and esteem go hand in hand. In attempting to analyze the four aspects of Karate and looking at developing self–confidence and gaining control over one's life, we must put these into functional and applicable perspectives.

One way to develop self–confidence is to work hard and develop physical and mental skills. This is what the Martial Arts have done for many people by providing a vehicle for the application and achievement. The more highly skilled a person is, the more valuable they become to themselves and others. It is also necessary to keep self–confidence in perspective. This is done by qualifying values and by instituting a system of mental self checks and balances. Martial Arts provide a most effective system for the achievement of this goal. Many people assume that because they think it is, it is. This is, as we know, not necessarily true.

A person who has his personal values set at a high level, but has no skills to validate his own beliefs, is not functioning in a state of reality. We often recognize these people as those who believe the world owes them a living. They are in a fantasy world and have set no method of checks and balances to see if they are thinking clearly. These individuals cannot gain control over their lives because they have not identified the reality of the nature of the universe. They do not think clearly and it reflects in their actions. Once an individual succeeds in this process, the confidence is greatly enhanced by the successes achieved. This is practicing Martial Arts with Heiho. The strategy of goal setting to achieve control, self–confidence and greatness. *Achievement* increases confidence and confidence increases the chance for success. Karate provides many opportunities for achievement and ultimately the building of confidence.

In order to take control of life one must have focus. *Focus* is the ability to direct the mind and concentrate energy for long periods of time on one subject or idea. Present time consciousness is essential for success. Taking control of one's life indicates a degree of self–reliance and the capacity to work or produce, the creation of value. *Capacity* is the ability to complete a certain amount of work. Each person's physical capacity is unique and dependent upon their physiological structure and psychological makeup.

Laying a foundation for success is critical if one is going to gain self–confidence and control in one's life. This requires the ability to follow through. Consistently laying the foundation for success must be based on reality, not fantasy. The laws of the universe such as the laws of cause and effect, the law of identity, etc. must be confronted and understood fully for the foundation to be laid. Those who remain subjective, emotional thinkers and refuse to realize that reality can and does exist outside of their own consciousness, can and will continue to fool themselves about who and what they are. Success will be elusive to them and control will be an unattainable mystery. Unless there is a series of accomplishments resulting from well laid plans, all will be arbitrary.

The concept of *creating opportunity* is something that most people do not know exists. This concept that one makes things happen in their lives, rather than letting things happen to them, is perhaps considered but rarely acted upon. Some may *feel* they are due certain opportunity, without the preparation. This is what occurs when a person is raised to their level of incompetence. This frequently happens in the Martial Arts. Many students would like to move up a belt rank, but perhaps they do not want to attend all the classes necessary, perform the academic and scholastic work and make a contribution to their Dojo or Art in the process of gaining the physical skills required for the rank. This is not functioning from reality, but from fantasy.

Associates and Friends

In attempting to increase the capacity, stay on track and achieve the goals, one must not waste time with others who waste time. Karate can be an excellent form of training one's self in time management. In order to gain control over life, one must gain control over the mental process and begin to think objectively. This may require that one analyze those people who are close to determine how much time is being wasted, whether or not they are absorbing the time with nonconstructive activities. It is imperative to stay on track and not lose sight of goals if the desire is to become achievement oriented.

Objective thinking requires that the relationship between reality and thought be consistent. The system of personal checks and balances with which to test physical performance, which is a manifestation of the thought process, must be objective. Kata is an excellent opportunity to implement an objective check and balance. Kata, to be done well, must be done well repetitively and consistently. There is no kidding one's self, it is either performed well or poorly. It either gets better or worse, or it stays inconsistent. To be objective has nothing to do with the speed of thought. Obtuse perception can still lead to success if it is based on objective criteria. Being objective has little to do with emotion or self–confidence and everything do with taking the time to analyze and think things through in order to validate them. When one knows he is functioning on valid facts, objectively and consistently, then self–confidence will soar. Being correct and functioning and directing the actions in a correct manner, will lead to more success.

Just because someone is confident does not mean they are right. Often confidence can be misconstrued as cockiness or egotism. Perhaps the more confident one is, the more important it is to be objective. Confident people often conclude quickly and erroneously without checking their premises. Objectivity requires that one do the homework and research. Often Martial Artists, by the nature of the organizational structure of studying (directly from teacher to student), will go by word of mouth or hearsay rather than hard, reproducible facts. Most Sensei will not invite the student to do their own research and self–evaluation before reaching final conclusions. They will say, "This is true because I say it is true." This can be pertaining to a technique which one's life may rely on, or with a philosophy of spirituality, or historical documentation.

Cognitive analysis will eliminate mysticism. In order to be objective one must remove emotional bias from the thought process. When qualifying data, especially when dealing with subjects such as Martial Arts, we must maintain our focus on observable phenomenon and provable facts. Define success before attempting to achieve it. When it comes to personal development this requires certain qualification of values with which to determine the content of success. One must define what success is for one's self. If one constantly changes the goal of success, it will be unrealistic to achieve any tangible goals. People start out with one goal in mind and before they achieve it or fulfill the success in it, they move on to another and then the next. These are the people who become dojo hoppers. They get excited about studying in a system or under a particular teacher. They stay for several months and then lose interest. They find something new to sidetrack themselves with and proceed with this method of self–limiting behavior, moving on to another dojo. This has become very trendy and is gaining in credibility amongst the modernists, or eclectic practitioners, especially those who follow the methodologies taught in the post–Bruce Lee era.

Philosophers Agree: Karate can be Objective

The four aspects of Isshin Ryu Karate Do are said to be: (1) developing the mind, body and spirit to the fullest extent, (2) developing self–confidence and gaining control of one's life, (3) developing self–discipline along with self–respect and (4) developing a way of defending one's self and one's loved ones. There may be only one problem with these four aspects as they are written; they are wordy in their statement yet short in definition. Ayn Rand, the philosopher, being the concise thinker that she was, seemed to have the unique skill of concentrating things down to the essence in words. If one were to ask a Martial Artist to define his philosophy, he would be disturbed by how imprecise and unsure the Martial Artist is in their definitions. Even more disturbing, if one were to ask a Martial Artist about philosophy, they would hear 3203A quotes and Buddhist clich s which are concise and short, but there is no underlying definition within them and most rely on a mystical, riddle–type of logic.

Ayn Rand, when asked about her stances on objectivism, expanded her meanings with some philosophical constructs. For the first construct of Objectivism: *Nature to be commanded must be obeyed,* or *wishing will not make it so.* Second construct: *One cannot have the cake and eat it too.* Third construct: *Man is an end in himself.* Fourth construct: *Give me liberty, or give me death.* Ayn Rand's quick definitions of her philosophy also contained four precepts at its essence, much like Grandmaster Shimabuku's four aspects. The similarities are immediately obvious. Each salient point is a study in itself. It is unfortunate that Grandmaster Shimabuku was not a writer. There is no detailed, recorded source other than him doing the eight Kata on video tape in 1966 in Tacoma, Washington and knowledge passed on from him directly to his students. That is why the patriarchs such as Master Harold Long are sources of information about Tatsuo Shimabuku. Master Don Nagle, Masters Steve Armstrong and Harold Mitchum and others who lived it and acknowledged the information first hand are so important to us today in studying this physical form of philosophy.

Reason and logic, checking the premises through deductive thinking versus inductive thinking. This is the appropriate way to perceive and integrate reality. To control one's life one must be focused on reality. When asked about her philosophy, she stated without hesitation: (1) Metaphysics — objective reality (we would say logic), (2) Epistemology — reason (we would say cognition or perception), (3) Ethics — self–interest (we would call these goals and objectives) and (4) Politics — capitalism.

Mysticism, which is opposite in nature to objectivism, finds its way into the Martial Arts frequently through a subjective thought process and through the structure of teacher–student or master–disciple relationship. Many who would argue for mystical concepts over objective reasoning and logic hide in the inconclusive, improvable elements of circular logic. We see this taught frequently today in the Martial Arts due to a lack of documentation, scientific experimentation and research. One will often hear a speaker say, "It must be because it says so here," quoting a source or teacher. This is circular logic. When there are inconsistencies to the factual aspects of theoretical discussion in the modern, educational setting, we would ask questions. In the Karate Dojo, a Martial Arts setting, it is frequently improper etiquette to ask questions. Therefore, we must place Karate and Martial Arts training into certain areas of study or settings that are conducive for the student to ask questions at the right times so that objectivity can become the basis for learning.

The humble follower of the mystic need not prove himself absolutely, with plausible facts or tangibility. After all, these are humble students, they are just human. They are not at the level of their guru, their shaman or teacher. This attitude only reflects the desire of the students of these people to remain in the dark, out of control and self–limited. Martial Arts must be based on solid rational thought and reason if it is to ever surface out of the feudal era of Japan or the tribalism of the numerous countries from which it comes. We can never accept circular logic or the avoidance of logic. Martial Arts philosophies must be provable and reproducible to be scientific. Whether it be a Kata, Kumite technique or training methodology it must be clear that it is worthless unless it is based on the law of identity. We are dealing with subjectivity in the Martial Arts and what has kept them from gaining the professional status and recognition as valid systems of education. Martial Arts training provides the methods which help increase productivity, develop self–confidence and self–worth in human beings. There are too many followers in the Martial Arts who believe in their guru, mystic or shaman and they put their faith in these people until the point that critical thinking is no longer necessary. They believe in the validity of the statements of the guru and the theories and philosophies involved are taken as absolute.

Martial Artists must research, study, validate and question. This means the acceptance of allegations without evidence or proof is mysticism. The mystic just knows. It is true because his teacher or spirit guide said it is so. This is how many of the mystical masters from Asia, India, Africa and Central and South America claim to have higher forms. Their training and meditation have taken them into some other realm, where they claim they reach a higher self and tap into a source of wisdom that only they are able to access. This claim to a non–identifiable source of knowledge such as the guru's is what makes the impression of the Martial Arts to many people a hoax. We see the interrelationship through many of these systems coming out of countries like Indonesia, where they use channeling and revelation along with meditation. Supernatural knowledge, they say, is received or perceived via some form of unnatural means.

In the pursuit of personal excellence and in following a life of Budo, we are not required to surrender our minds or our ability to identify reality. One must rely on hard work and discipline. There is no other way to reach the true end of self control and self worth. There are no shortcuts in real Martial Arts training, whether it be Shito Kan, Isshin Ryu or any other system.

On the path, following the discipline and constantly striving towards achieving personal excellence one may notice that more and more he is surrounded with like–minded people with nonconflicting goals. The longer we work and the harder we strive, the fewer people we will have around us who are not in accord with this. It becomes much easier to see mystics for what they are and avoid them. They are time wasters and the Budo practitioner will not waste time with people who waste time.

Intellectualizing Karate as a philosophy, practicing the physical Art of Karate and integrating these into life is what Grandmaster Tatsuo Shimabuku was referring to when he spoke of gaining control. When he spoke of self–confidence he meant turning the physical aspects of Martial Arts practice into a productive force to prove the theories and then turning it from theory into a fact. This is the creation of value and it requires action. The ultimate point in the philosophy of Budo and Martial Arts is that they are made up of both action and a science. Tatsuo Shimabuku's precepts and Ayn Rand's theory of objectivism rely on the same laws of nature and universal principles.

Aspect #3 of Isshin Ryu Karate Do: Self–Discipline and Self–Respect

The third aspect is to develop self–discipline along with self–respect. To develop discipline through Martial Arts training we use what is referred to as the power of reflex action or habit formation through proper thinking. Secondary reflexes equal proficient self–defense. This is where our defensive actions come from. When a student first begins Karate, it seems unnatural and difficult to just do a general workout. Somewhere within ninety days, the student realizes that if he or she wants the end result that is perceived (being in shape, wearing a black belt to reflect their abilities and wisdom, etc.), they will have to follow through with the work. Following through for at least ninety days begins a process of positive habit formation and discipline. In the process, the amount of work done will result in rewards in terms of the ability and achievement commensurate with the time, energy and effort put forth. To choose less in return than what is given would mean the value received was not equivalent to that of others who have preceded one and this would be a self–sacrifice.

I once asked Dr. Peter Urban, Patriarch of Goju in the United States, "What did the life of Martial Arts cost you?" He said, "Nothing. There was no loss. This would be a sacrifice. This would be working against the law of compensation." According to Ayn Rand, this basic concept of ethics comes down to self–interest, that every man is an end to himself, not the means to an end of others. Although their theories may not strike the favorable altruistic chord so popular in today's world, as Dr. Urban and Miss Rand point out, it is impossible to argue with objectivity.

In the Martial Arts we train for our own benefit, not for the benefit of others. But in doing so, others benefit from the brilliance of what we do. In a traditional Dojo the pursuit of an individual's own needs and happiness is not reliant on the sacrificing of others. This is consistent with the proper hierarchial structure of the Martial Arts. This does not mean one can circumvent the hierarchal system inherent of ranks and grades, junior–senior, Sempai–Kohai. However, one must be aware that there are unscrupulous mystics, gurus, or shaman.

Master Jigoro Kano, the developer of the ranking system in the Martial Arts, and Grandmaster Tatsuo Shimabuku were focused on knowledge and ability, structure and function and in complying with the laws of the universe. They were aware that these metaphysical principles existed and based their teachings and actions upon them, not the mystical aspects.

It was determined that for the first aspect, to developing the mind, body and spirit to its fullest extent, clear thinking was essential. Developing a thought process and working to fulfill things through controlled processing of material. In the second aspect, to develop self–confidence and the gaining of control of life, we found that we needed to put these thoughts into actions by setting goals and attaining these goals with consistent application of our Karate training. In the third aspect, we are working on developing self–discipline and positive habit patterns along with self–respect by showing ourselves that we are capable of absorbing the material through disciplined applications of training, or approaching it with a structure of learning it in a consistent way so that we have the achievement, we accumulate the material and we can put it into action.

Ayn Rand, in her discussion of the aspects of metaphysics, epistemology, ethics and politics, said her first aspect was objective reality and we said clarified thinking. Secondly, she talked about epistemology, cognition and perception.

Essentially, epistemology is a branch of philosophy, analyzing the origins of nature and methods of validating human knowledge. This means we are taking metaphysics, eliminating the mysticism and putting empirical knowledge to the test. In other words, how do we know that we know? Are the conclusions validated? That is where the vehicle of Karate comes into play. It is a physical means of grounding one's self in reality.

Things like the Makiwara, which we affectionately term the *Board of Wisdom*, give one the reality. I know how to do a vertical punch. Those who practice Makiwara can say, "I know how to stand. I have the knowledge of it. I have the basis and the physiological conditioning. I have the mental set and a state of consciousness for it. I can apply it and if I had to apply this technique in a life or death situation, would I be able to rely on my secondary reflexes to apply it?" Yes or no becomes immediately apparent when one applies the technique on the Makiwara. Then one knows that he is correct because it has been done consistently, day in and day out, through the training. It is through a process of accessing physical application, not by assessing supernatural power that correct action and thought are achieved.

It is important to understand that a system of cognition and analysis combined with reason is crucial in the Martial Arts. There is now a wealth of knowledge available in books and printed material where we can see authors theorizing about the Martial Arts. We are seeing people in the media who will study a little bit and then theorize a lot. They could literally revise history because there are so many accepted systems and approaches to it, few being of objective quality.

Despite those who would keep Martial Arts under the veil of mysticism, it will become apparent that there is a standard methodology for reaching success in the Martial Arts. The requirement of analyzing the methods and validity of the techniques involved and the educational material and philosophical nature involved will come down to the field of epistemology. This is where someone's work like Ayn Rand's is indispensable to the study of the Martial Arts because Martial Arts are daily life. They are integrated into daily activities for one to be a successful practitioner of Budo. So is the process of reason and the study of epistemology.

Reasoning indicates a power of faculty to think logically, draw conclusions and to make references. Today we are seeing Martial Arts zealots coming out of peripheral, obscure systems and inculcating us with mystical beliefs, philosophy and background which the average person may think is not based on sanity. These people appear mentally deranged and not capable of knowing right from wrong. They lack the values and the codes of ethics and behavior that are inherent in the Budo systems. This changes how we approach the Arts that we do. The consequences of their actions are not realized by these individuals because they are not functioning from a state of rational thought process. They have to be warped in their thinking or under the influence of drugs to maintain the beliefs that are inherent in some of these systems.

If we have a basic concept built on a lack of knowledge and experience, all plausible results and consequential conclusions will be faulty. This is what we see in these individuals. Their basic concepts are flawed about the Martial Arts. They have not put in enough years and have not been steeped in the basic training long enough. The philosophy without the technique put into action and the physiological changes that occur through years of the training, invalidate the theories.

The cognitive analysis and epistemological evaluation of a thought process, of an idea or a concept, disproves skeptics and disarms the mystics. Being cognizant, perceiving, knowing and proving the premises, has an effect that will be different than if one eliminates the cognition as the mystics would have us do. The result would be an attempt to accept consciousness as reality without evaluation. Reality would not exist outside of consciousness. The consciousness would become the reality, even if it was based on faulty premises. In the study of Karate Do, one should receive realistic rewards for the contribution, physically, financially and intellectually and then be able to integrate the concepts and theories and put them into action. One must have an action plan, not just a group of kicks and punches that one approaches every day. This is why one joins a Ryu Ha, or a style or a system of Karate Do and not just train with somebody down the street who works out in their backyard or their basement.

In Okinawa in the nineteenth century it was acceptable to teach in the backyard. The backyards were the Dojo. Even in the early 1950's, when there was no such thing as Dojo, the GI's like Master Harold Long, were taught in a back or front yard. Today, programs that are ill–defined leave one vulnerable to the whims of the teacher. If one is dealing with a teacher who is not a licensed instructor, if teaching credentials are not authentic and the teacher cannot produce anything more than a black belt certificate, reconsideration should be done as to the credibility of the teaching.

One of the problems in the Martial Arts is people join training centers thinking that they are going to dabble a little. "I will just try a little bit of this and if I like it I will continue on. I will seek a budget program, or a limited program such as a parks and recreation adult education program and if I like that I will go on." That is fine if that program leads to the higher levels, but frequently the instructors who teach in these programs are the ones that have not been able to be successful and who have not achieved very high levels of Mastery. Therefore, the student falls into the system and never rises up to the levels of excellence and standards that are possible and that one would expect out of professional instructors. At one time, in the 1960's and 1970's, these "low budget" programs were more acceptable. One should think twice about getting involved in these programs. Seek out a professionally qualified Sensei who has teaching licenses from a recognized organization or Sensei. Ill–defined programs lead to poor quality of physical and mental growth and educational frustration by both the student and the teacher, the Seito and the Sensei.

Guidelines for requirements for each level of performance should be available to the student, just as in college. For any degree, the course work is predefined and placed within a course catalog. For example, one may have to take thirty–five different classes to reach an associates degree, seventy–five classes for a B.A. degree, 150 for an M.B.A. and 200 courses to reach the doctorate. In addition, one has internships, clinical experience and adjunctive studies. This is the way Martial Arts should be approached. When a student looks at the Martial Arts, how are they going to make a sound, intelligent decision based on facts if there are no facts? This teacher says he is going to do this and that. How does he prove this? Does one spend ten years with this individual to find out? Where is the product? Some programs are designed to be just entry level. However, when one seeks a college degree with the intention to continue on and become a doctor, one does not seek the budget, lowest common denominator program at entry level, with plans to further pursue the doctoral knowledge somewhere else. Books, tapes, course work sheets and a required reading source list should all be available as well as a curriculum vitae of the instructor. There should be a traceable Keizu, or history and tradition of the instructor, including lineage and heritage. One can then compare and contrast the program with other programs.

The Fourth and *Final* Aspect: Self Defense

Going further into the aspects of Isshin Ryu Karate, number four regards the most physical and simplistic of them all. *To develop a way of defending one's self and loved ones.* Self defense can be taken, according to Dr. Peter Urban, patriarch of U.S.A.. Goju Ryu Karate Do, as survival. We can look at the self defense situations, one–on–one, or we can look at global war, as Miyamoto Musashi did in his book **Go Rin No Sho**. One could also look at surviving on a day–to–day or year–to–year basis. One can look at it financially, making a living to meet one's needs. At any level, Karate and Martial Arts philosophy teaches survival and encompasses all levels of survival. Not just of personal self defense. The theory involved in a training program should evolve as one goes up in the rank to higher levels of knowledge. This is the ultimate test of Martial Arts Mastery and the Sensei's knowledge and teaching ability. Karate and Martial Arts should be a course in survival in today's world. Not only the knowledge on how to survive, but how to adapt to changing social, political and financial environments.

Again we see common ground with Ayn Rand's four aspects in defining the essence of her philosophy of Objectivism. Her fourth principal was politics, i.e. capitalism. This is the financial infrastructure involved in a society. She summarized and defined this fourth point very clearly as "Give me liberty or give me death." This is what Warrior Spirit exemplifies and is the total culmination of all that we do as Martial Artists practicing Budo.

Many people today deny having any political inclinations. They will say, "I hate politics," not realizing that this in itself is a political statement. In the United States we see a trend towards **victim status** thinking. This is an immoral, valueless approach to life. It allows criminals to take the high ground morally over those who are productive in society. This is a crime against humanity and peace.

The true criminals are the altruists and the liberalists, those who advocate any form of taxation of others' production. Globalism and redistribution of wealth are crimes against the individual, who as Miss Rand pointed out *is* the largest minority. Individualism is not an ethnic nationality, it is not a religion. It is the individual and we must never forget that the individual right must reign supreme over any collective. Otherwise, the individual will continue to be an unwilling and sanctioning participant in their own enslavement. This will be true as long as altruism, liberalism, taxation and globalism are allowed to flourish under the guise of helping the victims. This is done through edict and governmental control, all under the guise of *protecting* the millions of nameless victims of society. Any law which infringes upon an individual's ability to have an autonomous existence for the person's own self–interest is a crime against humanity and freedom. We must never lose sight of this. Give me liberty, or give me death.

Those who preach antislavery, but place taxation on productive individuals, are masking the preaching of slavery to meet their own purposes. Slavery of body or mind, intellect or physical and any type of confinement or punishment by social or political edict by placing limitations on individuals is a form of political corruption. Ayn Rand states that the ideal state of political economics is laissez faire capitalism. This sounds simple and straight forward but it contains the necessary components for ultimate survival.

In the United States today we may see the government outlaw the Dogu, or traditional Okinawan weapons used in the Martial Arts. They may indirectly outlaw certain forms of contests by practitioners or certain forms of training by eliminating tools necessary for the training. Whether it be books, educational materials, radio shows, television, pay per view appearances of individuals, or outright banning of certain Arts, it is on the verge of occurring in this country. They may also use zoning to keep individuals out of certain areas, not allowing them to lease buildings for the teaching and education of their Arts. We see a parallel to the feudal era of Japan and Okinawa where the Okinawan people were overtaken and it was demanded that they cease using all forms of weapons and Martial Training. It is only capitalism that will keep this type of oppressive legislation from coming into being. It is only the capitalistic ideals that will allow the individual to survive and have the means of survival in the future.

Capitalism is the only system of economics appropriate for the survival and to further the happiness of the individual. In traditional Budo Martial Arts systems the capitalistic structure is in place; everyone starts at the bottom, everyone pays and everyone works. Anyone who does these things gets the rewards equal to their efforts. This is the hierarchial matrix upon which Martial Arts seniority is based. Not seniority based upon time alone, as is found in the union mentality of today, but one where a consistent amount of work and application, knowledge and ability, structured into layers so that one can rise up and get recognition exists. This is the original process of the belt ranking Dan–Kyu system. To thwart those who would just put in time, show up in the training center and expect to receive accolades for theiru mere presence.

Master Tatsuo Shimabuku and other founders of Karate Do lived in a different state of society and political government. Many of the Martial Arts came out of very oppressive and feudalistic systems. Therefore, their perspectives on politics are far removed from our current process of politics and socialization. However, they had similar results as we have here in the United States today: oppression of the individual for purposes of those with higher levels of force. The Martial Artists devised a system by which they could protect themselves from this oppression. In the work force we work for perceived rewards. Perceived rewards in the Dojo are the belt ranks and the status that goes along with it. But even in the Dojo it is not permissible to use physical force against somebody if one is not a willing participant. There are consistent guidelines within the philosophy of Budo, which means to stop conflict, and the capitalistic ideals.

On a personal level, or on a global level, there are guidelines and restraints that we must use voluntarily. After the United States dropped the bombs on Hiroshima and Nagasaki during World War II, there was a general global thought that the U.S.A. had gone too far. The debate still continues today on whether it was necessary to destroy so many unwilling participants as a means to reach our ends. It has caused years and years of contemplation.

Likewise, in the Dojo during Kumite, there are guidelines and rules. There are lines that one does not step over, where one becomes violent in behavior rather than controlled in demeanor. During Kumite, in which two people voluntarily participate in matching techniques, they are expecting the other individual to respect their personal rights and not to infringe on them by breaking the rules or going beyond in aggressiveness. This is practicing Budo. If someone goes beyond and gets excessively violent or aggressive, or attempts to cause injury in what should be a in a non-volitional situation, then that person subjects themselves to disciplinary action, possibly dismissal from the Dojo. We have seen this occur in situations where tempers fly and self control is not used. In Shito Kan, Isshin Ryu, or any Budo system we are attempting to control ourselves with discipline and self-respect while maintaining control. This produces the Warrior Spirit, yet keeps it at a level that is moral and just. Guidelines for Kumite in the Dojo are standardized, where on the street it is a different set of rules and conditions. There, it is the rules of no rules. One must be well-versed in these. Behavior that is acceptable on the street is not acceptable in the Dojo. In war, certain acts of violence are acknowledged as acceptable that would not be justified on the streets of a general society in the United States. This must be well thought out by every practitioner of the Martial Arts. One must stay within the constraints of the law, but still act in the cause of justice, liberty and individual rights at all costs.

The hierarchial structure of the Dojo only remains intact to preserve and protect the individual's rights who train there. There is no free ride in the Dojo. Individual rights are the right to work, produce and own what is produced; not the right to welfare, not the right to automatic ranks, not the right to buy a belt rank, not the right to not do Soji (cleaning of the Dojo) and not the right to not have to turn around one day to teach a class and pass on the knowledge. A ranking structure only works when there is a consistent environment of reason, logic and adherence to the objective process. Ayn Rand recognized that under a political structure, if one removes the ability to live and produce for one's self then there remains no personal freedom. Also, without proper economics, one lacks the resources to survive and defend one's self. When looking at this fourth aspect of Grandmaster Shimabuku, Martial Arts training is at the most primal level of survival. When all else is lost, one always has the physical skills to rely on. The inherent value of the Martial Arts at the core level is always personal survival.

When it comes to the right of self defense, we are faced with the consideration of laws and governmental intervention. Politics play a role in self defense and the right to protect one's self, loved ones and property. Having the complications of a judicial system run by advocates of socialistic viewpoints and governmental intervention results in policy that states that as an individual one does not have the right to defend one's self with swift and permanent punishment being administered upon the felon. The right to self defense extends also onto the level of property and country. In this country, the individual has lost his property rights. In most states there are property taxes, which are an infringement on the right to full ownership of property. It is another word for leasing or renting the property from the state. The loss of private property ownership and the ultimate, exclusive right to the property, including mineral rights, content and air passage rights, is infringement on us as individuals and is an outright assault on individualism.

In addition, each country's rights to self–protection entail considerable discussion raising the methods in questions relative to the self–determination of nations and the right to maintain its freedom autonomously from other nations. Regardless of whether it is an individual, a state, a city, or a country, the right of self protection does not include the freedom to commit criminal acts or to violate the rights of others. Unfortunately today many law abiding, tax paying citizens are beginning to feel their own country is violating the rights of its citizens, stating that in the cause of justice it is a "moral imperative" to place restrictions on segments of its population. The individual's rights and the corollary ability to defend themselves, comes down to survival. Self defense infers protecting the life. "Give me liberty, or give me death," as Ayn Rand was quoted, is quite a striking gesture for one who did not practice Martial Arts, but understandable from someone who lived in repression in a communist country. To most Martial Artists the concept of self defense may first appear to entail only defending oneself from an obvious attack of a punch, kick, knife or gun. However, underlying the right to defend one's life is the right and ability to earn a living and the right to own property. If someone assaults the right to earn a living or the right to own property, they are assaulting our life just as surely as if they try to punch us in the nose. If one tries to develop self–discipline, self–respect, self–confidence and gain control of life, but he has someone removing perhaps 40%, 50%, or 60% of what he earns involuntarily via taxes, his efforts will be thwarted. The greatest assault from which one must protect one's self from today is not necessarily the thug on the street who will steal his wallet, but the thug in the bureaucracy who will steal the means of having a wallet and all that it would ever be filled with.

Others cannot own the body as their personal property. The body is the ultimate personal property. Oppression and repression begins with a taxation on the personal property, then moves to rules, restrictions and guidelines on what one can and cannot do. Since all material goods and land are earned by using physical and mental labor, any form of wealth is a byproduct of the individual's labor and therefore should be regarded as part of that individual. This is proven by the law of cause and effect. Study this carefully. The act of extracting the intelligence and physical products of an individuals labor may not take the form of physical shackles or slave ownership papers, but it exists today in greater mass than ever before. We, as Martial Artists, must recognize these individual rights or we will eventually lose the right to practice our Art as has been done in every Asian country in the past. History repeats itself. Most Martial Artists are busy fighting what they call "political battles" between themselves. While Martial Artists are busy being jealous of each other and vindictive against one another, fighting the battle to conquer and become king of the mole hill, their rights are being usurped right out from under their noses. Soon they will be prohibited from continuing their Martial Arts as they see fit. "Society" under the direction of an "action group" will soon define Martial Artists as overly aggressive and violent and push for legislation that controls or eliminates them. Although this may sound radical and extreme, there is a tremendous amount of precedence and case history to verify and validate this potentiality. By allowing the media to define what the Martial Arts are we sanction their right to condemn what we do and control our actions. By condoning others who redefine the Martial Arts, blurring the edges and reconstructing the philosophy of Budo, we contribute to our own demise. Martial Arts do not need state, federal, city or any other kind of regulation. The Martial Arts need laissez faire, free enterprise capitalism. They need the Dojo infrastructure, the apprenticeship systems and the hierarchial structure known for centuries. Teaching certifications and ranking systems should come from the autonomous associations which have built their organizations through their own labor.

The only correct way for one individual to obtain goods or services from another is by mutual consent. The individual must come in and purchase training in the Dojo on an apprenticeship basis, keeping all Dojo Kun (policies and procedures) intact. This is the moral, ethical approach to individual freedom in life. It is known formally as laissez faire capitalism. If we begin the process of federal funding for Martial Arts programs, or subsidized programs through the government, then we are going to have the federal, state, local or city governments dictating what is taught in these programs. We are already seeing this process evolve. The parks and recreation and adult education programs have compromised their training. They have compromised their educational material. They have to standardize their materials to the university level acceptance of what other *sport programs* are. Therefore, we have the adult education and park and recreation programs that are government funded and subsidized by accrediting bodies which have no recognizable status to accredit the Martial Arts. No governmental agency in the United States, or any where else, has the authority to accredit Martial Arts training. Only the Soke, the familial patriarch and founder of a style, has the authority and knowledge to license and accredit his program. They may voluntarily form associations for the recognition of their fellow Martial Artists for their own edification, standardization and fulfillment of furthering their Martial Arts training.

When the freedom and the rights to labor and thought are infringed upon, it is every bit as much of an assault as would be a robber holding a gun to one's head. When one hears about the growing need for Martial Artists to be more aware of their surroundings for their own protection, be aware that this goes much deeper than having a defense for an assault on the street. Martial Artists must expand their consciousness, not by submitting the mind to mysticism or by wasting the time with pure materialism of technique. Those who fail to grasp a bigger picture of what the great Martial Arts leaders and masters like Tatsuo Shimabuku, Gichin Funakoshi, Morihei Ueshiba and Jigoro Kano were expressing, may find they will no longer have the right to defend themselves, their loved ones and their property.

A Final Analysis of the Four Aspects of Isshin Ryu Karate Do

The "trichotomy" of the mind, body and spirit is one of theoretical notions used for exploitation by the mystics and should only be considered of value to those who train in the Martial Arts for definitional purposes. Dividing the human being into parts and considering any one of these as more important than another is disintegration and is therefore detrimental to the result we are attempting to achieve by training in the Martial Arts. Our spirit and mind could not exist without our body and the body would have no animating force, character or will without the spirit and mind.

Grandmaster Shimabuku's first aspect of Karate Do was to *develop the mind, body and spirit to the fullest extent.* He was specific in naming the parts of the human being that he considered essential to develop, i.e. all of it. But it was necessary to name them, for without being specific and including the mind and spirit many practitioners would and do concentrate only on the body. Without the mention of the body, the mind and spirit would be the only emphasized parts and the body then becomes weak and ineffective. There is balance necessary for one to become competent as a human being and this is seen so poignantly in the Martial Arts.

The second aspect, *to develop self–confidence and control over life* describes the process which should occur to youngsters early on in life, but unfortunately often does not. In Martial Arts training, we expect this to happen early on in the life of the student. In the Shito Kan Karate Training Centers there is an analogy drawn between the human developmental stages of infancy, childhood, teen years, early adulthood and adulthood and the developmental stages of training. First you learn to sit up, then crawl, then walk and finally run. Throughout these stages you learn to have self–confidence. This is very similar to the concept in the third aspect of self–respect, however this is much more fundamental. There must be a certain amount of security and confidence created within the student for him to desire to go on in the grueling task of forging a Martial Artist out of himself. The mechanism to have control over one's life must come early on in the training. Prioritizing life activities and time management are parts of the young Martial Artists repertoire. Without this initial phase of control, no commitment can be made and no true goals can be set and achieved. Having this first stage of control over life is essential for the Martial Artist to gain ultimate control over all aspects of his life.

The third aspect is *to develop self–discipline and self–respect*. This is key to becoming a fully self–actualized human being. Being productive and happy come from having the ability to be self directed such that plans are laid and goals are attained. Self–respect is that which occurs from having a deep knowledge of who and what we are and knowing that we fit into the world as an integral part, that we have the *right* to be here and to live. Self–respect is fostered through the Martial Arts and Karate training by achievement and mastery.

The fourth aspect is one which has gained much of the attention given to Martial Arts. To *develop a way to defend one's self and loved ones*. This is such an incredibly complex concept, much more so than perhaps even Grandmaster Shimabuku imagined. One's life, liberty and ownership of one's productive force and result are at stake here when speaking about the defense of life. For what is it really that we defend when we keep ourselves from physical harm at the hands of perpetrators of personal crime? Of what point would it be to protect that which we love and value, our own life and that of those around us, if we had no means by which to enjoy it or live it to the fullest? It is the particular means of defense that we learn in the Martial Arts and Karate, but it is through Budo training that we see the deeper aspect here, that of personal liberties and freedom.

Chapter 3

The Twelve Key Points of Isshin Ryu Karate Do

There are twelve key points which identify the differences and nuances of Isshin Ryu. When Tatsuo Shimabuku founded the system of Isshin Ryu he was in a research and development mode of thinking and evaluating his technique in the Martial Arts. He studied principally with Chotoku Kyan, Chojun Miyagi and Choki Motobu. There were others, such as Gajoko Chioyu and Urshu Matsumura who taught Shimabuku. Grandmaster Shimabuku made the decision to express himself with what he had learned. He was going through the Shu Ha Ri process and in the Ri stage is where he formed the Isshin Ryu system. His Sensei were passing away and the era was post–World War II. When Master Shimabuku developed his techniques of Isshin Ryu, he found some things to be universally true of Martial training. These are the Twelve Key Points of Isshin Ryu:

1. The elimination of fancy and frivolous techniques.
2. Isshin Ryu was a combination of Shorin Ryu and Goju Ryu.
3. The kicks of Isshin Ryu were all low kicks. Some Sensei, essentially the sport–minded teachers, attempt to get the kicks higher to look impressive. This is very dangerous for defense.
4. Short, natural stances. There had been a trend in Karate to get very wide Zenkutsu Dachi and Kokutsu Dachi stances. The older systems of Karate from Okinawa had shallow stances. The Chinese, very flowery in their application, had different geographical territory and therefore had low, wide stances. The Japanese, who were sports orientated after the 1920's, developed very low stylized stances in the university systems of Karate.
5. Equal use of hand and foot techniques. For instance, Korean stylists use 80% feet and 20% hands. Master Shimabuku was competent in both and felt it a necessity for a complete Martial Artist to have equal emphasis on the techniques of the hands and feet.
6. Emphasis on close range techniques and closer in fighting.
7. Snap punches and snap kicks.
8. Hard and soft blocking techniques.
9. Blocking with the muscular portion of the forearm.
10. The vertical fist, with the thumb up higher on top of the fist.
11. The vertical punch versus the full reverse punch.
12. Multiple purpose techniques.

Elimination of Fancy Techniques

Over the years and for many reasons, Karate has accumulated many superfluous and obscure techniques, or flashy, fancy techniques. With the elimination of some techniques the meanings of many of the very old Kata were lost. Many of the masters who were killed during World War II in Asia had only a few students and many styles continued to use these techniques, never having been taught their purpose. They just did them for the sake of it. Elimination of many of these techniques was common for this reason. The practicality of this is that there is only so much time in a lifetime to learn this and over a period of thirty or forty years, there is only so much one can absorb. When one starts combining systems, time spent on frivolous material that has no meaning is a waste. This is the evolution of Martial Arts and what Master Shimabuku did when he started forming Isshin Ryu. Grandmaster Shimabuku went through the Kata, step by step, removing the superfluous techniques while maintaining those with practicality. Many of the less utilitarian meanings of the techniques, the Bunkai, were removed. At some time and place, all of the techniques had meaning, depending on the training and the individual. After the war, there was a ban on Martial Arts training. Many of the techniques were disguised in Kata. Grandmaster Shimabuku felt that the hidden techniques were unnecessary when Karate became legal on Okinawa. The hidden techniques, or Kakushite are learned just as are Bunkai. Some of the techniques we are learning may have taken ten years of study in the past for a student to learn.

Isshin Ryu: A Combination of Shorin Ryu and Goju Ryu

Shorin Ryu came from Shuri, Okinawa. The practitioners from Shuri called what they did simply Shuri Te, Te meaning hand. Goju Ryu came from Naha Te, out of Naha, Okinawa. Grandmaster Shimabuku took the techniques from Shorin Ryu that he learned from Chotoku Kyan and Choki Motubu and combined those with the Goju Ryu of Chojun Miyagi. Isshin Ryu only uses eight empty hand Kata, wherein Shito Kan Karate we use twenty-four empty hand Kata. There is quite a difference in the amount of Kata from one system to another. For instance, Uechi Ryu, which is from Naha, Okinawa, used three Kata, however, one would spend approximately three years learning each Kata. If one looks back in the history, it seems that is the correct way, that of combining things that one learned. The foundation of nearly all styles and systems today is that of combinations of other styles.

There are also great differences between Shorin Ryu and Goju Ryu. Shorin Ryu has no defined breathing mechanisms. One does not see deep inhalations and exhalations, In Ibuki and Yo Ibuki, or the Yin/yang breathing that is typical of Sanchin Kata of Goju Ryu. However, the breathing is a natural regulating method and there has been a long battle between Shorin Ryu and Goju Ryu practitioners as to how effective the breathing is and whether one need learn it.

Gichin Funakoshi, in his book <u>Karate-Do Kyohan</u>, stated that Shorin Ryu had faster and lighter, more agile movements than the Shorei Ryu or Naha Te systems, which were heavy, muscular and slow moving. As soon as that was written, there came instant debates as to whether he even knew what he was talking about. The aficionados of the Martial Arts would pick Funakoshi's argument apart most definitively. Eventually, one will study everything in a complete system like Shito Kan Karate Do including Kokyu Ho (breathing techniques), speed and power techniques, Nage No Kata (throwing techniques) and Gyaku Te (joint reversal techniques). All techniques are incorporated in any advanced system if one stays with the Master long enough to learn them.

The Low Kicking of Isshin Ryu Karate Do

The kicking of Isshin Ryu is all low which is indigenous to Okinawa. The Okinawan people were on a sandy island. Being fisherman and agrarian by nature they used stances more like we would use. Where we have ice and snow, they had sand. They did not have firm footing everywhere they went. If they got into a wide stance, their feet would slip out from under them. So they used narrower stances. The Japanese, although they were on an island, had more mountainous areas and their stances were developed more for training in a regimented, systematic military approach. The Koreans use extremely wide stances, as do the Japanese, particularly in sport Karate.

All styles of Karate utilize all kicks, low level, mid-level and high. The exception for an Okinawan would be the kick to the head. The idea would be to lower the body down by kicking the legs out from under the opponent then kick to the head. Most people do not have the flexibility to kick someone's head and this is especially true as we get older. Grandmaster Shimabuku emphasized kicks below the waist. But in reality, although it is translated as a low level kick, it is generally from the floating ribs, from the bottom of the ribs down. Kicking is very effective along the solar plexus and the rib cage. However, when

Grandmaster Shimabuku, who was only approximately 4'11" and 110 lbs., worked with the GI's, a *high* kick for him would be the floating rib. If he worked with someone like Master Long who is over six foot tall, his kicks were waist level on Master Long. The true emphasis in Okinawan Karate is to keep the kicks low for effectiveness.

Short, Natural Stances

In Isshin Ryu the short, natural stances accompany the intent behind the use of low line kicks. More balanced stances are not only for surer footing, but also for faster movement and moving in and out quickly with the use of a simple shuffle step. Grandmaster Shimabuku knew that in a self–defense situation mere seconds would often be the difference between life and death. The stances of Isshin Ryu were designed to put time on the side of the practitioner. Moreover, he found that they worked well with the physique of the Occidental.

All of the Tenshin Waza (body shifting movements) patterns used in Shito Kan Karate are based on maintaining a stable stance with a set gap between the feet. The shorter stances also enable one to get in close quickly. Shito Kan Karate uses an extensive stance pattern. The beginnings of the Shito Kan Tachi Kata began in 1969 and 1970 at the Karate and Judo Schools of America in Detroit, Michigan. I had learned stances in Tang Soo Do from Ricardo Smith, but they were not the classical Tang Soo Do stances. Having been in Special Forces and having had to literally apply his skills physically, he automatically eliminated all of the superfluous material and stayed with effective techniques. At the Karate and Judo Schools of America there was a grouping of seven original stances and three ready stances taught. At that point the Malo Brothers had developed a pattern similar to that which Koei Kan Karate used in their Tachi Kata (stance pattern). When I went to Lansing and opened the first Shito Kan Karate Dojo in 1974 I added more stances that were relative to the Kata that I had developed. Stances are integral to full knowledge of movement, balance, power and speed.

Equal Use of Hand and Foot Techniques

Tang Soo Do uses 80% kicking. Korean Tae Kwan Do, even the Olympic form, uses predominately kicking techniques. The emphasis between hand and foot techniques has always been indigenous to Okinawa. The Chinese use either more hand techniques or more kicking techniques depending on the geographical location from which each style originated. Grandmaster Shimabuku wanted equal emphasis between the use of hand and foot techniques. Most people would agree that in practical application this is very wise. Many systems emphasize that which came easy or best to its founder. This is where we find the great imbalance in some systems of training, leaving the student without knowledge or experience in valuable techniques. Moreover, it is as important for practitioners to work on their weaknesses as well as strengths. The strengths develop in the course of training, but the weaknesses do not.

Tatsuo Shimabuku developed two technique charts. Chart Number One was the hand techniques and exercises and Chart Number Two was the kicking techniques. The charts incorporated the low kicks and originally there were eight kicking techniques in the charts. But those who studied with Tatsuo Shimabuku personally, like Master Long, report that he did all kicks.

Close Range Techniques

The short stances of Isshin Ryu are very important for shuffling close inside of an opponent's guard and for moving in and out quickly. In teaching smaller people to deal with large people, larger people to deal with smaller people and equal size people to deal with each other the use of Maai (distance) and Riai (timing) are critical. The self defense effectiveness of using those tools and techniques such as elbows, knees and the vertical punch is very evident. Learning to use techniques with the feet and legs to keep opponents at a distance and the hands and elbows when an opponent is very close is one important aspect of Isshin Ryu Karate.

Snap Punches and Snap Kicks

Most of Isshin Ryu's punches and kicks are called snap techniques. The difference between a snap kick versus a thrust kick is how quickly one retracts the kicking leg. With a thrusting kick, one locks the kick and holds it out, focused, for a longer period of time. In the snap kick of Isshin Ryu, the heel is pulled back quicker versus pulling it back in at the same speed that it is kicked out. This speed results in a change in the amount of force applied and also the length of the focal time. One hits and pushes through the object with both types of kicks; the Keage, snap kick and the Kekomi, thrust kick. The thrust kick focuses through the object further and moves in a linear fashion. The snap kick takes more of an arch and has a shorter focal distance into the target.

When we speak of snap kicks, they are faster because they are retracted more quickly. However, the focal point is the shorter depth on the body surface and one has a shorter period of time to work with. One would have this effect with the so–called "snapping" technique of cracking a wet towel. There is a whiplike action versus using a baseball bat to strike, for example, that would be a thrust technique. The force is applied differently and there is a time and place for both. Master Shimabuku wanted to emphasize the speed and snapping, agile movements for Isshin Ryu. With snap kicking techniques the practitioner has to be very accurate and specific, there is less room for error. On the other hand, since the kicks are faster one can get in and out more quickly and safely. The thrusting kick, being more linear and having a great deal of focus is very powerful and devastating, yet is more cumbersome to stop or redirect. It is like the difference between hitting a heavy bag and hitting the makiwara with the technique, each has a purpose and each has its positive aspects.

There is an appropriate time for both the thrust and snap kick. But the ideal kick, just like the balance between hands and feet, is a balance somewhere in the middle between emphasizing all speed versus all power. Each individual has a different body type and nerve fiber structure. There are slow twitch fibers and fast twitch fibers. One must learn to use the best techniques in self defense situations, yet at the same time working the weak aspects in training. If one is fast, he needs to emphasize power. If one is powerful, he needs to emphasize speed and agility. Remember, always work the weaknesses. The strengths will develop on their own over a period of years.

Hard and Soft Blocking Techniques

This is one of the most misunderstood aspects of Karate. Back in the 1960's and 1970's, ten to twenty years after Karate was introduced to the United States, Martial Artists began to discover that there was more than one type of training. As we started to look at each other, this argument of hard and soft came about. Soft, flowing circular techniques were emphasized on the Kung Fu television series and this came to be synonymous with Kung Fu or Chinese Arts. This is how rumors start and why there is so much misconception today about the content of different styles of Martial training. Every system of Karate and every Martial Art has hard techniques and deflective or soft techniques. Every system has linear techniques and every system has circular techniques. Every system has the thrusting technique and every system has the snapping technique. It is how it is emphasized that stylizes the technique into being the most recognizable aspect of each system.

A master in any Art can apply all of the techniques and that was the concept behind Shito Kan Karate Do. We do not know just hard or soft or circular or linear. We know them all, attempt to master them all and to perfect them all. One would not go into a skilled trade, for example carpentry and say, "I am only using a saw and a hammer. I am going to be the best there is with the hammer and that is the only tool that I am using." One needs a level, a plane, ten different screwdrivers, ten different saws and ten different hammers. One needs every tool available. The Karate Ka needs to learn everything about Martial Arts that exists. For every technique, one needs to experiment with it and work with it. In Shito Kan and in Isshin Ryu, there is a system that makes learning the techniques logical and simple. The techniques are set up in a structured system to maximize the learning capacity. They are categorized into concepts so that one can learn them more quickly. They are put into groups of relative material, each one is not learned merely independently, with no organized logic. The practitioner could spend his whole lifetime and not know if he knew it all.

Blocking With the Muscular Portion of the Forearm

Grandmaster Shimabuku focused upon blocking with the muscular portion of the arm rather than bone on bone with the side edges of the arm. After having practiced Ko Tekki Tai (arm conditioning techniques) one knows that those bones get hard and tough and that like the saying "a block is a strike, a strike is a block," they can break things. They can break another arm with the conditioned arm. Grandmaster Shimabuku saw arms being broken and also saw that the disparity of size would work against even the most conditioned arm. He realized that one could condition the arms as well, muscle to muscle. In the Isshin Ryu Kata, one will see blocking this way, with the Te No Ura (back of the arm). There are techniques and Kata movements that are included in Isshin Ryu which retain the use of the hard edge of the arm blocking. However, Isshin Ryu has become recognized as using deflective type blocking primarily with the muscular portion of the arm.

The Modified Vertical Fist

The major trademark of Isshin Ryu today in the United States is curling the fingers and setting the thumb right up on top of the vertical fist. This is very remarkable as is the Hiki Te (pulling hand) which is placed palm in instead of palm up at the hip. When working with the vertical fist position, it is said to strengthen the fist by bringing up the tendons on the side of the arm where it is weak. Aligning the first two metacarpals with the ulna bone of the arm gives strength to the vertical punch. It works very well and many times one will find untrained people will naturally punch like this, as did the GI's. Therefore, Grandmaster Shimabuku felt that the vertical punch was more natural. It worked very well with his emphasis on speed and deflective techniques and it does make anatomical sense. The Japanese and the Korean form of making a fist is to roll the fingers in and pull the thumb all the way down over the second bone of the first two fingers, thus making the fist turn into a ball or block. Their concept is balling the fist tighter, strapping the muscles around the bones and bringing out the Ken Saki (fist tip) striking area.

The Vertical Punch Versus the Full Reverse Punch

The vertical punch was somewhat revolutionary, in that the Hiki Te came palm in rather than palm up, as in the Japanese systems. However, Isshin Ryu does use a full reverse punch. It is a myth that it is not in Isshin Ryu, but again, the emphasis is toward stylizing and Grandmaster Shimabuku wanted his own system stylized. Therefore, any Isshin Ryu practitioner uses the vertical punch, but so many will say, even today, that the reverse punch is not there. One can look at Grandmaster Tatsuo Shimabuku on tape performing Sanchin Kata and there is a full reverse punch.

William Duessel, a 9th Dan in Isshin Ryu states that in 1964 when he studied with Grandmaster Shimabuku for the first time in the United States he was teaching the reverse punch. Evidently, there was so much conflict on the island of Okinawa over the reverse/vertical punch controversy that Grandmaster Shimabuku was wavering in teaching the vertical punch exclusively. When he came back to the U.S.A. in 1966, Sanchin Kata was taught with a reverse punch and all other punching in Isshin Ryu was done with a vertical punch and Hiki Te. He had taken another step in the evolution and the decision was made based on the strong support in the U.S.A. He felt that he had the power he needed to go ahead and institute his ideas against some of the old thinking in Okinawa. So today, Isshin Ryu has the vertical punch and Hiki Te.

Multiple Purpose Techniques

Tatsuo Shimabuku wanted all techniques to have multiple purposes, i.e., that a technique could be converted at any point to another technique. He wanted a block to be a block and a block also to be an attack. That a block become a strike and a strike become a block at the slightest command. All of the great Martial Arts Masters understood that each technique could be used for different purposes. The most classic example is the sword edge hand could be used for blocking and it could be used for striking.

As another example, at certain points in the mechanical transition of kicking technique, the knee up position particularly gives one the ability to change the technique completely at any instant. If one brings the knee up the same way, one could throw a front kick, an Otoshi (squat kick), a side kick or a back kick from that same up position. And one could also knee block, leg block and deflect from that same position. There is a world out there waiting to be discovered in multiple purpose techniques. Multiple purpose techniques also means to be able to change a confrontation from a defensive action to an offensive action and visa versa. This is necessary as one evaluates a situation and realizes that it is either more than one expected or less dangerous than the initial reaction indicated. If the practitioner is unable to make this type of mental change from defensive techniques to offensive movement or escalate the moves from defensive to more aggressive he may find that he is unable to handle the situation appropriately. There are levels of escalation to every self defense situation and these must be understood and used correctly. Inappropriate use of force could result in severe injury to the defender or attacker and it must be in the cause of justice and defensible if it is to the attacker.

It does no good to be a master if that mastery does not apply to all situations. To be a master means one can do it under any conditions. One could apply technique in the shower in the morning, or on the street or on the deck of a boat in shoes or bare footed. One can do it blindfolded or upside down. This is the mastery. This is what multiple purpose techniques are about.

Chapter 4

The Code of Karate

The Code of Karate is known throughout all the styles of Karate. Every style that originated in Okinawa or Japan had some philosophical guidelines to follow. These are somewhat esoteric to those Martial Artists who practice only the physical aspects of their training.

It is important to understand that Japanese and Okinawan are two different languages. The Hogan or Okinawan dialects were not well understood in Japan and when the Martial Arts Masters traveled from Okinawa to Japan, they had to employ the use of interpreters. This was a great problem around 1922 when Master Gichin Funakoshi took Shorin Ryu Karate Do to Japan. Gichin Funakoshi was not the first Karate Master to bring Karate from Okinawa to Japan, however, he was the first to formally present it to the Emperor of Japan and the first to write about Karate as a Japanese form. He was fluent in Japanese and communicated well without the aid of translators. His etiquette and behavior were suitable for Japanese society. The previous Martial Artists who had been to Japan were considered crude island fisherman or peasants and they did not have the refinement to make formal presentations to the Emperor. Therefore, Funakoshi Sensei has been given the credit of delivering the great Okinawan Art of Karate to the Japanese and the world.

As we study different styles of Karate, each one has a *code* and they all seem to have originated in the book of **Bubishi**, also called the **Wu Pei Chi**. The **Bubishi,** or Way of the Warrior or Samurai, has been translated into many languages. Sensei George Alexander is the author of one English version. As practitioners meet and train with one another, they find that Martial Arts and specifically Karate Do are very similar even across the different styles.

The Code of Isshin Ryu Karate Do is:

1. The heart is the same as heaven and earth.

2. The blood circulating is similar to the moon and the sun.

3. A manner of drinking and spitting is either hard or soft.

4. A person's imbalance is the same as weight.

5. The body should be able to change direction at any time.

6. The time to strike is when the opportunity presents itself.

7. The eye must see in every direction.

8. The ear must listen in all directions.

These require some explanation and it is unfortunate, but the majority of Martial Artists spend very little time on their *codes* of conduct and belief in their training. If these codes were self–explanatory there would indeed be a different phenomenon occurring in the Martial Arts world today.

The Heart is the Same as Heaven and Earth

This relates to man's role in the universe. Because of his major developments, man has become a very strong force. The power of man's mind has made him the superior animal on the planet. We rule and we dictate. Yet we are not more powerful than the universe, although we think we are. Ego and greed, which come from incorrect and inappropriate thinking, have made man very weak. Man must not disrupt life and must be in harmony with all that is around him, despite the overcrowding of the planet. Harmony with nature, harmony with other animals and harmony with other people.

The Codes of Karate Do were written before World War II following the era in which we saw the end to the Warrior Arts known as Bujitsu in Japan and the formulation of Budo. It was a concept that had occurred in the early 1900's when Karate Do came out of secrecy from the repression of the Satsuma clan. This was the time during which Yasutsune Itosu and many of the other major Sensei, such as Kanyro Higashionna and Sokon Matsumura, started to bring the public a form of Budo, or personal development, not just Warriorship.

The end of feudalism occurred in the late 1800's in Japan and Okinawa. The Samurai lost their purpose. With no Feudal Lords or Emperors to protect and with the advent of firearms which rendered the Katana (sword), the soul of the samurai, almost impotent, the Martial Artists of that era found they needed to alter their *Way*. By 1936 Karate Do was fully established.

The heart is the center of Budo, which is not always a gentle concept. Budo can be very forceful, but the true concept of Budo is parallel to that of Isshin Ryu, the One Heart, One Mind method. In the first movements of Kushanku Kata, the opening of the hands represents the universe or the heart of all things in Isshin Ryu. The heart or the spirit are also the center of the human being and his universe. To build character in Karate Do one need to forge the spirit through hard training. This is the more direct application of "the heart is the same as heaven and earth."

The Blood Circulating is Similar to the Moon and the Sun

The moon and sun, in constant motion, symbolize life which is constantly changing. Motion is extremely important to the body, as seen through the circulating of the blood. Change is the only constant we know in life and often this is overwhelming to us. We must move to circulate the blood and the blood must move to keep us alive. Equally, the universe must move to function properly. If a thing were to stop, it would die. There is nothing that can exist motionless. We must function consistently with the laws and forces of nature. We can train very hard, we can forge our spirit and we can practice Misogi (cleansing training), as long as we stay within the laws and forces of nature. If one were to go outside those parameters, one would know it. They are not etched in granite like curbs on the road to guide the way. These laws are evident to those who wish to learn them and use them to their benefit. Those who train realize these laws with much greater ease than those who do not practice Karate Do.

The Manner of Drinking and Spitting is Either Hard or Soft

The third Karate Code brings us to the In/Yo or the Yin/Yang concept within the Martial Arts. The manner of breathing is also either hard or soft, as are most other things in life. There is a "hard" side or *way* and a "soft" *way* to every action and thought. In Karate there is hard and soft *blocking*. Twenty or thirty years ago there were discrepancies and debates about hard and soft blocking. Even today as we are coming into a new century, we are still hearing this discussion about hard and soft *styles* of Karate. These debates are reignited by those whose education is from a Sensei not yet beyond the *Shu* or beginning stage of training. Anyone who is at least to a Shihan level, would agree that there is both hard and soft in breathing and in blocking, indeed in every technique. When one looks at or meets Masters from different systems around the world it is not hard to realize that all styles have hard and soft. Even the softest styles have a focal point in their technique, at which time it becomes hard. What the novices are referring to is linear blocking and striking versus circular, or striking with the hard striking surfaces, such as the Kensaki (the first two knuckles), the Teishu (palm heel) or the Tegatana (sword hand). Hard systems are often referred to as the linear, rigid, aggressive type of Karate Do. On the other hand, even within styles like Goju Ryu, which is the hard/soft system, or Uechi Ryu, which is a hard/soft system as well, they have both linear and circular blocking. They consider the hard and soft as equivalent to internal and external training. It is also referred to as internal and external *systems*. The simplistic explanation of this concept is given by and for the people who focus on the physical skills. The deeper meaning, the meaning of this code goes beyond the body and into the spirit and mind of the practitioner. It centers around those who focus on the internal healing and energy direction, or the Ki (internal energy) development within the human being, This is not to say that one has more merit than the other, both aspects are connected and of equal importance. It is only when one is made the sole attention at the expense of the other that imbalance occurs and the individual will then be incomplete in their training.

Can one separate the mind, body and spirit? Can one have hard without soft? According to the Yin/Yang or the In/Yo (Okinawan for Yin/Yang) one cannot have light without dark or soft without hard. Therefore, they cannot exist separately. Whoever is making these statements may just be quoting rhetoric or dogma that has been handed down, rather than analyzing the concepts themselves. Nothing can be hard all the time. Nothing can be soft all the time. How could one have a Martial Art, a defense system which comes down to survival, that is soft? One will not hug opponents to death. At the same time, how can there be a personal development tool which is all hard? Should the self–confidence and knowledge be beaten into all the students?

In Goju Ryu and Uechi Ryu, they refer to the breathing being hard and soft, which generates the internal force of Ki. Sanchin is hard breathing, or Tsuyokuhaku Kokyu Ho. It is considered a hard technique. Yet, when these same techniques are done with Shinsen Kokyu Ho, meditative breathing, they have a calming and rejuvenating effect on the mind and spirit. There is no such thing as an all hard system or an all soft system in existence. To a lot of people it has become marketing, a play on words to make the training enticing for the mystically focused individuals and those who want the image without doing the work. The concept of *spitting* either being hard or soft is to illustrate that in every action there is the hard or the soft aspect, depending upon how it is done.

A Person's Imbalance is the Same as Weight

In the purely physical aspect of this Code we find that the more one is off balance, the more weight he is required to have control over. Isshin Ryu Karate relies upon the balance of equal weight between front and rear foot stance. This allows the body to be centered about the Manaka, the center line or point of the body. If one moves off of this center point, he will feel as if he weighs twice what the actual weight is. Being in control of the body weight is critical to having mastery over one's technique. Just as important is the concept that imbalance is something one attempts to have happen to one's opponent. We draw the opponent off balance into technique so that there is a head–on collision of forces. Force coming in which is stable, solid and rooted and the opponents force which is spinning out of control onto the end of a punch and kick. This is one of the aspects of developing the ultimate Ikken Hissattsu, one blow, one kill. If a person is off balance, then striking them with full force becomes hitting them with their own weight as well. That is why a small person like Gichin Funakoshi or Tatsuo Shimabuku could be effective against people who were 6'4." They handled them like they were children, because they were able to use Kuzushi (to break the opponent's balance). Balance in relation to training regimens are important to keeping the body healthy and the skill levels high. Balancing training between Makiwara, Kata (forms), Kihon Waza (basic techniques) and conditioning drills is critical. As we look at a broader picture from one training session to the next there must exist the balance to complete all of the necessary components that is required to become a well rounded and fulfilled Martial Artist. There are times when the training goes at a frenzied speed and there are others when it remains quite calm. For example, one shifts gears in brown belt to achieve black belt. The training necessarily takes on a different complexion and balance to reach new heights. When one goes into black belt, it changes again. If one were to continue to work out like a white belt, one would stay at the white belt level. One has to constantly change and stay balanced with training. There are other aspects that, when out of balance, seem as weight to the practitioner of the Martial Arts. Diet and general health are two of these. This is the reason for the Spirit Honing Diet, a one–day fast combined with specific preparation and foods. Balancing foods and fluids for our workouts, keeping our balance of vitamins, minerals and other essential nutrients in check is crucial to overall health and therefore to overall balance.

There are other aspects of imbalance besides simply the physical. There is the balance of thought and spirit that when off cause trauma and disturbance of mind and mentality. Bun Bu Ichi is an important ideal to the Martial Artist; *Pen and Sword in accord.* It is well and good that we become healthy, vibrant and skilled physical practitioners. However, without the mind to support and direct behavior we would be lost to whims and emotions. A Martial Artist is nothing who cannot express himself, who cannot teach and give back to the world that which he has gleaned from his training. Where would we be if Gichin Funakoshi had not been scholarly? What would Martial training be like if Miyamoto Musashi had not forsaken his sword for the brush? And where will the Martial Arts be in the future if we do not take the time to balance our training with scholastic endeavors and education? We would be weighted down by all of the physical knowledge in the world and as we grew older and infirm it would become a lead ball and chain around our necks.

One Should be Able to Change Directions at any Time

The ability to be physically mobile depends upon one's skill and dexterity. Isshin Ryu is designed with ease of movement and quickness of body shifting from one direction to another. Seisan stance and in the Seisan Kata these aspects are particularly notable. It is in Seisan Kata especially that one can learn and perfect this concept. Psychologically, being able to change the direction of one's attention depends upon not mentally anticipating but reacting to events as they present themselves. This is valuable advice in self defense situations as one can never plan for the unexpected event. However, with skilled instruction and diligent, perfect practice the Karate Ka can have those techniques and abilities honed such that they are automatic responses to the cue of danger or threat. It must be kept in mind, however, that just reacting without thought does not show mastery. The final decision to execute a harmful or lethal technique must be made with proper judgement. This takes split second evaluation of the situation and the consequences of all actions.

Changing directions can be thought of in the sheer physical sense of positioning one's body to deal with techniques. Being able to change directions can also be taken to higher levels of consideration. Just as the levels of training take place as we move up through the belt levels and teaching levels, change is concurrently going on within us at all times. The attainment of new levels could be compared to the shifting of gears on a car. In the initial stages of training it is like the lower gears, moving slowly with high RPMs and great strain on the engine. Into the middle gears and intermediate levels of training there is a gaining of speed and less strain. The training is less hectic, the body has some basic conditioning and skills. Into the higher gears and more advanced levels of training, the Yudansha (black belt) levels, there is a firm foundation of conditioning and strength, usually three or four years of experience and thousands of repetitions in basic techniques, Kata and Kumite. This is where the vehicle goes into overdrive and the training takes on a seemingly new direction. In overdrive the Yudansha is moving at high speed with little strain. The anxiety of Shoshin (beginners mind) is something that is sought after, not feared. The effort is to go deeper into the meanings of techniques and the meaning of Budo rather than simply to accumulate more material. Rank consciousness and the focus on testing diminish at this level and the practitioner settles in for the long haul. However, this is no time for relaxation or to slow one's rate of progress. It is here that the realization comes that all things in training and in life are constantly changing. It is here that being able to change direction at any moment, in physical technique or in mental state becomes invaluable. Many things effect us on a daily basis. Without the solid foundation of Budo training we would not have the stability to withstand the changes that are thrown our way. How we handle changes in direction that will occur in life is directly proportionate to how well we have prepared for opportunities. It is closely linked to how integrated we have made Budo into our personal and professional lives. All those who practice the Martial Arts should strive to have the ability to adapt to change and be prepared for the unexpected. If we prepare for it we will find that we are ready to change direction in life

The Time to Strike is When the Opportunity Presents Itself

This means *preparation makes opportunity*. To create the time to strike is the ultimate in being in control of one's destiny. Striking does not necessarily mean hitting. Of course it could mean just that in the physical realm, however, there are other ways it can be interpreted. It can refer to opportunity of opening a new Dojo. The time approaches, the opportunity presents itself and the time to take advantage of it is either used or lost. It is rare that an opportunity returns. Once it has gone the preparation must begin anew and the time must pass just as for the first opportunity. This applies in the Dojo, in our personal life and in business. One must seize the moment of opportunity. Prepare, prepare prepare. Train, study and act when the time is right. In Kumite this means not hesitating when an opening is seen. One may have to create the opening. When one is fighting an equivalent opponent, it is harder to create an opening. Matching with an opponent of lesser skill allows for the creating of many opportunities to strike. Kumite with an opponent of greater skill challenges one to prepare for even the thought of an opportunity.

There is also the idea that there are moments in life that are appropriate for certain things and others that those same activities would not fit. The opportunity for certain types of training is better at different times. Summer is great for building stamina and endurance as well as flexibility. Winter is good for perfecting technique and monitoring problem areas of the training. It is important to tune in to the different seasons and the times of our lives and utilize these changes for optimal training.

The Eye Must See in Every Direction

When we talk about the eye seeing in every direction, we are not just talking about visual acuity. "One cannot see the forest for the trees" would be a good statement to analyze that. In Karate we call it Metsuke. One must be visually aware of everything going on. One must utilize peripheral vision as well as specific focal vision. One must see the subtleties of the motion of an opponent, utilizing vision to read the body language. One must see more than just part of the visual scope available, otherwise one risks missing some vital piece of information. To be locked in on the detail is to be easily set up. For example, in Kushanku Kata there are two foot stomps. One Bunkai (practical application) reflects the intent to draw the person's attention and away from the real attack. If the opponent were to direct all their attention to this one small item, they would be hit in a blind area never having seen the technique coming.

The ability to focus clearly and see what is important is also based on having a clear mind. It is very difficult for one to focus attention and see clearly when distracted. We have all had times when we are mentally overwhelmed. A crisis may have occurred and we cannot get our focus. During these times we are not seeing clearly and attention span is poor.

Vision is also affected by having preconceived ideas. A simple analogy is in Kumite. A person may use a particular kicking combination every time they Kumite (two person matching technique). While practicing Kumite they may do it once or twice and the opponent will assume they will continue to execute that kick. Then they do something totally different and then blow the opponent away with a technique that they have never seen before. The assumption was that since it had been *seen* over and over, it was *expected* to be seen again. Preconceived ideas and notions come in all sorts of packages and settings, not just Kumite. The whole idea of being well balanced is to be able to utilize all skills equivalently. When we know someone is *reading* us, we change what we do. But we must be aware that it works both ways.

Having vision also means to be on what we call *Amber Light*. This is an extremely important concept in today's overprotected and controlled world where violence and criminal acts can occur anywhere. When we least expect it (and that is precisely why) a criminal who has designs on our life or property appears. It is not enough to have the six week self defense course under our belt. This concept of *Amber Light* must be practiced and honed just as any other finely tuned skill. Every instant is a potential problem and without that idea solidly planted in one's mind the eye will not see in all the directions necessary to save us from the unexpected.

The eye seeing in all directions could also construe a much more philosophical and long range view. Remember, when these codes were written the times were very different for the Warriors of that era. No longer did they have the purpose of battle and need of deadly skill. They were becoming scholars and needed to have vision of the future to secure their continued place in history. They also spent a great deal of time contemplating, even before this era, the deeper meanings of life and death. Having a long range vision about the future and being able to see in every direction is critical for one who wishes to become a Master of the Arts.

The Ear Must Listen in All Directions

One must not only have the obvious hearing factors, but there is also something to be said for being quiet at times and listening. Many times people talk continuously. We have all been in lectures or in classes when students will interrupt and ask questions before they hear everything. They have stopped listening and do not know they have not gotten all of the information that was there. Listening is a great skill and plays a major role in communication. One can still train in the Martial Arts if hearing is one of the faculties not available. What we do not want to do is get to the point where we tune out some of the senses, losing the overall perspective. One must hear it all and analyze what is being said and the meaning. We have to constantly upgrade knowledge of words to enhance the level of comprehension. At the same time, if we are dealing with someone who is using improper vocabulary or speaking in a different language, it makes simple listening difficult if not impossible. This is exemplified by the Japanese and the Okinawan communication problem. The Okinawans say the Japanese do not understand Karate. They claim the Japanese misinterpreted it from the beginning because they did not speak Okinawan. The Japanese claimed the Okinawans were merely peasants and did not have the language or scholarship skills to propagate such an Art as Karate. How were they going to understand this Art if they could not communicate? It is very important that we work on clear denotation and definition in our words. That is why textbooks are so important. Concepts that are not properly understood must be clearly defined in order to communicate effectively.

Know the Code

The Isshin Denshin or direct transmission is the spirit, the eyes, the hearing and the communication from person to person. These are all aspects of these eight codes inherent within what we do and share as Martial Artists. It must be put into an intellectual or academic format because then we have another dimension of understanding and clarification. A Dojo that has no written material cannot pass all of the needed information on completely through Isshin Denshin. One can study from an instructor who does not speak his language. But every layer and every dimension that one can add to this to shorten the different perspectives and to explore it from a different venue is going to contribute to presenting a clearer message.

In Master Harold Long's book, **The Dynamics of Isshin Ryu**, published by the National Paperback Book Company and available through Isshin Ryu Productions, he has put these eight codes together in a quick memory format. It reads very quickly and with this format one can memorize the codes utilizing rote memory. One can become a pro at rote memory and not know the content of the material. However, given the choice of using rote memory versus not knowing anything about a subject, we will take the rote memory.

Here is how it reads:

1. Be in harmony with all things so that...
2. Movement...
3. Can be either blocking hand or deflecting foot...
4. Without being off balance...
5. So that one could change directions at any time...
6. And strike when the opportunity occurs...
7. As you look and...
8. Listen in all directions.

Without the numbers, it reads like this:

Be in harmony with all things so that movement can be either blocking hand or deflecting foot without being off balance, so that one can change directions at any time and strike when the opportunity occurs, as you look and listen in all directions.

That brings it down to a paragraph that one can rote memorize. All that is left is for one to grasp the meanings of all eight points and then integrate them into daily life and training.

Devote Yourself Only to the Way of Karate: Think of Nothing Else

Chosin Chibana was the founder of Shorin Kobayashi Ryu. He trained under Yasutsune Itosu and Kosaku Matsumura. His main student and instructor was Katsuya Miyahira who taught Sikichi Iha. This is one of the base systems to Isshin Ryu, Koei Kan, Shito Ryu and others. Master Chosin Chibana was a very famous Sensei. He said some things that should go hand in hand with our training and thinking. He said, "When you train, you have to devote yourself only to the way of Karate. Think of nothing else." The Way, the Do, the path, the methodology to "Think of nothing else" is what he was saying. This does not mean just think of a few things and perhaps only during class. He meant all of the time.

Many of the old Masters only had a half dozen students, if that many. The students who were fortunate enough to train with these Masters dedicated most of their lives to their Art. For example, in 1974, Dr. Mike Walters was a young boy who started training at seven years old. He trained side by side with me. He was teaching and living at the first Shito Kan Dojo. I feel personally responsible for contributing to the highest quality times of his life, because living the Dojo life and sleeping on Tatami mats is an excellent experience for everyone. I can vividly remember him getting up from his sleep in the middle of the night. Thump, thump, thump, thump, "Kiosuke (line up)!! " Thump, thump, thump, "I said Kiosuke!!!" And hearing him running around and counting, "Ichi, Ni, San. Get that fist tight. Get the knees up" throughout the night. Those who have devoted themselves to Karate have all had similar experiences. When one devotes themselves entirely it does not mean skip meals or miss work. That does not mean there are not other things to be done, but in the spare time. Priority should be primarily on training. That was probably what Master Chibana was referring to. Direct one's self to become a professional instructor. It is within the grasp of anyone who devotes themselves.

It is critically important that one grasp the magnitude of what this is. In this soft society today, we have people who will drop out from a lecture. Not from the Makiwara training, they did not even get to that. The talk about it scared them out. This is how soft society has become. One can scare someone with a discussion about training. Things are changing and to devote one's self to one direction requires much more fortitude than it did in the past, when the work ethic was strong in this country and people understood working in a constructive, positive direction. One must grasp the magnitude of Karate Do: The hard and soft, the codes and concepts, the philosophy, the ideas about clarifying the thinking, being a philosopher and a scientist. It is about having the ability to change; for someone to go from being a soft blob of protoplasm or the Pillsbury dough boy, reconstructing themselves as an adult into a Samurai with a brain, with a mind and with an intellect as sharp as a Katana (Samurai sword). To realize that it is the ultimate preventative medicine; that it stimulates the immune system, builds and strengthens musculature, ligaments and bone structure. That it lowers blood pressure, changes cholesterol ratios and prevents disease in the body. One can actually heal the body through breathing exercises. This is an awesome program to offer people in this world, something that people need. The more technologically oriented we become and the softer society gets, the more they need this. People go to health spas, where there is chrome, neon, plush carpet, saunas and whirlpools. They spend more of their time soaking, massaging and sunning than they do working out. They are doing the insignificant things that others make millions and billions of dollars off, yet never get healthier and never get devoted enough to stick with one activity.

Think of Nothing Else

"Think of nothing else." Here is a critical statement. This is very difficult for our society to grasp, but it is so important. "Do not think of others or what they may think." Wouldn't we like to imprint that in the mind of every seventeen–year–old who is having difficulty in school right now with peer pressure? "Do not think of others or what they may think." How many times and how many students have quit because of peer pressure? I heard from one of the Sensei today that after my last lecture and brisk round of Renzoku, two robust, well-built, bodybuilder type students dropped out of our Dojo. One of them dropped out because he did not feel he should abuse himself by being sore the next day after a workout. He asserted that there are too many other ways to exercise that do not leave one sore. The other strong, masculine individual was told by his wife that he was not returning because *she* did not think it was appropriate that he should go through hard training like this. Since they were friends, they did not return. Apparently they did not read Chosin Chibana's precepts. They did not listen to what the Master had to say. "Do not think of others or what they may think." Those who do not devote themselves do not know, those who do not train have no clue. If they share the experience, then they would come to understand. Everyday is a whole new experience in the Dojo. The dropouts failed to realize the flaw in their thinking. They think that every class will be the same as the few classes they have experienced. Has anyone ever said there is Kumite every night in hell week? No. Had these young men returned, they would have known that. But they jumped to rash conclusions with preconceived ideas, listening to what other people said and did not do their homework. They did not think clearly.

"One must develop the ability to focus mind, hands and feet strongly," continues Master Chosin Chibana. There is no doubt that he was a Makiwara and Kata Master and that he understood thoroughly all the concepts of training. The term *focus* is not a loosely used word. Focus is a very precise aspect of training. Having experienced direct transmission, Isshin Denshin and shared common experiences of training and Makiwara, one can understand what focus means. Focus means more than what we hear in schools today. It means more than "look up here" or "pay attention, Johnny." One must not only learn body movements, but also research and study. Analyze what we are doing and why we are doing it. One must grasp the *big picture* as the developer of Chiropractic, B.J. Palmer stated. The timing, the balance, the rhythm, the breathing, the vision and the hearing all go together, developing into the Ikken Hissattsu which is where the ultimate in focus is exhibited. It takes many years to develop Ikken Hissattsu. We have ridden the coattails of these Masters and had access to much of their knowledge. They practiced and trained in secrecy. They did not know what the person six huts down was doing in their training in the middle of the night. Today we know globally what is going on in training and we are sharing that training amongst different Masters. Master Chibana said, "We trained the Karate as a Martial Art. Now they train Karate as a gymnastic sport." He was comparing the training of the late 1800's and early 1900's to the 1930's. If he could only see it today, what would he think?

The Samurai vs. The Weekend Warrior

Every legendary Master that we respect for their wisdom of the Arts taught students who have transmitted the Art worldwide. Every major Master felt that Karate should not be trained primarily as a sport. They all had their reasons. It must be a Martial *Art*. Here is how one must train: Fingers and the tips of toes must be like arrows, palms must be like iron, kicks are lethal. One must visualize the techniques and their applications. When doing a Kata, one cannot *play* it like a sport. One will not develop from this and intrinsic force will not rise up to the levels of mastery.

In doing the Martial Arts, if the idea is be a weekend warrior, participating in the latest demonstration team circuit to show off in fancy silk Kimono (robes) and four color uniforms with fancy patches and whistling Nunchaku realize that the training will never reach down into the depths of soul and create greatness. The tournament circuit does not teach the most vital aspect of the Martial Arts; how to overcome the fear of death. Some people are big and strong, tough, rugged, rich, powerful and intelligent. They can buy anything. They can influence anyone. But no one can change the fact that we are all going to die. That is the entire basis of the Code of the Warrior. Training as the Samurai trained meant confronting death at a moment's notice for the cause of justice. They were willing to die for the cause of their Shogun, Emperor or prince. The bodyguard theory. Anyone who has ever been a bodyguard has taken the oath that they will throw themselves in front of a bullet to save another human being. That is their code. That is the Code of the Warrior. Until one confronts the reality that one can die at any moment, one has not even begun the journey as a Warrior. That is why severe training is important and harsh testing for black belt is necessary. If one thought black belt test was going to be a walk in the park, one would never confront the fear of death and will never make the change.

If we practice gamesmanship or sportsmanship for a little tag on the weekend, the fingertips will not be like arrow tips. One will not be able to thrust and kill if one is not using the Makiwara. Training and preparation make opportunity happen. If one trains incorrectly and confronts a life or death situation the preparation has not been made for that opportunity and it will turn out poorly. It is moral obligation to intercede, to take a life to save the life of an innocent person if necessary. That is the true use of Karate Do. No other use is correct. Not feeling egotistical and going to a tournament to hurt somebody. Not hurting somebody in training. Not getting mad and hurting somebody. Those are not correct uses of Karate Do. Master Chosin Chibana knew that. If one punches one must thrust to kill. If one strikes, then strike to kill the enemy. This is the spirit one needs in training. Do not use technique *ever,* unless it is that critical. It does not matter how embarrassing the situation is or how intimidated one is by somebody on the street. Do not use it unless it is a life and death situation. Then use it with everything one has. Use every bit of force one has ever been trained in. Do it from the depths of the Warrior Spirit and do not stop until it is safe. That is Karate Do.

Children with black belts does not reflect true Karate Do. Children do not have the emotional capability of understanding codes of Karate. Effort and maturity is required. How many people do not understand this? Great things require great effort. Master Chibana said, "Years ago, I wished to leave my name in Karate Do and I trained very hard to do that." He knew that he had a destiny. Someone did not come up and say, "You are going to be great, Mr. Chibana, if you put forth great effort."

He did not say, "I am no good. I am nobody. Please do not mention my name." He said, "I wanted my name to be left in the ages. I wanted to go down in history. I wanted to leave my mark." One has to understand this, pride is not wrong. Humility, misunderstood and misdirected is an insult to achievement, accomplishment and to self–worth. Humility can be a very manipulating term used to control people. The Masters understood there is a difference between being boastful, a braggart fantasizing about skills that one does not have and being proud, confident, self–assured and having self–esteem. This man had enough self–esteem to say that he wanted to leave his name in Karate Do. But he also said he trained very hard to do that. He said that not only do we need physical training, but we need to think for ourselves. Study and research the Kata and their applications. Look deeply and research. Whether one becomes great depends on two factors only. Effort and study is what separates one from greatness. That is all. Consistent hard work and focus. One has to stay on the path in the correct direction. One can expend huge amounts of wasted energy if one is traveling in ten different directions or very fast in the wrong direction. Moving forward and putting the effort, hard work and study in a constructive focused direction will create greatness.

Chapter 5

The Strategy of Mastery & Destiny

All of the Martial Arts systems are on different standards of behavior today. There is no one consistent value system which drives all styles of training. However, there are certain organizations who are consistent with high standards. The classical Martial Artists practice what we call Budo. There are Martial Artists who do eclectic Karate, based on aspects other than traditional Martial Arts training and the philosophy of the Warrior. These are the people who generally adhere to more sociological trends. They have things like Martial Arts birthday parties for children to enhance the family atmosphere in the Dojo. They will sponsor events like kick–a–thons. The student pays to attend certain consecutive classes and perform one thousand kicks and get a new patch as a reward. The motivational methodology of these commercial programs bait potential students with a carrot–on–a–stick approach for small, short term rewards. There are also those who do other physical activities and combine a few Martial Arts moves or cliches and will then say that they "do the Martial Arts." These things are not necessarily *bad,* however they are just not focused on what the Code of the Warrior should be, or on the standards of Budo or Bujitsu have been throughout history. It is revisionist and it corrupts the name of Martial Arts.

Character, self–esteem, pride and values. These are the areas that are integrated into life through traditional Martial Arts training. The student progresses along the path of Budo, the path of discipline and the path of resolving inner conflict as well as outward violence. Budo is not a "warm fuzzy" concept where everything is nice and like Mr. Miyagi, the movie character, is always sweet and gentle and kind. Chojun Miyagi, Gichin Funakoshi, Morihei Ueshiba and Jigoro Kano were not gentle, sweet and kind. They had compassion but they were disciplinarians. They were tough. They were Martial Artists to the core, they were Warriors. They could give a beating and they could take a beating. They forged their spirit with hard training. There has never been a traditional concept Dojo where Budo meant *soft.* It has always been hard. Driving the self for personal excellence.

There are very few Americans in this country who are elite enough physically, mentally, or philosophically to qualify as a Martial Arts masters. Yet today it is quite frequent that people claim rank they do not deserve and have not earned. Standards of behavior and skill are gone, putting the emphasis on money, not on technique, not on training and not on the individual. Yet, many great Sensei are scared to take a stand and challenge this trend by stating plainly, "These people are wrong. Their standards are not high enough, they are not tough enough and they do not have the knowledge it takes to be a true Martial Artist." As Martial Arts Masters, when we see someone espousing incorrect information to a point below competency, it is reasonable and responsible to point out the error. We are on the verge of seeing many Martial Artists, nationwide, willing to become judgmental, with group consensus. Not a democracy, but a group of individuals who have a like–minded purpose and standards that are high. They look at an individual and, by observation, can tell that this person's kicking mechanics are incorrect. Warriors such as Miyamoto Musashi placed great emphasis on physical skills, dexterity and being competent in battle. One cannot be a great Master if he is incompetent physically. Training is not only a class in theory. Martial Arts means practical application and one must be competent, which means he must train hard. One must train severely to reach the levels of the seniors who have attained mastery. It cannot only be talked about, it must be done. It is something that must be continually done for the whole of one's life.

As the Masters age and mature, we often see a change in their character and outlook on the Martial Arts. We use a more direct method of dealing with incompetent people who want to lower the Martial Arts to standards with the lowest common denominator and claim high esteem and status. As Dr. Peter Urban would say, "Immediate and swift justice or punishment" is necessary for those who do not comply with the standards. The truth of the matter is that becoming a Martial Arts master and one who is able to shape the future takes much more than a hard core attitude, it takes hard core training. Those Masters that we have heard of and see today who *seem* too intense or too harsh are actually the very people who keep the standards of excellence high. That does not happen by playing at Karate or any

Martial Arts training. It comes from intense, sincere and serious repetition over a period of years. Forging not only the mental process and the spirit, but the neurology as well. It is casting a mold for Mastery and vision. Every achievement in our lifetime is a culmination of thought and action. Tomorrow is an accumulation of what we did yesterday. Character is moral quality, strongly developed and strikingly displayed. There are all levels of character. In Shito Kan Karate Do, the character developed through personal excellence training is a specific kind of character. A component of that character is integrity. We display it in the Dojo with politeness, etiquette and Giri (debt of obligation) on time. Remember the old days, when a handshake meant something? Notice that the traditional Dojo works the same way as the handshake. A man's word was his honor. When a Dojo reflects this ideal then contracts and sales pitches are not necessary or desirable.

Be as well versed in the art of the pen as the sword is the translation of *Bun Bu Ichi*. This book is part of the Bun Bu Ichi. One can kick and punch forever, but if he does not develop a philosophy that follows him out of the Dojo, he will not continue training over a period of years. It will become boring. It is through the daily execution of technique and thought together that makes one a Warrior. Not executing physical techniques over and over again mindlessly.

Character is qualities or features, that together define or identify someone or something. A character can be eccentric. They can be amusing. If they have remarkable personalities and behavior, that is all part of character. That is why we have a certain stereotypical character to a black belt. There are expectations of the way a black belt stands, walks and behaves. People can be out of character. Every black belt has told me at some time or another they saw a black belt who was out of character. A 9th degree black belt will telephone and request that he be addressed as "John." That is out of character for a black belt and it is inappropriate. This man has not integrated his Art. We have all seen it, a black belt with a stomach out so far he cannot see his feet. It is out of character for a black belt to be that out of shape. One cannot earn a black belt and be out of shape.

Mastery exhibits certain *characteristics*. There are certain traits that all masters have. This means that people who think clearly, rationally and logically when dealing with the same subject will reach the same correct conclusion. There is a right answer to a problem. There is black and white in an issue. Yet we see all kinds of unprofessional thinking about the Martial Arts from "black belts." Is there a certain expected *aura* to a Karate Master? Certainly there are basic characteristics expected from them: physical competency, mental focus, knowledge about their Art, philosophical background in their study, correct teaching methodology and the ability to transmit the message. Do we expect an eight–year–old to be a black belt? It is ridiculous to have an eight, nine, or ten–year–old black belt. It is a fictitious, commercial aspect and a fraud perpetrated on the true Martial Arts black belts in this country. There is no real Warrior, no true black belt that will ever say that an eight, ten, or twelve–year–old can have the maturity to understand the concepts, ideology, philosophy, discipline and rigors required to be a black belt. They cannot even clean their rooms yet. How are they going to be black belts? This raises questions about people who put black belts on children. We have actually had Martial Artists who call themselves great Sensei, who will take the titles, yet they are scared and inhibited. They will not come forward to enlighten other people. A person's contribution to the Arts is a reflection of character.

Dabblers & Fakers

There was a student who was video taped after his Shodan test talking about his reactions to the test and his new rank. He stated that it took him longer than others to get to black belt because he dabbled in and out of training. When he took his test, he stated that it was not bad and he was not scared of anything. He went on to say, "I thought I was going to go through changes. Really, it is not a big deal to test for black belt. You can all do it. It is wonderful. I had a warm feeling during my black belt test. I felt love for everybody." What kind of test was this? This was not a real black belt test, not a test such as the Shito Kan Karate Do tests. One cannot become a black belt with the character of a Warrior by getting warm and cuddly during a black belt test! One must overcome the fear of death to become a black belt in the standard of the great Masters. This is the difference today. Do not expect other people to understand this idea. Do not expect Martial Artists who have not gone through it to relate to the concept of Warriorship. Expect them to claim to be the same in rank.

That is why training under a Master who has vision and perspective is important. Hard work, whether building character, self–esteem, pride or values is the foundation of personal excellence. Hard work creates self–esteem and improved self image. The student will know why he trains so diligently and will receive the greatest of all rewards; self knowledge. Those who trained hard to become masters are confident, outspoken and will take a stand. We seek their guidance as mentors. If they do not set the prerequisites for excellence, what are we going to shoot for? What are we going to use as a target? If a teacher's standards are low, where are the student's standards going to be? If the instructor is a cowardly, weak Martial Artist who does not train, what will his students become and what will become of his Dojo and eventually his system?

The status of Hanshi, Master Instructor, requires many things. The title of Hanshi indicates there are teaching credentials that have been received along with the standard ranking in technical skill. Over black belt, there are ten levels or Dan ranks, originally designed by Jigoro Kano, a professor from Japan. He had originally included twelve degrees of black belt, however, only ten have been used. Teaching certifications are earned by people who have put in a great deal of time in instruction. Some black belts will be students, yet they will not teach. These individuals earn grades of black belt and go up in proficiency level however, they cannot get instructor licenses unless they are contributing to the art and furthering their knowledge and skill through instruction. Requirements of teaching include participation in demonstrations, organizing exhibitions, operating a Dojo and promoting the Art. The Master instructors are ambassadors for the Art. It takes many years of working with students to master teaching and that is what the levels of Shidoin, Renshi, Kyoshi and Hanshi are about. Each level has a certain degree of accomplishment and intellectual skill.

The Dai Nippon Butoku Kai's original concept was to regulate and standardize the Martial Arts. Ryu Ha are the family or traditional Martial Arts organizations. The Japanese tried to make it a military concept. The Okinawan Karate systems were not the Bujitsu systems found in Japan. Which explains why, in Shito Kan Karate and in Isshin Ryu Karate there are Soke, or head of the family. They are not military organizations based upon garnering nationalistic spirit, but Budo systems designed to bolster the individual spirit. However, the Dai Nippon Butoku Kai granted the first teaching licenses, or Shihan Menjo. They were authorized by the Emperor of Japan himself. That is why Chojun Miyagi of Okinawa and founder of Goju Ryu did not give out black belts and would not grant teaching licenses. Gogen Yamaguchi requested Hanshi status for his contributions to the Art in Japan and Chojun Miyagi refused, saying, "Only the Emperor can grant Hanshi status." At that time, it was true. The Dai Nippon Butoku Kai's values for teaching licenses were based on honor. They did not say much about kicking and punching. These were the instructors licenses, the professor level degrees, in Martial Arts. Values were based on honor, respect, gratitude, discipline and integrity. The purpose of their institution was to foster the Japanese acceptance of such concepts. They desired greater values within their people. This had been a feudal era and the people were not well educated or developed. The push was on to industrialize, to come up to speed with the rest of the world. Educational standards also had to rise. Literally, being a Hanshi was like being a full, tenured professor in the university system today.

The Emperor also established the Budo Simon Dai Gakku, out of which came the Martial Arts Technical College. In 1907, the Butoku Kai became the foundation of the Martial Arts educational system and Budo training was stressed for all youths along with Judo, Kendo and Naginata. Between 1907 and 1910, the Dai Nippon Butoku Kai developed a system of the distinguished titles of Renshi, Kyoshi and Hanshi. Originally, Renshi was not incorporated. That fell under the title of Shihan. Menkyo were master's licenses. Promotions to these titles focused on the achievement of goals in *Budo*. Between 1906 and 1907, Professor Jigoro Kano founder of Judo and who is credited with the change in the Martial Arts from Jujutsu into a form of Budo, developed the Dan–Kyu ranking system. These two events, the incorporation of teaching titles and certifications and Kano's Dan–Kyu ranking system were not done together. Still today, one can earn degrees of black belt and not get teaching licenses.

Initially, Professor Kano did not award a black belt, he gave a black sash. The black sash represented the beginning of advanced training and studies. That level was considered post graduate training. It is like being in Shoshin, the beginner's mind all over again. In 1907 at the Kodokan, the headquarters for Judo, Professor Jigoro Kano designed the Judo Gi (uniform). This is the standard uniform used in Judo today. Concurrently, they established a black belt as the rank standard. The sash system came out of China and at this time Japan was preparing to go to war with China, so they were attempting to eliminate things that were Chinese. At one time Karate practitioners used black Keikogi (practice uniform) to differentiate themselves from those who practiced Judo. Most of the pictures of the Masters of old show them in black Keikogi or Haori (traditional Oriental robe). Today, the black Gi is generally reserved for 3rd Dan and higher.

It was not until 1936 that Karate became included in the Dai Nippon Butoku Kai. It was called Ryu Kyu Tode Jutsu. Ryu Kyu is the name of the Ryu Kyu Island chain archipelago from which Okinawan Karate has its origin. Tode means Chinese hand and Jutsu is art. Gichin Funakoshi spearheaded the movement to get Karate accepted into the Butoku Kai. Funakoshi was a Renshi and fifth Dan when he went to Japan. There are very few Renshi in the world today and even fewer Kyoshi and Hanshi. The challenge for the Okinawan Martial Artists was to meet the prerequisites established by the Butoku Kai. This historical chronology is important because it is the heritage of all Karate Do. The Dai Nippon Butoku Kai attempted to organize many separate factions of the Okinawan Martial Arts. That is what had to occur before the Karate Ka from Okinawa could be accepted in the Japan Federal Licensing Program, which was sponsored by the Emperor through grants and funding. That is why there was such tremendous, rapid growth of the Martial Arts in Japan. It was not because it was a popular hobby, like it is here, but because it was pushed by the governmental powers.

The All Japan Budo Kai was a nonprofit foundation. The Okinawan Masters were against the Kanji change of Tode Jutsu to reflect something other than China. If you have read Gichin Funakoshi's **Karate-Do, My Way of Life**, he wrote about it and was given some credit for changing the Kanji (Chinese or Japanese written characters) from the Tode to Karate, empty handed way. Chomo Hanishiro is credited with the original idea of the Kanji change, however, Gichin Funakoshi popularized it.

The Okinawan Martial Artists did not support the change. After all, they had been subjugated by the Japanese. The Satsuma Clan took away their weapons and abused these people for several hundred years by this time. They were not interested in submitting this 1,000 year old Art of Okinawa Te to the Japanese only to have it changed. This Art had been passed on from generation to generation, through families in secrecy. It was the last line of defense they had against the Japanese. To turn it over to the Japanese giving them credit for it was not at the top of their agenda.

Needless to say, the name was changed from Tode Jutsu to Karate Do. Fortunately, the Okinawan Masters were able to add the "Do" to give it a philosophical or spiritual meaning. It extended the concept to include more than self defense. They sought to include enlightenment, wisdom and knowledge through training. Incorporation of the standard Karate Gi was also necessary for inclusion into the Butoku Kai.

Many of the original Karate Gi were made out of flour sacks and burlap. Standards for Dan–Kyu testing were incorporated into Karate Do from Professor Jigoro Kano.

The final requirement to have Okinawan Karate to be accepted, licensed with certified instructors and funded with grants as a nonprofit discipline and classical "Budo" or Ryu Ha (styles) through the Butoku Kai was sport. Of all things, it had to have a sport component as did Judo or Kendo. The requirement was for rules and guidelines to foster competitive spirit. This step was too much for many of the Okinawan Martial Arts masters of the time. Imagine Sokon Matsumura or Yasutsune Itosu being told they had to go play tag in a ring. The Okinawan Martial Artists, the older generation, were anti–Japanese to begin with and did not forget the suppression of their people. There was never complete consensus on the sport aspect of Okinawan Art and there still is not today. The Okinawan Martial Artists in their Ryu Ha were focused on the art of self defense and improvement.

They practiced it as an Art and a way of life. They practiced Karate as a discipline with their main focus on its effectiveness as a defensive *art*. Karate Do can be a very lethal defense. Those who practice the lethal art of Karate Do versus those who participate in the sport aspect alone have two very different perspectives about their training.

Classical techniques of Ryu Kyu Tode Jutsu and some original forms still exist today. Today, in the United States, there is growing concern about the lost Art and values of Budo and Bujitsu by the senior black belts who train traditionally.

Throughout history there have been age guidelines for the granting of instructor titles and Dan ranks. These are general standards and there have been and are exceptions. Many Soke have inherited Ryu Ha at very young ages. Chojun Miyagi inherited his system from Kanryo Higashionna. He was one of the forerunners of our system and one of our ancestors. Eizo Shimabuku, Fuse Kise, Kichiro Shimabuku, Yamaoka Tesshu, Miyamoto Musashi and Bokuden all inherited an Art when they were very young. However, all of these Masters proved their worth over the years and the existence of their Arts today shows their vision. Once they reached Mastery in the Arts they could master anything. Musashi, Tesshu and Bokuden went on to be great artists and sculptors. They transcended the physical, realizing the intellectual and spiritual. This is integration of the art into life.

That is what we are seeking with Budo. That is the wisdom we are looking for. It comes through hard training, long hours, Makiwara and tremendous contemplation. Is enlightenment the main requirement? Is that what we should be looking for; the wisdom and the synergistic quality of the individual? Yes, but not instead of physical accomplishment, understand that. To get through the repetitions it takes to forge the spirit, to transcend the physical changes through programming neurology one must be physically competent and do thousands of repetitions. This is what is misunderstood by the politically correct, new age crowd, that one could bypass the physical requirements. Being peaceful, kind, sweet and gentle is not the way of the Warrior nor the road to self discovery or enlightenment. It is certainly not the road to competence in self defense or the way to understand the universe. When we think of enlightenment, we picture some monk up on a mountain top in a cave.

Walk the Same Path

Walk the same path as the Masters walked, what does that mean? It represents that by doing the same training as the Masters did one can become what they were. Did the greatest minds and bodies in the Martial Arts "kick back" on Sunday morning because they were a little beat from the week? No, they got out there and trained and trained every day. One cannot be Miyagi or Musashi by training once in a while or when it is convenient. One must train constantly; mentally, physically, awake or asleep. Enlightenment means to be given or have knowledge or wisdom revealed. It is revealed through the training. The instructor can point the path or direction, but he cannot *give* it to the student. The Master can demonstrate the concepts, but they will not be grasped until the training is done. Even then, enlightenment may not occur.

Enlightenment: An 18th century philosophical movement characterized by rationalism, skepticism of traditional doctrine and empirical methods in science. In other words, they were skeptical of induction versus deduction. Induction is a method of arriving at a general conclusion based upon limited data. Someone comes in and sees three students working out, two green belts and a white belt struggling along. Because the students are not competent at that level, the conclusion is made that the entire Dojo is incompetent. That is induction, making a conclusion based on a limited sample. Deduction is making a decision by testing every example that comes before and after in a consistent order, proving the theory by showing it holds to the first number and all other proceeding.

We cannot allow Martial Arts theory and philosophy to become an indoctrination based upon induction. Enlightenment is reproducible. It is not intangible. It appears ethereal and esoteric to us, but once experienced it changes the consciousness. Then it is reflected physically. It is only ethereal or esoteric or intangible to someone who has not been through it already. Those who have been through it not only recognize it in someone, they can take someone else through the process. This is when Mastery is proven, when an instructor can point the way and the student reaches the same conclusions.

Remember, enlightenment is not religion. It means to be given or have knowledge or wisdom revealed to you. It means to be delivered from prejudice, ignorance or superstition. If one believes that he can get enlightenment by some supernatural form, magic vs. training, then he is dealing with mysticism. If wisdom or knowledge is gained through training, it is metaphysical. It is reproducible, physiological changes in the body and consciousness. Not many Martial Artists ever analyze any aspect of this. They will train. But ask them where they are going, what they are doing, to define their purpose. They will respond, "I want to break through. I want to get enlightened." Meanwhile, they are doing drugs on the weekends and undoing what they did in the Dojo all week. A drunken stupor is not enlightenment. People who are intoxicated with power are not enlightened. Because they can beat somebody up does not mean they are enlightened. There is always someone bigger and tougher coming down the road, who has never trained, who will thump these people. It can happen to anyone, no matter what level.

Why would we want to base promotion and teaching licenses of Renshi, Kyoshi and Hanshi on these intangibles? Because they are not intangible. They are reproducible, verifiable and obvious. It is misinterpreted by people. The greatest cause of failure in anything is the lack of follow–through by individuals. Initially, we were talking about character and then went through the origins of grading values and skills in the Dojo. Now we are talking about the roots of teaching licenses. They are linked directly through the physical skills, but based on values, ethics and principles, demonstrable knowledge and contribution to the arts.

Man is a rational being. He has the ability to think creatively and realize when he is not. He *sometimes* has the ability to know when he is getting off track. That is why guidance is so important, often someone needs to point out to us when we are off track. This is why a Sensei is so important. We see people who, with a little training, drop out thinking they can go off by themselves and have the breakthroughs. "Does a person stumble onto greatness and great thoughts or is it a process of preparing that occurs over a lifetime?" Preparation meets opportunity. If one wants to be great, he must prepare for it, it is a process. It is just a process. Once the value of self–esteem and personal greatness is grasped, all that is necessary for its accomplishment is preparation and hard work. What difference does it make if we allow Martial Artists who have low standards to sell belt ranks and con people with artificial things that are not relative to the Martial Arts? We lose the capacity of all these human beings. We lose their breakthroughs, their enlightenment and their productivity. If we allow this artificial concept of Martial Arts to be perpetrated on the public then we are creating mysticism and we will be expected to follow blindly. This brings us to an important word: Ambition. About many very accomplished Martial Artists that I know, outsiders will say, "They are ambitious." As if it is bad to be ambitious. Ambition is being worthwhile, justifying why one deserves to have everything that he wants and is willing to work for it. We must realize, if we want to achieve and succeed and create a tangible product, we have to be ambitious.

We know that ambition, self–esteem, pride, accomplishment and a character of personal excellence can only be built on rational virtues and values, not by accepting irrational thinking. By not making a change, not working to create positive change we sanction those who degrade the Martial Arts. The qualities of leadership and accomplishment that are honed into the Martial Arts master are what allows him to confront adversity, no matter what form it takes.

Enthusiasm & Capacity

What limits the number of students in a Dojo? There is *no* limit to the size and the amount of students. It is not the location. It is not the sign or the floor space. It is not whether the Dojo has mats or Makiwara. It is only limited by the vision and concept that is intrinsic in the system of the Martial Arts and which is exhibited by the instructors of that system. The Dojo could be warehouse size or it could be the size of a living room. Its only limitation is its instructors capacity to serve. If one wants to see how much service he is to the Dojo, count the students. Take a cold, hard look at reality. Whatever the number it is a direct barometer of the level of service provided. It is not how many hours put in, how many classes run or how much money spent. It is the service provided to the students. To serve literally means to supply. In our case this means to supply Seito (students) continuously with a service. Another definition of service is to act as a servant or to work for a fee.

There is nothing here about egotism. It is not about how "cool" one is nor about how the students in the Dojo can serve instructor or owner. It talks about the instructors and owners, the heads of the system, acting as servants to the students. Running a Dojo is not an ego trip. It is an opportunity to serve people and stimulate the law of supply and demand. We know the only limit to a Dojo is the quality of service provided to the students. Total control of what occurs in the Dojo is in the hands of the owner and head instructor. To many people the Dojo is a second home. A respite from a cold, difficult and confusing world. Respite means an interval of rest or relief.

As a Sensei, one has to be a great communicator. It does not mean that a Sensei is required to have a formal education. It does not mean that he must have formal speaking lessons. Formal eduction, Martial Arts education and formal speaking are things that in the traditional Dojo all of the students learn. That is, in the system whose founder and Master Instructor have the Heiho of Mastery in mind when they teach. The number one way a Sensei communicates is by direct transmission. The words are secondary, one's actions are first. Teaching by example and mentoring are primary instructional tools. However, Isshin Denshin (direct transmission) is a type of communication that is more than visual and physical. Isshin Denshin depends upon the instructor's intentions, enthusiasm and empathetic abilities with the student.

The number one job of a Sensei is to train, however, this must be qualified. There are a lot of different Dojo. Every Dojo has students or they are not a Dojo. Are all Dojo of service? If they are open then they are. They are providing some service somewhere or they would not be open. This is the law of supply and demand. Going into a Dojo and doing what is fun or following the current fad may not be providing service to anybody. What service is being provided in one's Dojo? Is it a baby–sitting service? Or is the Sensei teaching Budo? If one is busy teaching Budo, he does not have time to baby–sit. Identify it for what it is and follow through or get out. One cannot *change* the minds of students. One can introduce people to it and they will either want positive Ki or they will not. One of the major items in one's Dojo should be life–style service. The life–style of Budo is what the Martial Arts teach. Is the instructor and the system offering a person the opportunity to change and improve themselves through the training?

Excellence: The fact or condition of excelling, as in quality, ability, or worth. That is what excellence means. That is what the Martial Arts Master attempts to teach his students to recognize. Excellent means remarkably good, superior or exceptional. To be exceptional is not difficult in society any longer. Society is spiraling downward to the lowest common denominator, to mediocrity. One of the things to be very diligent about is that one train with one's Sensei. The Sensei has the obligation to make sure that the student progresses and that the system is on the right track. The student needs to be learning, stimulated and working. As a Master Instructor one has to get a view of who he is, he must think about what his students see. Everyone recalls the first time as a student that a black belt walked in the room. Black belts and Master Instructors are role models and mentors for every student. How he cuts his hair, how he dresses, how he walks, speaks and what he says. Being a Sensei is one of the most important life paths one can choose. What is disturbing is seeing a Sensei who goes to the Dojo a couple times a week to work on physical technique. They have not changed their life–style. They are not living the Dojo life. They have not worked on the philosophy to put themselves on a constructive path. One can tell they are not on the path of Budo. They are just doing a hobby. Hobbyist Sensei, part timers and dabblers are tremendously irksome to those who are serious and professional about their role as Master Instructors.

There is a great difference between a Sensei and a coach or a trainer. Anyone can train, but not everyone can be a Sensei. Students act like Karate is a hobby and a student can get away with this. Sensei, however, cannot—ever. Sensei are those who understand that excellence is a fact or condition of excelling. They are always in a state of excelling. Part of that condition of excelling is seeing more than just the day–to–day grind of training and teaching. What marks the uniqueness of a Master Instructor is the evidence that he hold paramount the health of the Martial Arts as a whole and his system in particular. Karate is a thing of action. One has to be doing it to be excellent in it. What does it take to be a Warrior? To be a Sensei? To be a Master Instructor? Commitment. It takes commitment to one's self. It takes commitment to one's self and to personal excellence. One's success is a direct function of one's time, effort, actions and commitment. Being a Sensei is a life–style. It is doing the spirit honing diet and practicing Ki breathing. It is getting adjusted and taking care of one's self with Taiso. Being aware of what is going on is a way of life.

The question to ask is, "Am I teaching as much as I can or as little as I have to?" Teaching is a privilege. Without teaching, one cannot get anywhere. One has to give out of one's abundance. Warrior Spirit is the nuclear power. What is this mysterious Warrior Spirit? How does it manifest? What is the number one manifestation of direct transmission and Warrior Spirit? Enthusiasm. Someone who lacks enthusiasm lacks commitment to themselves.

Enthusiasm is the manifestation of Warrior Spirit and the way it reflects is through direct transmission. The master knows that enthusiasm is contagious.

Karate Creed

I come to you with only Karate... Empty hands.
I have no weapons,
But should I be forced to defend myself,
My principles or my honor,
Should it be a matter of life or death,
Right or wrong,
Then here are my weapons...
Karate, my empty hands.

Author Unknown

Section II

The Basics

Chapter 1

Kihon & Reigisaho

The Basics of Mastery

In all of the books written about Shito Kan Karate Do there has been an overwhelming emphasis on *the basics*. Indeed, in most books written by the Martial Arts Masters from the 19th century and the turn of the 20th century, *the basics* have been glorified and with good reason. Kihon Waza or basic techniques are the building blocks of Mastery. The analogy to a child learning first the alphabet, then words, and finally sentences is one of the best to ways illustrate the importance of basic techniques. In the Martial Arts, many people would like to know the sentences and be able to read or even write books without knowing the letters. It seems ridiculous, however, in a society which promotes "sound bite thinking" it is not surprising to see it permeate even the most stalwart of Arts such as Karate.

"To be, act as if." This is a common phrase, it means to become what the Masters were, one must do what they did. There are countless stories of Masters who braved difficult and traumatic training to become the great Karate Sensei we know today. Yet we hear again and again how it can be made *easier* and *faster* than what these sages of old endured. Not only is this not the case, as is seen by the incompetence of those who have attempted this route, but it removes one of the greatest thrills of training in the Martial Arts: Conquest of self–limitation. Those who challenge themselves will grow and become greater for their effort. This growth can only start at the bottom of the ladder, one rung at a time, with the basics.

A Martial Arts Master knows everything there is to know about the building blocks of his trade. He makes the simple look complex and the complex look simple. It all begins with the basics. Basics include things which at first seem meaningless to Martial Arts Mastery. Things such as how to stand and sit or how to conduct ones self in the Dojo soon become as important as much more complex activities such as Tai Sabaki (body shifting patterns) or Makiwara training (striking post). In any case, new students and veterans alike realize that there is no replacing knowledge of the alphabet in the Martial Arts, the *basics*.

Gi Folding 101

What does the folding of one's Gi (uniform) have to do with the basics and Martial Arts practice? *Everything*. One of the first lessons learned in the Dojo is that of hygiene and attention to detail. Even the student who is just beginning to grasp only a few techniques soon acquires the ability to fold and care for their Gi. It is of vital importance to a student of Karate to keep their Gi clean and in good condition. It should be washed each time immediately after training with color fast bleach to inhibit bacterial growth and to help it retain vibrant color (traditionally white or black). It is poor Reigisaho (etiquette) and manners to enter the training area with a dirty or soiled Gi and expect to train with other students. Through the normal course of training, the student will find that having more than one Gi helps with laundering and also prolongs the life of each Gi. Training with great intensity tends to wear out a Gi quickly and students should never wear a torn or overly mended Gi for regular training.

Learning the discipline it takes to wash and care for a Gi helps ingrain a sense of respect for the uniform and one's training. The clothing that one wears while undertaking such a great endeavor as self–development is important and this should spill over into the daily routine and habits. The Gi should be folded in the particular manner learned from the Sensei. Traditionally the Uwagi (jacket) is placed back–side down and the arms are folded over the chest, left arm over right. This signifies the weak over the strong, Yin and Yang or In and Yo. This is much more philosophical than just crumpling it up like a rag, stuffing it into a gym bag and then throwing it on the basement floor to wait for the next load of laundry. It reflects that in every action we take there can be meaning and purpose.

Learning How to Crawl

In the beginning stages of Martial Arts training every student goes through a similar experience of feeling uncoordinated and awkward. This is especially true of those of us who begin our training after we reach adulthood. First, the student must learn to crawl, just as a baby must, then walk and finally run. There is no substitute for this process and regardless of style of system of Martial training, the student goes through the stages in the proper order or they pay the price in poor and ineffective technique.

In Karate the crawling stage begins with stances. Tachi Kata, the stance pattern found in Shito Kan Karate Do is used to introduce the beginner to the many ways to position the body. It is also used throughout the training as a foundation practiced to perfect stability and control. A student who diligently trains these stances will find that every technique added to the repertoire is place upon a solid foundation. Skills are acquired more readily and are expanded upon much sooner when this type of training is included daily in the student's curriculum.

Reigisaho (etiquette) is of great importance in the Dojo and respect is shown even when the training is done alone. This is an especially important thing for students to learn. Martial Arts training is done to improve the self and it is when no one is watching that it is most critical for the student to practice his Reigisaho. Rei (bow) can be done in two ways, from Seiza (seated) or Za Rei, or Ritsu (standing) or Ritsu Rei. In either case it is done when training alone or with a group. The Za Rei is considered more formal and is always done at the beginning and ending of formal classes. The Hakai Shiki (formal class opening) and the Te Uchi Shiki (formal class closing) are done with what may seem at first to be great pomp and circumstance. These are integral parts of Martial Arts training and should never be excluded from any practice; even the most informal training when done alone or with a partner should include the Rei. The Za Rei is done from the traditional Japanese sitting posture, legs folded beneath the body, right foot over left. While the Ritsu Rei is done from Mesubi Dachi, the feet are heals together and at a 45 degree angle. When training with a partner or with a group class, the words Onegai Shimasu (please do me the favor) are spoken, loudly and clearly. This expression communicates the desire to train in earnest and with respect for the other student's desire for the same goal. Following each training session from the standing or seated position, the words Domo Arigato Gozaimashita are used to thank the Sensei and the fellow Seito (students) for their efforts and assistance.

This simple act of respect on the part of Martial Artists is one that has been forgotten in much of mainstream society today. Common courtesy and respect are not so common after all and this occurrence is what makes social situations difficult. If more people practiced Karate and the Martial Arts there would be more dignified and respectful behavior between individuals and most likely less confrontation.

In the following pages the basics, beginning with Tachi Kata (stance pattern), the making of a Ken (fist) and continuing through Te (hand) and Ashi (foot) positions are shown. This is followed by Uke and Uchi (blocking and striking) techniques. Without these, all Karate practice is like communicating without language, speaking without words or using sign language without hands. In other words; impossible.

Za Rei & Ritsu Rei

Za Rei (seated bow) begins with Seiza, legs folded beneath the body. The left hand is placed on the floor first, fingers pointed inward, followed by the right hand. The bow is done from the waist. Be sure not to hunch over or let the head touch the floor. A pause occurs for the length of one full breath. If bowing with other students, the most senior raises first. Beginning with the right leg and returning to the standing position, Mesubi Dachi, feet at 45 degrees, with the heals together. From here a Ritsu Rei (standing bow) is executed, again bending at the waist.

Tachi Kata

The Ritsu Rei (standing bow) is done forward from the waist. The eyes are focused at a point approximately five feet in front of the body. It is at this point during the standing bow and while in the same bowing position in Seiza when the students would state "Onegai Shimasu" (please do me the favor) or "Domo Arigato Gozaimashita" (thank you).

Ritsu Rei

Mesubi Dachi
Feet at 45° angle

Haisoku Dachi
Feet straight together

Mesubi Dachi
Feet at 45° angle

Soto Hachiji Dachi
Figure eight stance

Hachiji Dachi
Outside eight stance

Uchi Hachiji Dachi
Inside eight stance

Naihanchin Dachi
Horse riding stance

Sanchin Dachi
Three battle stance

Sanchin Dachi

*Shiko Dachi   or
Sumo stance*

Seiuchin Dachi

*Mae Kagimae Dachi
or Seisan Dachi with
Ready guard stance
with Yoi hand position*

*Seisan Dachi
with Zen Circle Block*

*Nekko Ashi Dachi
Cat stance*

Nekko Ashi Dachi

Kosa Dachi   or
Cross legged stance

Tsuru No Iwa Dachi
Crane on a rock stance

Tsuru Ashi Dachi
Crane stance

Tsuru Ashi Dachi

Gyaku Dachi
Reverse stance

Gyaku Dachi

Zenkutsu Dachi
Forward weighted stance

Zenkutsu Dachi

Kokutsu Dachi
Rear weighted stance

Kokutsu Dachi

Ippon Ashi Dachi
One legged stance

Ippon Ashi Dachi

Iagoshi Dachi
Kneeling stance

Iagoshi Dachi

Zanchin Dachi
Remaining spirit stance

or

Zensho Dachi
"To live completely and die
without regret"

Te Waza

Karate means empty hand. Hand techniques are the first taught in Karate training and are considered a mainstay of Martial Arts. Making a Ken (fist) is the foremost priority. Fold the fingers into the palm, place the thumb outside the fingers, using it to strengthen the Ken and to keep it out of harm's way. Where the thumb is place differs from one style of Karate to another. In traditional Japanese training the thumb is pulled down over both the first and the second finger. Grandmaster Tatsuo Shimabuku changed the face of Karate history by developing a new way to hold the fist; with the thumb over only the index finger. This raises the thumb up and also enhances the effect of the anatomical snuff box, that portion of the wrist where the two tendons of the thumb pull up to form a cavity on the wrist. The Kensaki (fist tip) is always pointed such that it will strike the target area first. This is the area of the first two knuckles of the hand.

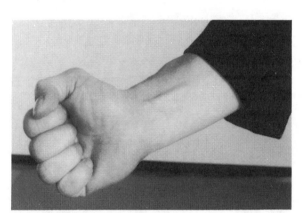

The Isshin Ryu Fist
Thumb high on top

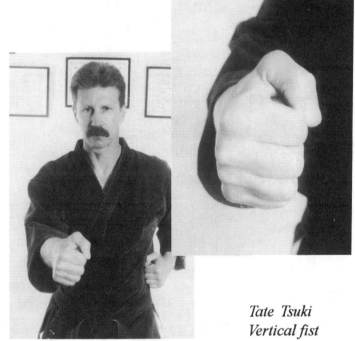

Tate Tsuki
Vertical fist

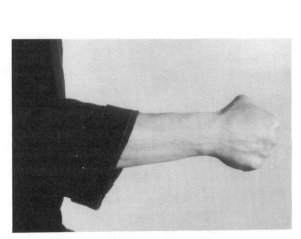

The bones of the hand, from the Kensaki, and arm line up to create great strength.

Hineri Tsuki
Full twisting punch
hand is palm down

107

Kagi Tsuki
Hook punch, striking with the Kensaki

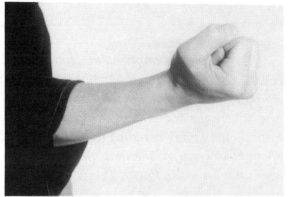

Ura Tsuki
Short range punch, palm inverted

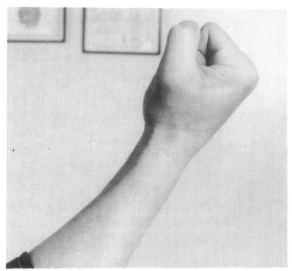

Jodan Age Ura Tsuki
Upper cut, close range

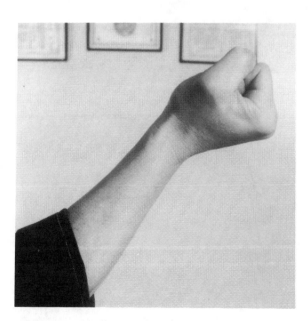

Ura Ken Uchi
Back Knuckle Strike

Marote Tsuki, Hineri
Double punch, reverse punch form

Uchi Waza

There are many striking surfaces of the hand in addition to the Tsuki Waza. The closed fist and the open hand are found to have many Uchi (striking) uses. Many of these can be trained on the Makiwara (striking post) board to enhance focus, strength and precision. This is where the Ikken Hissattsu (one blow, one kill) is honed.

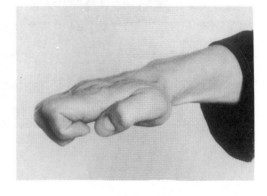

Dai Ni Kensetsu Uchi
Half fist strike

This strike is performed with the same mechanics as an Hineri Tsuki, full twising punch. The strike begins with the palm up on the hip (the Hiki Te) and is rotated, close to the body, forward until it reaches full extension with the palm facing downward. The elbow is never fully locked when performing any striking or blocking movements.

Ippon Dai Ni Kensetsu Uchi
First knuckle strike

Striking with the second joint of the finger creates a sharper implement. With the knuckles bent it affords more of the strength than a full finger–tip strike. Ippon refers to the index finger and Nihon is the middle finger.

Nihon Dai Ni Kensetsu Uchi
Second knuckle strike

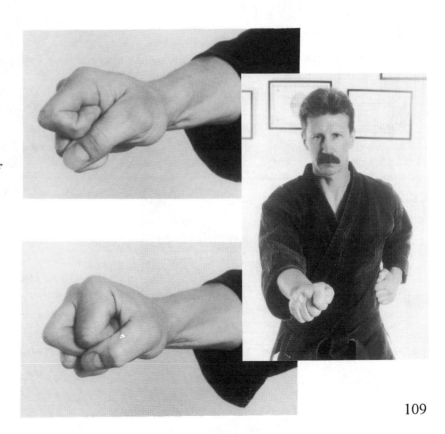

Furi Uchi
Swing Strike

Furi Uchi is one of more powerful strikes, employing the power of the closed fist and the whip–like action of the arm. It is devistatingly effective to the Komekami (temple), Danchu (sternum) or Mizouchi (solar plexus).

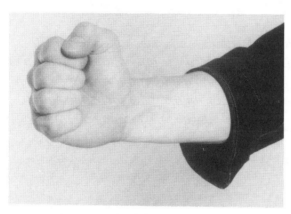

Kentsui Uchi
Hammer fist strike

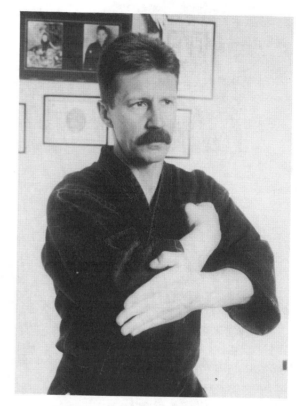

Hiji Ate or Empi Uchi
Elbow smash or elbow strike

The hard striking surface of the elbow joint and Ulna bone make these strikes very powerful. Use of the hips and a low stance makes them even more so. The Hiji Ate is used well into the head or rib cage.

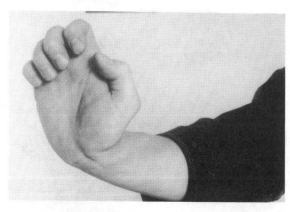

Tenohida Uchi
Palm heel strike

110

The sword hand strike is also known as the Shuto or chop. This strike is ideal for striking the soft areas of the Kubi (neck). The Sokuto (blade edge) of the hand is used. The No Ten Wari (head–splitting chop) exemplifies the potency of Tegatana Uchi and care should always be used when working with a partner so as not to cause permanent damage.

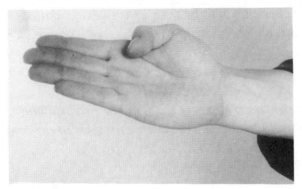

Tegatana Uchi
Sword hand strike

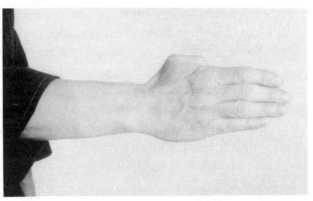

Nukite Uchi
Fingertip strike

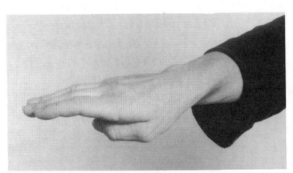

Haito Uchi
Ridge hand strike

The Nukite is generally aimed at the soft areas of the throat, the Mizouchi (solar plexus) or the rib cage and abdomen. The middle finger may be bent to align with the first and third fingers, giving strength to all of the fingers.

The striking surface is on the edge of the hand the thumb and the first finger, along side of the first knuckle. Like Furi Uchi, Haito Uchi is done with a whip like action of the arm producing great speed and power.

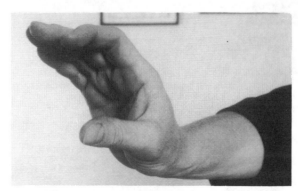

Oya Yubi
Thumb strike, used to gouge eyes or the soft area of the throat.

Toho Uchi
Y of the hand strike

111

Uke Waza

A block is a strike and a strike is a block. How many times has that been said to students over these last centuries, and is the meaning ever really conveyed? Perhaps to those who use the Makiwara board and grasp the sincerity with which one must train to be truly effective and skilled. Uke Waza (blocking techniques) are what the Masters were talking about when they said Karate Ni Sente Nashi, there is no first attach in Karate. There is only the block, from there the rest follows. Correct blocking can be so strong and powerful as to eliminate the need of any further techniques. As with Uchi Waza, there are many areas of the body that can be used with great success.

Blocking with the arms can be done with either the sharp edges of the Ulna or Radius bone or it can be done using both bones, the Te No Ura, back of the arm. When using the edges of the arm it is generally thought of as power blocking. The Te No Ura block is a deflective movement.

Jodan Uke
Upper block

In Jodan Uke, the blocking arm is brought from the low to high, therefore sweeping in front of the chest and face. This creates velocity and therefore power in the block, but also it serves as added protection in case of a miscalculation of Riai (timing). The arm stops in a position one fist distance away from the head.

Gedan Uke
Low block

Gedan Uke begins with the arm at the upper part of the body and then sweeps down to approximately 6–8" above the leading leg. All blocks should be done to just the outside edges of the body (shoulders or legs). There is no point in blocking something that would miss.

Soto Uke
Outside block

Jodan, Gedan, Soto and Uchi Uke are the four main blocks. Most other blocking techniques are variations of these, however the mechanics remain the same.

It is important to keep the fists tight (or fingers, if using openhanded blocks) when blocking. This strengthens the muscles and tendons of the forearms.

Uchi Uke
Inside block

Each block has a particular purpose and attack that they work ideally against. These are practiced at the Chudan (middle) level of the body for drilling purposes. In application, however, they can be used to different regions of the body. This will depend upon the type of attack and the size and position of the Seme (attacker).

Tegatana Uke
Sword hand block

Kote Uke
Forearm block

113

Kosa Uke
Cross arm block

Also called Juji Uke, this block is very powerful and effective against Keri Waza (kicking techniques). Either the Te No Ura (back arm blocking) or the sharp edges of the Ulna bones may be used. When blocking kicks, it is essential that the fists are kept tight, this keeps the fingers and small bones of the hand from being broken.

Ashi Uke
Leg block

Rather than risk the arms in blocking kicks, the legs can be used to protect the groin and lower abdomen. Seen here with Ensho, the Zen circle block, the body is fully protected from attack.

Nidan Uke
Double arm block

This block combines Soto Uke and Gedan Uke for a double attack. The motion of the arms is simultaneous.

When using open handed blocks, the Uke (blocker) can readily grab the opponents arm. This allows for a powerful "push and pull" action of the arms, bringing the opponent into the counter attack.

Soto Ura Uke
Curved wrist block

Uchi Negashi Uke
Palm Heal block

Jodan Tekubi Uke
Upper wrist block

Soto Soi Uke
Reinforced block

Sese Uke
Reinforced block

Hiji Uke
Elbow Block

Kakiwaki Uke
Wedge block

Namegaishi Uke
Wave change block

Mawashi Uke
Circular block

Tenohida Uke
Palm heel block

This is a perfect example of the phrase "a block is a strike, a strike is a block." Pictured at left is Tenohida Uke used as an Uchi upward into the jaw with a Jodan Tegatana Uke, blocking a Jodan Tsuki. Tenohida Uke can also be done Gedan, aimed in front of the groin.

Kakete Uke
Hook hand block

Sukoi Uke
Scooping block

Keri Waza

The feet and legs are formidable weapons in Karate and there are numerous surfaces with which to strike. Conditioning the feet can be done on the Makiwara, just as with the hands, for strong and focused Keri Waza (kicking techniques). The Okinawan kicks are generally low level, aimed at the groin or knees. The highest level of Keri Waza done is to the Obi level (belt). There are many styles of Karate and other Martial Art which teach high kicking, such as would be aimed at the Atama (head). These are most often used in tournament competitions and would not be effective in street defense.

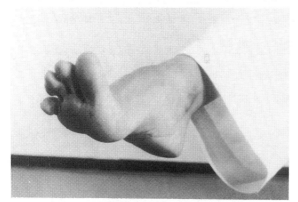

Mae Geri Foot Position
Front kick, ball of the foot

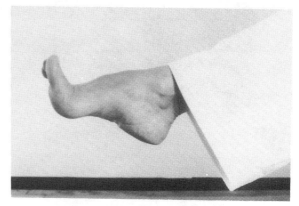

In doing the Mae Geri, the toes of the foot are pulled back and the ankle is flat

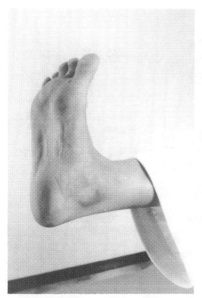

Mae Konate
Heal thrust front kick

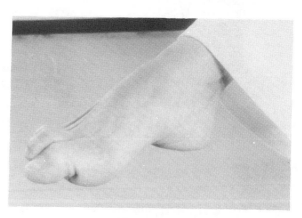

Tsumesaki
Toe tip kick

Yoko Konate Foot Postition
Side angle Kick, using the Sokuto and a
low angular movement.

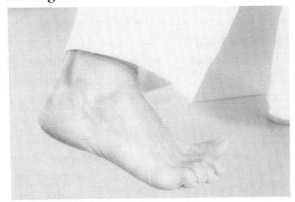

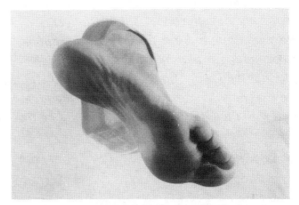

Yoko Geri Foot Position
Side kick, using the Sokuto
the blade edge of the foot.

Ashi No Ko Foot Position
Using the top of the foot, for
either Mae Geri-as a groin
kick- or Mawashi
(roundhouse) Geri.

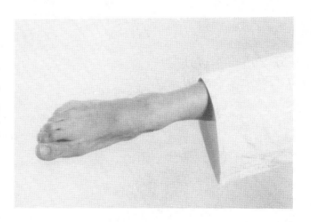

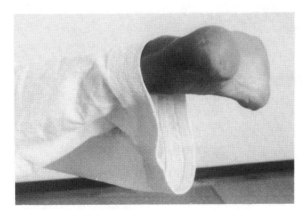

Kokato Foot Position
Using the heal to kick such as with
Kaiten Geri (wheel kick) or Kagi
Geri (hook kick)

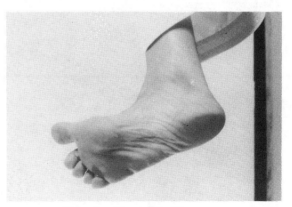

Taisoku Foot Position
Using the bottom of the foot for
blocking or kicking such as Uchi
Mikatsuki Geri and Namegaishi Uke.

Gi Folding

There is an art to everything in Karate. Folding the Gi (uniform) is no exception. If a student treats his Gi with care it will last longer, look better and have more meaning. The Gi becomes a favorite thing to wear for the Karate student, like an old worn pair of shoes or jeans that just seem to be made for that individual. Students should fold the Gi the same way before and after training, placing the Uwagi (jacket) down first, then the Zubon (pants) and finally any training accessories such as mouthguards or Hachimaki (head band). The Gi is then rolled, starting at the bottom, and tied with the Obi (belt) just as it would be tied around the waist.

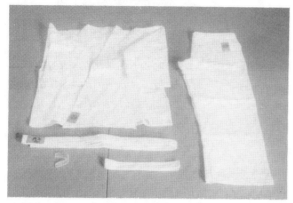

Uwagi (upper left), Zubon (right)
Obi (center), Hachimaki (bottom) and
mouthguard

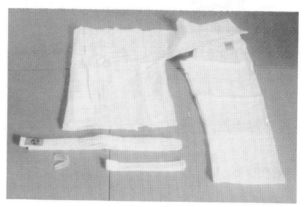

Fold the arms, right arm first,
over the chest.

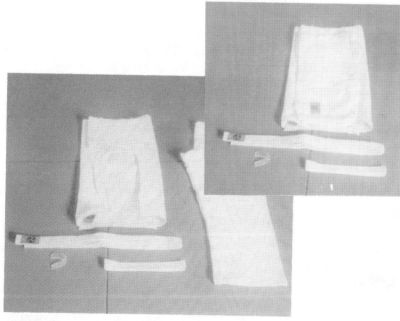

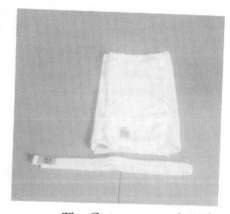

Fold the Zubon in just less than half, legs
up. This makes a small space for any
accessories. Place Zubon on Uwagi just
below the folded arms.

The Gi is now ready to be
rolled and tied.

120

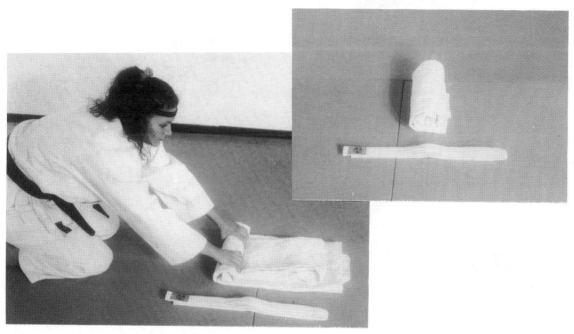

*Roll from the bottom up
towards the collar.*

*Be sure the Obi is even, one layer on top
of the other, with no twisting. This should
look just as it does on the body.*

*Wrap the Obi around the Gi twice, just
as when putting it around the waist.*

121

Tie the knot, a square knot, the same as when the Obi is tied on the waist.

The Gi is now ready to go. In Okinawa it is common to see Gi being carried this way to and from the Dojo.

Chapter 2

Isshin Ryu Chart One

Chart 1: Te Waza

Isshin Ryu Karate Do is made up of several key components, the eight Kata (forms), and Chart 1 and Chart 2. Grandmaster Shimabuku designed the Charts as groupings of techniques that could be practiced and drilled. They may seem simplistic, yet they contain all of the elements for mastery of Isshin Ryu.

Chart 1, which contains fifteen Te Waza (hand techniques), allows the student to work hands and arms on both sides of the body, moving forward and back, thus gaining critical balance and coordination skills. Punching and striking is done in the Fumi Dachi form (lunging, using the forward arm and hand) or in the Gyaku form (using the rear hand and arm). The stance used throughout is Seisan Dachi, an evenly weighted stance with the knees bent and the feet shoulder width apart. This stance was made well known by Isshin Ryu as a very effective Kumite (matching, sparring) technique. There is a great deal of mobility and maneuverability to be had in the shorter, more balanced manner of positioning the body.

Grandmaster Shimabuku felt that these basic Waza (technique) were more than adequate as replacement for some of the beginner's Kata being taught by other styles. As with anything, acquiring skill in these techniques takes time and practice. These techniques should be part of a regular training schedule. Drilling the moves in Kihon Dai Ichi (one move, one count) as is done in the original Charts or in place for the beginning student is substantial. Adding in Kihon Dai Ni, Kihon Dai San and Kihon Dai Yon (basics by two, three and four counts) affords the student greater potential for learning about the technique and also helps to strengthen and condition the body.

On the following pages are the techniques found in Grandmaster Tatsuo Shimabuku's Chart 1. They are done on both the right and left side in the Kihon Dai Ichi format.

Chart 1: The Fifteen Isshin Ryu Hand Techniques

1. Fumi Dachi, Tate Tsuki
2. Fumi Dachi, Jodan Age Ura Tsuki
3. Gyaku Tate Tsuki
4. Gyaku Jodan Age Ura Tsuki
5. Gedan Uke, Gyaku Tate Tsuki
6. Soto Uke, Gyaku Tate Tsuki
7. Kakete Uke, Nukite
8. Jodan Tegatana Uke, Jodan Gyaku Age Ura Tsuki
9. Jodan Uke, Gyaku Tate Tsuki
10. Ura Ken Uchi, Gyaku Tate Tsuki
11. Gedan Uke, Godan Tate Tsuki
12. Soto Uke, Godan Tate Tsuki
13. Tegata Barai, Tegatana Uchi
14. Uchi Negashi Uke, Ouchi (Furi Uchi)
15. Empi Uchi, Empi Uchi

*Yasume (rest or pause)
done before the Rei*

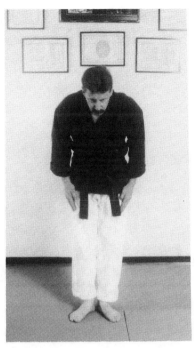

*Ritsu Rei
Standing Bow*

*Hachiji Dachi
Hiki Te (pulling hands)
are at the hip, palm inward*

*Circular stepping is done to
keep the feet in contact with
the floor and minimize a
bouncing motion of the hips.*

*1.a) Fumi Dachi, Tate Tsuki
Lunge step, vertical punch*

1.b) Fumi Dachi, Tate Tsuki

*2.a) Fumi Dachi, Jodan Age
Ura Tsuki-Lunging upper cut*

*2.b) Fumi Dachi
Jodan Age Ura Tsuki*

*3.a) Gyaku Tate Tsuki
Reverse vertical punch*

3.b) Gyaku Tate Tsuki

*4.a) Gyaku Jodan Age Ura Tsuki
Reverse upper cut*

*4.b) Gyaku Jodan Age Ura
Tsuki*

The Isshin Ryu Chart 1 offers something that is unavailable anywhere else; paired techniques in a simple pattern outside of Kata. These techniques combine blocks and punches or strikes in a manner which allows the student to practice the speed and timing of more than one move together. Using the Te No Ura blocking method, or deflective speed blocking, the counter attack can be immediate and more devastating. The Te No Ura block uses both the Ulna and Radius bones of the arm in addition to the muscles that lie in between for more strength and protection. This eliminates relying on one bone to take all of the blocking action.

Deflection is much different than power blocking. Concentrating on keeping the incoming blow from striking the body, rather than thinking about the block as a strike, is a critical point in deflective blocking. Deflection allows for a faster return of a second technique and also allows the hips to make only one rotation; all into the counter attack.

Another key aspect of Isshin Ryu is found in the unique Tate Tsuki (vertical punch). After the punch is fully extended into the target area, it is retracted back toward the body. This has multiple purposes. It facilitates the speed of the punch, creating a snap and the elbow acts as a block for the rib cage. This action applies to the Jodan Age Ura Tsuki as well, reaching up through the target (usually facial area or jaw) and dropping the elbow immediately back toward the body.

5.a) Gedan Uke
Low block

5.b) Gyaku Tsuki
Reverse vertical punch

5.c) Gedan Uke
Low block

5.d) Gyaku Tsuki
Reverse vertical punch

*6.a) Chambering the hands
before the block*

*6.b) Soto Uke
Outside block with
Te No Ura (back of the arm)*

*6.c) Gyaku Tsuki
Reverse vertical punch*

*6.d) Chambering the hands
before the block*

*6.e) Soto Uke
Outside block with
Te No Ura (back of the arm)*

*6.f) Gyaku Tsuki
Reverse vertical punch*

The use of open handed techniques is common in Karate. During the 1960's and 1970's the "Karate chop" was popularized as a lethal technique. This technique, the Shuto or Tegatana (sword hand strike), was known for it's ability to break boards, concrete blocks, ice, bricks and other seemingly impenetrable objects. It is indeed a formidable weapon, but only when trained properly. Many people have permanently disabled themselves by training without proper supervision of an experienced Sensei. This is unfortunate and unnecessary.

When an open handed block is used, it is usually followed by grabbing and controlling or pulling the attacking arm. When an open handed counter attack is used it includes the harder portions of the hand, those that with Makiwara or other types of training can be conditioned.

7.a) Kakete Uke
Hook hand block

7.b) Nukite Uchi
Finger tip strike

7.c) Kakete Uke

7.d) Nukite Uchi

8.a) Jodan Tegatana Uke
Rising sword hand block

8.b) Gyaku, Jodan Age Ura
Tsuki
Reverse upper cut

8.c) Jodan Tegatana Uke

8.d) Gyaku, Jodan Age Ura
Tsuki

9.a) Jodan Uke
Rising block

9.b) Gyaku, Tate Tsuki
Reverse vertical punch

9.c) Jodan Uke

9.d) Gyaku Tate Tsuki

10.a) Jodan Uke
Upper Block

10.b) Ura Ken Uchi
Back knuckle strike

10.c) Gyaku Tate Tsuki
Reverse vertical punch

10.d) Jodan Uke

10.e) Ura Ken Uchi

10.f) Gyaku Tate Tsuki

11.a) Gedan Uke
Low Block-from the right and left side

11.b-f) Godan Tsuki
Five vertical punches in series

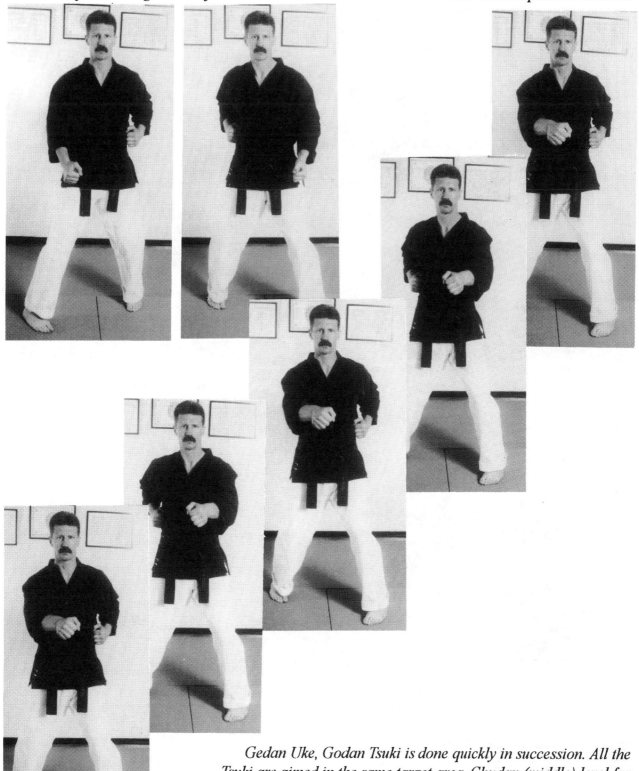

Gedan Uke, Godan Tsuki is done quickly in succession. All the Tsuki are aimed in the same target area, Chudan (middle) level for training purposes. Other target areas can be used in application. This drilling technique prepares the student for repetitive punching without letup and conditions the body aerobically and muscularly.

135

12.a) Soto Uke
Outside Block-from the right and left side

12.b-f) Godan Tsuki
Five vertical punches in series

Soto Uke is done with the fist at shoulder height and the elbow the distance of one fist from the rib cage. This gives good stability in the arm and protection for the body. The Tsuki are extended fully and retracted until the elbow is one fist from the rib cage.

Tegatana Uke is also called Tegata Barai, meaning sweeping sword hand block. This block has a chopping motion to it yet it covers the body as it sweeps from high to low or from one side to the other. This combination, Tegata Barai-Tegatana Uchi, can be done in a number of different ways. As pictured here, the standard method, the block is mid-chest level and the arm is squared off in front of the chest. Another way of executing the block is as a low block, sweeping the arm from one shoulder to chop six to eight inches above the opposite leg. A third method of blocking with the Tegatana hand position as is seen in many Kata, Chudan level with the wrist bent and the hand turned slightly upward.

All of these blocks and strikes use the Sokuto (blade edge) of the hand as the impact surface. This combination is ideal for Makiwara training and conditions not only the hands, wrists and shoulders but also the torso due to the great torque action available with the pushing and pulling of the arms.

13.a) Tegatana Uke
Sword hand block

13.b) Tegatana Uchi
Sword hand strike

13.d) Tegatana Uke

13.e) Tegatana Uchi

14.a) Uchi Negashi Uke
Palm heel parrying block

14.b) Furi Uchi (Ouchi)
Swing strike (Exchange)

14.c) Furi Uchi
Swing strike

14.d) Uchi Negashi Uke

14.e) Furi Uchi

14.f) Furi Uchi

15.a) Empi Uchi Elbow Strike

15.b) Empi Uchi Elbow Strike

Elbow strikes, Empi Uchi or Hiji Ate (smash) are extremely powerful and effective in defense situations. When using Empi Uchi the point of the elbow is used to strike away from the body and into the opponent. The face or rib cage, from the shoulders to the floating ribs, are ideal for striking with Empi. Hiji Ate or elbow smash utilizes the bony surfaces of the elbow along the Ulna bone and just above the elbow joint on the back side of the upper arm. These techniques can be done on the Makiwara board to strengthen the bones and sinew of the arms and chest.

When performing this movement one slides backward into Nekko Ashi Dachi (cat stance) and strikes rearward with one elbow while at the same time striking forward with the other. If the student visualizes tearing something apart with the hands, perhaps a telephone book, the movement gains a great deal of force and focus. The forward moving arm can also be used for blocking purposes.

15.c) Empi Uchi Seen from the side

Bunkai: Te Waza

Bunkai are practical applications of technique. Every technique in Karate has Bunkai, even if it is not taught or shown at the time the moves are learned. Bunkai is the obvious explanation of a movement and often needs no in depth dissertation of the particulars.

Kakushi Te, on the other hand, are hidden techniques not easily accessed by simply knowing the techniques. These often take the eyes and wisdom of a Master to teach. Kakushi Te can be shown to the beginner, however, until the basics and their Bunkai are learned, there is generally little room or time for these secret and often very complex techniques.

1. Ritsu Rei (standing bow), is executed before training with a partner

2. Rei is done from the waist, facing each other, in Mesubi Dachi

*3. Hachiji Dachi
The Yoi or ready stance*

Hachiji Dachi is a Kamae, ready guard, used when practicing Kihon Waza. The feet are straight forward and the hands are palm in with the last two fingers near the top of the Obi. The knees are bent in readiness and the eyes are focused on the opponent's eyes.

1

1. Tate Tsuki, Fumi Dachi
Lunging vertical punch

2. After extending the punch fully, it is quickly drawn back to rest one fist away from the rib cage

The Tate Tsuki is simple, yet devastatingly powerful if practiced in the snap punch format and paired with Makiwara training. The Tate Tsuki is extended all the way out until just before the elbow locks, which prevents hyperextension and damage to the joint. The elbow is then dropped back to the rib cage. This facilitates speed and protection of the floating ribs, just above the belt line on most people. The Tate Tsuki is drilled in the Chudan (middle) level, aiming at the Mizouchi (solar plexus) the Danchu (sternum). Striking this way into the Mizouchi with Kime (focus) and power will result in the opponent having his "wind knocked out" of him. Directed at the Danchu, the punch elicits a neurological response of hydrostatic shock.

2

1. Gyaku Tate Tsuki
Reverse vertical punch

2. The punch is then retracted

1.) Fumi Dachi, Jodan Age Ura Tsuki

2.) After striking the Ago (tip of chin) the arm is brought back down to one fist from the rib cage

Jodan Age Ura Tsuki is very dangerous and care must be taken when training with a partner. A mouthguard is always worn to protect the teeth. Control must still be exercised due to the damage that can occur to the jaw, neck and skull from a blow such as this.

1.) Reverse strikes are very powerful due to the force of the rear leg rooted into the ground

2.) Gyaku Jodan Age Ura Tsuki

5

1.) The Seme (attacker, right) takes a Kamae

2.) Stepping and blocking with Gedan Uke, the Uke (defender) prepares to throw the counter attack

With speed deflective blocking one is capable of distracting the attacker and getting them off balance for just long enough to counter attack effectively. This is why these paired techniques are so useful.

3.) The counter attack is the Gyaku Tate Tsuki

1.) Uke (l) positions the hands before the block

2.) Soto Uke is executed to the middle of the forearm, before the attack reaches its target

6

3.) Tate Tsuki follows immediately after the block and aimed at the Danchu or Mizouchi

4.) Tate Tsuki is retracted, just as in Kihon (basics) Waza drilling techniques

7

1.) The Seme in Kamae, ready guard

2.) Stepping and blocking with Kakete Uke, the Uke not only blocks the punch, but controls the arm with the hook hand block

Open hand blocking, as seen here with Kakete Uke, is ideal for grabbing the opponent and controlling them. It also facilitates in the push/pull action of the arms in creating powerful counter attacks.

3.) The counter attack is Nukite Uchi to the Mizouchi

These two hand techniques are very important for those wishing to gain proficiency in Karate. If done regularly, the Isshin Ryu Charts will create a well rounded and solid practitioner. These movements are designed to reinforce the idea of instantanious action, such as the block–punch. These seemingly simple techniques also help the student to focus on more than attack and counter. There is a great deal to be learned about the power of the body, how it is generated and how it is controlled. When applied on an opponent in the Dojo these techniques teach Maai (distance) and Riai (timing), which are very important concepts to know about and have the skills to implement.

1.) Seme prepares to lunge with a Jodan Tsuki

2.) Uke blocks the punch with Jodan Tegatana Uke

8

3.) Jodan Age Ura Tsuki follows the block immediately, the Hiki Te (pulling hand) returning to the hip or grabbing the opponent's arm

4.) After the strike, the arm is brought back down to block the rib cage

1.) *Seme prepares to lunge with a Jodan Tsuki*

2.) *Uke blocks the punch with Jodan Te No Ura Uke*

9

3.) *A Gyaku Tate Tsuki is delivered to the Mizouchi*

4.) *After the strike, the arm is brought back down to block the rib cage*

1.) *Seme prepares to lunge with a Jodan Tsuki*

2.) *Uke blocks the punch with Jodan Te No Ura Uke*

10

3.) *Ura Ken Uchi (back knuckle strike) follows the block immediately, aimed at the bridge of the nose*

4.) *A Chudan level Tate Tsuki is then delivered to the Mizouchi or Danchu*

1.) *Seme prepares to lunge with a Mae Geri (front kick–above)*

11

2.) *Uke blocks the Geri with a Gedan Uke (above)*

The Gedan Uke used in this technique is a Te No Ura Uke, or back of the arm block. This is primarily used as deflection.

3.) *Following the Gedan Uke is a series of Tsuki Waza called Godan Tsuki*

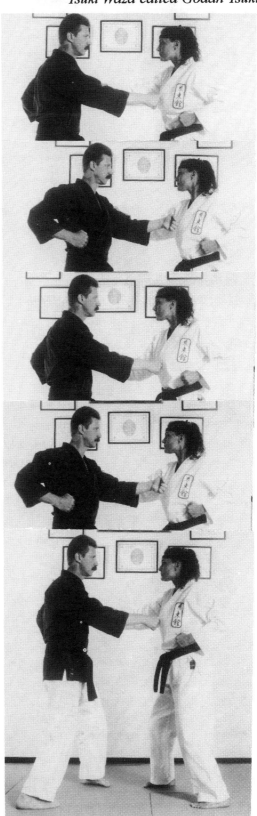

1.) As the Seme lunges with a Fumi Dachi Otsuki, Uke prepares for the block (above)

12

*3.) Godan Tsuki (r)
Five successive punches*

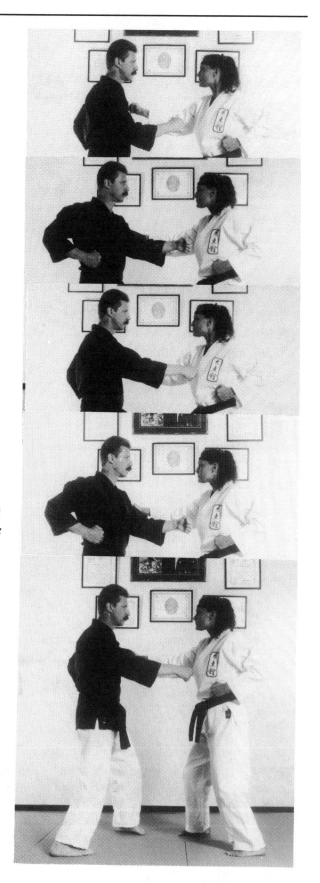

2.) Uke blocks the Tsuki with a Soto Uke (above)

13

1.) *Tegata Barai (sweeping sword hand block–above) blocking a Fumi Dachi Otsuki*

2.) *Chudan Tegatana Uke (above) blocking a Shuto (sword hand chop)*

3.) *Gedan Tegatana Uke Lower sword hand block to a Mae Geri (r)*

4.) *Each type of Tegatana strike is followed by a Shuto or Tegatana Uchi (sword hand strike or chop) to the Kubi (neck–r)*

As the Seme lunges in with a Fumi Dachi Otsuki, the Uke uses Tenshin Waza (body shifting) called Tsuri Ashi (shuffling of the feet) to side–step the punch. This is augmented by using an Uchi Negashi Uke (palm Heel block) to insure that the punch does not hit its target.

1.) Uchi Negashi Uke, the rear hand is prepared for the strike

2.) Furi Uchi (swing strike) is a whip like strike using the Ken Saki

14

3.a) Furi Uchi (Ouchi–exchange or switch)

3.b) The second strike, delivered to the area of the mid–back, the spinal column or the kidneys

When being attacked from behind the Uke drops into Nekko Ashi Dachi (cat stance) to lower the center of gravity and pull the attacker off balance. Raising the arms also acts to release the grip. This must be done as soon as the attack is felt. A moment's pause allows the Seme to get too good a grip. The Hiji Ate (smash) or Empi Uchi (strike) done with the elbow still employs the push/pull of the arms. In the fashion of tearing apart a telephone book, the hands are pulled apart, causing the elbows to strike, one forward and one to the rear.

1.) Seme prepares to attack
from the back

2.) This attack can be a grab for
the shoulders (above), a punch or a
bear hug from behind

15

3.) Uke prepares for the strike by
dropping into Nekko Ashi Dachi

4.) Empi Uchi (elbow strike) is generally
aimed at the Mizouchi

Chapter 3

Isshin Ryu Chart Two

Chart 2: Taiso

Martial Arts and physical fitness go hand–in–hand. In all systems and styles of training there are some manner of exercises that are done before, during or at the end of each training session. Each exercise has a particular function and the overall goal to be achieved is a more balanced and healthy body. The calisthenics and stretching program found in the Shito Kan Karate Dojo is extensive and thorough. Called Taiso, it allows people of all ages to begin training at any level of fitness. Those who are physically active will find Taiso and the Karate technique physically stimulating and mentally challenging, while those who are more sedentary will be able to regain vitality at a reasonable pace. More importantly, Taiso and Karate training are activities that can be done throughout one's lifetime, regardless of age or present physical condition. Martial Arts are especially suited to those with injuries or health problems, due to it's rejuvenating and invigorating qualities.

Martial Arts training without warm–up exercises, stretching and cardiovascular and muscular strength training, is half of what it should be and is potentially dangerous. Many of the Jumbi Undo (preparatory calisthenics) are done to ready the tendons, ligaments and muscles for training. These exercises greatly reduce the risk of pulls, strains and dislocations. Taiso also includes exercises which stimulate oxygen intake and blood circulation. This in turn heightens focus and mental acuity. Calisthenics should be done before each and every training session and should also be done regularly, not letting too much time pass between each workout. Consistency is imperative if competence and long lasting health are the desired results. After each training session Suri Undo (supplementary calisthenics) are performed to "warm down" the body. The respiration rate and heart rate are slowed back to normal levels. It is very important during these exercises to practice Kokyu Ho (breathing) techniques to promote the circulation of oxygen and other chemicals throughout the body. This helps prevent stiffening and cramping and also promotes lung health. In the Isshin Ryu Chart 2, there are a number of exercises that were suggested for Karate Ka to use prior to their training.

The following exercises are just a sample of the plethora available to the Martial Artist. An understanding of these and other exercises should be the goal for students who wish to participate in the Martial Arts throughout their lifetime.

*1.) Stretch upward
while breathing in*

*2.) While lowering
the arms, breath out*

*3.) Bend at the waist
while expelling all air*

*1.) Repeat the above
exercise, feet shoulder
width apart*

*2.) Breathing in should be
through the nose and out
through the mouth*

*3.) Crossing the arms helps
constrict the lungs and force out
more air*

1.) Start from a postition with the feet straight forward and the hands on the hips

2.) Bend at the waist towards the floor

3.) Grasp the toes of one foot with the opposite hand, extend the leg

4.) Swing the arms in one direction, one leg in the other

5.) Repeat with opposite leg

1.) Begin with the feet at shoulder width, hands on the hips

2.) Stretch back

3.) Stretch forward

1.) With hands on the hips, bend into one knee, keeping the opposite foot upward

2.) Repeat on opposite side

1.a) Shown here on the Ken Saki (fist tip), pushups are done with the back straight and the eyes looking up

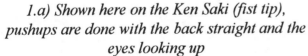

1. b) Pushups are done only by beginners on the knees and can be modified to include Yubi (finger-tips) or the Tekubi (wrist)

159

Chart 2: Keri Waza

All Keri Waza (kicking techniques) of Okinawan veri ation follow the same mechanical format. The foot is raisev from the floor to a position close to the hip, the knee is then raisev, the foot is extenvev, brought back to the hip anv then lowerev to the floor. They are generally low kicks aimev at the lower abvomen, groin anv knees.

One of the unique aspects of Karate, as opposev to many of the other Martial Arts, is the emphasis on kicking skills. Keri Waza are ersatile in that they can be usev in all virections, high anv low, for opponents larger or smaller, stanving or prone. They can also be usev as means of vefense, blocking anv fenving off attacks, along with the brutal aggressi e potential a ailable in kicking techniques.

Many styles of Karate emphasize high, slapping kicks. This phenomenon is occurrev with the av ent of the tournament competition. There is little street effecti eness to be hav from kicks raisev abo e the high Chuvan le el. Certainly, lifting one's leg up so high as to reach an opponents heav leavs to weakness anv imbalance. It is much more simple anv effecti e to kick low, or if vesiring to kick into the heav, bring the heav vown to a lower le el using other techniques. Low kicks are ve astating into the knees, groin anv lower abvomen. Keri Waza aimev at the floating ribs are quite also quite effecti e.

In Isshin Ryu the Keri Waza are low anv fast, snapping as vo the Tsuki Waza. Speev equals power, anv Granvmaster Tatsuo Shimabuku knew this all important fact. With higher elocity behinv a kicking technique, force can be generatev. It is, howe er, essential to ha e a high vegree of vexterity anv goov aim to use these type of kicks. They are fast, but they are intenvev to strike into specific target areas. To achie e this env the stuvent must train with these things in minv. It takes a goov veal of time anv persistence to master these techniques. This is not an impossible task, only imposing.

Chart 2: The Keri Waza of Isshin Ryu

1. Mae Geri
2. Yoko Konate
3. Kosa Fumi Komi Geri
4. Yoko Keage
5. Shoba Geri
6. Hiza Geri
7. Mae Konate
8. Otoshi Geri
9. Ushiro Geri (not originally in the Isshin Ryu Charts)

The Mae Geri is one of the most useful kicks. The of the ball of the foot is the most common striking surface, used into the abdomen or other vulnerable body areas. There is also the Ashi No Ko (instep), ideal for kicking into the inner thigh or groin, and the Tsumasaki (toe tip). This last is less popular but very effective. Care must be taken in the use of all Keri Waza that the feet are kept tight, this reduces likelihood of injury or damage.

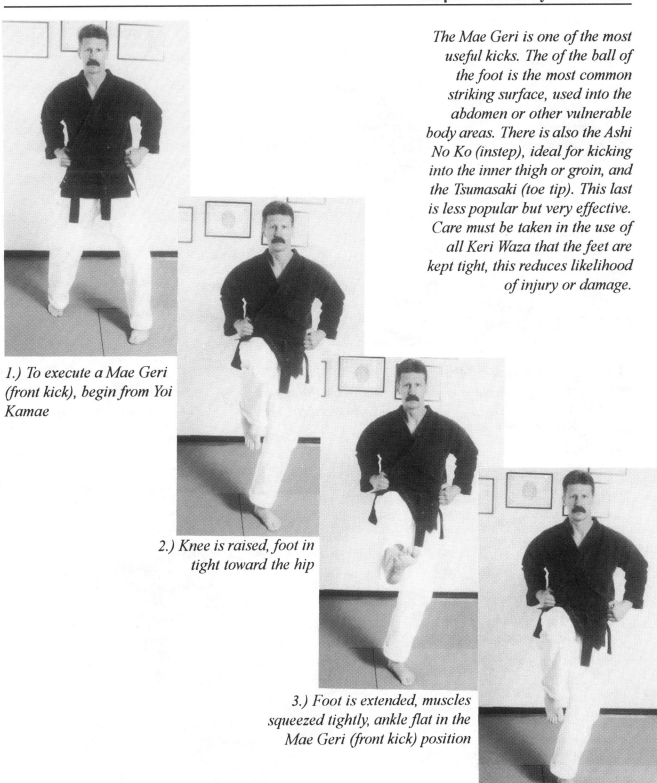

1.) To execute a Mae Geri (front kick), begin from Yoi Kamae

2.) Knee is raised, foot in tight toward the hip

3.) Foot is extended, muscles squeezed tightly, ankle flat in the Mae Geri (front kick) position

4.) Heel is pulled back with the knee still up (this acts as an Ashi Uke–leg block)

1.) *Mae Geri from the side, the heel is brought up as tightly as possible to bring the striking surface (foot) close to the power source (hip)*

2.) *The leg is extended, being careful not to hyperextend the knee*

3.) *The Isshin Ryu Mae Geri is a snap kick, not a thrust kick, the foot is extended and retracted very quickly*

The knee comes up pointing toward the front of the body for all kicks (l). The opponent would not be sure what kick to expect, a Mae Geri or a Yoko Konate (above), side angle kick, which thrusts the Sokuto (blade edge) of the foot at 45° angle.

The Kosa Fumi Komi Geri (cross stomp kick) begins with the knee raising up higher than other kicks (l). The leg then extends, across to the opposite side of the body, striking with the Sokuto (r). The leg mimics the motion of a piston, thrusting down then retracting back up to the same position.

1.) Yoko Keage (side snap kick) is begun from the same position as the Mae Geri–knee up, heel in

2.) Using the Sokuto, the Yoko Keage is a snap kick, the height of the kick is determined by the height of the knee prior to extending the leg

2.) *Pivoting to the side into Nekko Ashi Dachi*

1.) *Shoba Geri (ball of the foot kick to the side) begins in the Yoi Kamae (here seen as Migi Kamae–right guard)*

3.) *The knee is lifted and the heel is pulled in, just as with other kicking techniques*

4.) *The leg is extended and the striking surface is the ball of the foot, toes up, ankle flat*

5.) *The foot is then retracted, heel in and the body is returned to the Yoi Kamae position*

1.) Hiza Geri (knee kick) is a very powerful kick and is begun from Yoi Kamae

2.) The hand is extended palm down, this is the stabilizing hand, to hold the target while the knee drives in

3.) The knee lifts up, striking into the palm, the heel is pulled up toward the hip as in other Keri Waza

In the Hiza Geri, the hand does not slap down–it is the knee that rises up into the hand. The hand is used to grab, pull down and stabilize the object to be kicked. Pointing the toes downward strengthens the leg and creates a more powerful kick, effective into the face or abdomen. The Hiza Geri can be done in place, lunging or even Mawashi (round house).

4.) The Hiza Geri from the side

5.) The toes are pointed downward

1.) Before the Mae Konate (front stomp or thrust kick) the stance is Mae Kagami Dachi (ready guard) which is a Yoi stance and is also called Seisan Dachi

2.) The knee is raised very high toward the chest

3.) The foot is thrust outward, heel first

1.) From the Side, Mae Konate begins as do other kicks, the knee is brought higher

2.) As the heel is thrust forward it is important not to hyperextend the leg and damage the knee

3.) After every kick, without exception, is the same retraction; heel in, foot back down to the floor

1.) Otoshi Geri (squat kick or side angle kick) begins in a Zen Kutsu Dachi (forward weighted stance)

2.) The hands are "stacked" on the opposite hip from the kicking leg

3.) The foot is brought up, heel in toward the hip, knee pointed at the target

1.) The Otoshi Geri uses the Koshi (ball of the foot) or the Ashi No Ko (instep)

2.) Once the kick has struck the target, usually the groin, inside of the thigh or lower abdomen, the foot is retracted. This should be done with speed.

The Ushiro Geri (back kick) completes the range of kicking, however it was not originally in Chart 2. The kick begins as do all others, knee up, foot in (l). Looking over the shoulder to see the target.

The leg is extended and the Kokato (heel) is the striking surface (r).

The foot is retracted after the kick (r). Quickness in this action keeps legs from being grabbed or too easily blocked. All kicks can and should be practiced on the Makiwara board, however, only under the supervision of a qualified instructor. As with any technique, misuse can be damaging. Without Makiwara training, Keri Waza will lack the focus and strength required to be effective.

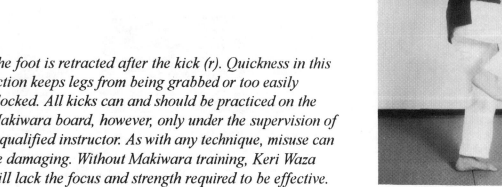

Bunkai: Keri Waza

1.) After the Rei (standing bow), the Seme and Uke begin Bunkai (practical applications) from Hachiji Dachi (r) and Migi Kamae (l)

Mae Geri

2.) The knee is raised and the heel is brought in, aiming the knee at the target area

3.) The Mae Geri with the ball of the foot is aimed at the Mizouchi or lower abdomen

169

1.) The Seme will begin from Hachiji Dachi (above) then step in toward the Uke (r), the knee is brought up and aimed toward the Seme (r)

Yoko Konate

2.) Yoko Konate is a side thrust kick using the Sokuto (blade edge of the foot) and aimed generally at the knee joints

1.a-b) From Kamae the Seme performs Fumi Dachi Otsuki (lunge punch) which the Uke blocks with Kakete Uke (above l & r)

Kosa Fumi Komi Geri

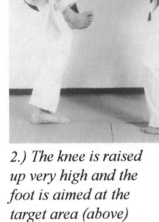

2.) The knee is raised up very high and the foot is aimed at the target area (above)

3.) The Kosa Fumi Komi Geri is done with the Sokuto, stomping into the knee joint, the knee lifts again after the kick

1.) The Seme and Uke begin from Hachiji Dachi (above), Seme will attack from the side (r), Uke blocks the punch with Kakete Uke and raised the knee for the Yoko Keage

Yoko Keage

2.) Yoko Keage uses the Sokuto to snap into the vital areas of the body, the rib cage or abdomen, exceptionally high kicks can be aimed at the chest or throat

1.) Taking a Kamae to the side, the Seme performs Fumi Dachi Otsuki (lunge punch)

2.) The Uke pivots into Nekko Ashi Dachi to face the Seme

Shoba Geri

3.) The knee is raised and is aimed at the target area (above)

4.) The Shoba Geri is a snapping Mae Geri with the Koshi (ball of the foot) into the groin, lower abdomen or Mizouchi

1.) The Seme reaches to grab the Uke by the shoulders–Hiza Geri is ideal for close attacks such as this from the front

2.) The Uke breaks the hold with Kakewake Uke (wedge block) using the Tegatana hand position

Hiza Geri

3.) The Uke then strikes the Shofu (side of the neck), this strike is extremely dangerous due to the nature of the target area

4.) The knee is lifted, using the muscles of the hips for power and the Hiza (knee) is aimed at the face, chest or abdomen

Mae Konate

1.) The Mae Konate (heel thrust kick) is very powerful due to the force of the hips and the piston action of the leg. The Uke raises the knee up very high prior to the kick, pulling the heel in tight

3.) The target area is Chudan level (middle) into the Mizouchi, lower abdomen or the Danchu for higher level kicks. The Kokato is the striking surface, the heel only is used, not the full length of the foot. This adds focus and depth to the Mae Konate

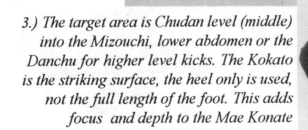

1.) Seme takes a Kamae (r)

2.) Seme attacks with Fumi Dachi Otsuki Lunge punch

Otoshi Geri

3.) As the Seme attacks, the Uke leans out and away to avoid the punch into a Zen Kutsu Dachi (forward weighted stance) with the hands stacked on the opposite hip.

4.) The knee is lifted and with the heel in tightly to the hip. The foot position can be a Koshi, toes up or Ashi No Ko (instep) toes pointed and ankle flat.

5.) *The Otoshi Geri is a squat kick, thus the deep Zen Kutsu Dachi.It is aimed at the lower abdomen, the groin or the inner thighs.*

6.) *After the kick the leg is quickly retracted.*

1.) *From the opposite side the Hiki Te is clearly seen, also the knee is over the tips of the toes in Zen Kutsu Dachi*

2.) *The feet must be tight for the kick to be effective and so that they are not injured.*

1.) The Seme stands in a Yoi Kamae to the rear of the Uke, who looks over the shoulder to see the target

2.) The Uke raises the knee and pulls in the foot in preparation for the Ushiro Geri (back kick)

Ushiro Geri

3.) The the leg is extended and the heel is driven into the target, here, the Mizouchi

4.) The Ushiro Geri can be done low, like a Konate into the knees or shins, middle level into the abdomen or Danchu or high into the throat or face

Chapter 4

Shito Kan Chart Three

Chart 3: Goshin Jutsu

Throughout the history of the Martial Arts students have learned what their Sensei have taught, grasped its deeper meaning and then expanded upon it with a unique perspective and understanding all of their own. Is it the student who achieves the *Ri* or stage of Mastery alone, or is it also the system which he creates that passes through these stages? *Shu Ha Ri* process occurs within a system of Martial Arts, just as it does in individual students. The student who reaches the *Ri* stage and is said to be of Master level will then go on to take his style though the same changes and growth. Although this process is highly sought after from both the Sensei, who desires to create great students, and also by the student themselves, who wish to become great Martial Artists, it is also ridiculed when in action. For example, many of the peers of the Martial Artists that we consider great today were criticized severely for striking out on their own with their own system. Even when these individuals had the blessing of their teachers, often the highest commendations, Menkyo Kaiden ("all passed down," meaning all has been passed from Master to Student; both knowledge and responsibility), they still were denounced for having the "nerve" to think that they were good enough to offer the world something. As time passed and these Masters and their peers died, so did the prejudice and condemnation. They soon were recognized for what they were and not simply young upstarts who had the brashness to "go it alone." This happened for a number of reasons, none of which is as important as the fact that as time passed, what these downtrodden Masters taught was finally seen as worthwhile. This is no less true in the Martial Arts world of today. Many Masters who have trained for 30, 40 or even 50 years are finding it difficult to garner the recognition for their efforts and contributions. This is especially true in the Occidental world, where there has always been a certain mystique and prestige to Oriental Masters or those who have trained with an "Oriental Master." In reality, there are many fine Martial Arts Masters of all nationalities who are struggling just as hard as Gichin Funakoshi or Tatsuo Shimabuku did for recognition. They will receive their due, if they have the "nerve" to persevere and their systems are based upon solid technical and philosophical ground. Unfortunately for the uninitiated in the Martial Arts, it is difficult to discern the true Master from the charlatan who has made an art out of imitation.

Goshin Jutsu: Self–Defense

Today, there are self–defense classes and Martial Arts training facilities on every corner. The telephone book is loaded with claims of greatness and Mastery. Every advertisement proclaims the instructor's unparalleled ability to take the student from zero to Superhuman in six weeks for the price of a cup of coffee. There is, however, no replacing what the Martial Artists of old have found to be true; hard work, repetition and years of training in the correct manner are the tools to become superhuman. If the claim of instant Mastery with little effort seems too good to be true; *it is*. What the modern day "quick self–defense experts" teach is not at all the same as what the Masters taught, which is called Goshin Jutsu. Practicing a technique a few times for several weeks will not create the physical ability nor the mental agility to command a real self–defense situation. Perhaps in role playing these fancy moves taught by the Gurus of Gimmick would work. Let time pass and it becomes plain to see that the body and mind do not keep what is not practiced and what is not practiced correctly with correct intention will never yield correct results. Moreover, if the techniques themselves are not correct from the start then the student will run a million miles an hour down the wrong road, only to find himself very proficient at worthless movements.

The Shito Kan "Cocktail Waza"

The Goshin Jutsu found in Shito Kan are natural extensions of the fifteen hand techniques found in Grandmaster Tatsuo Shimabuku's Chart 1 and the nine kicking techniques of Chart 2. It was therefore natural to call these techniques *Chart 3*. Known colloquially as *The Cocktail Waza*, due to the realism found in these techniques, they are nonetheless true self–defense Waza (technique).

There are fifteen Goshin Jutsu in the following pages. First they are shown as Waza to be practiced without a partner. Subsequent to the student's ability to do the individual techniques found in Charts 1 and 2, they must be proficient in these techniques grouped together in small units before moving on to practice with a partner. All Goshin Jutsu have "stages of escalation" or points at which the practitioner must, through a process of critical judgement, arrest the progress of the Waza during a real encounter. These techniques are very effective and must be used only by those willing; a) to accept the responsibility and consequences, and who are b) able to determine what degree of force is necessary for the situation.

In training with a partner care is always taken not to injure the person who so graciously has allowed us to borrow their body so that we may learn. This is one of the reasons why, before we begin training with other people, whether in one on one practice such as with Goshin Jutsu or in group training, it is standard procedure to bow to each other and verbally state our thanks and hopes for a good training session. *Onegai Shimasu* is what is said when bowing in before training with a partner. This means "please do me the favor." In other words, please let me borrow you and your body so that I can learn these techniques. After the training is finished the two partners or the class as a who state loudly and clearly, *Domo Arigato Gozaimashita*, which denotes the highest level of thanks. It is not enough that we train in earnest and that we attempt to help each other in our quest for competency. Especially during practice with partners, it is crucial that the Reigisaho or etiquette remain at its peak. This results in civil and controlled training with little risk of severe injury or bruised emotions. Often times, Goshin Jutsu practice can get frisky and the utmost care must be taken to keep a state of dignity and decorum in tact.

With that in mind...Onegai Shimasu!

Yasume (rest or pause)
done before the Rei

Ritsu Rei
Standing Bow

Hachiji Dachi
Hiki Te (pulling hands)
are at the hip, palm inward

Circular stepping is done to
keep the feet in contact with
the floor and minimize a
bouncing motion of the hips.

Seisan stance is used for all Goshin Jutsu, as it is used in all
of Isshin Ryu practice. It is excellent for maneuvering and
also a great source of power. The knees are bent the feet are
shoulder width apart and the feet are parallel.

1a.) Fumi Dachi, Tate Tsuki
Lunge step, vertical punch

1.b) Jodan Age Ura Tsuki
Lunging upper cut

1.c) Gyaku Tate Tsuki
Reverse vertical punch

2.a) Gyaku Tate Tsuki

2.b) Gyaku Jodan Age Ura Tsuki
Reverse upper cut

2.c) Fumi Dachi Tate Tsuki
Lunging vertical punch

3.a) Hachiji Dachi
Hiki Te (pulling hands)
are at the hip, palm
inward

3.b) Kosa Dachi, Tate Tsuki
Cross legged stance, vertical
punch

3.c) Naihanchin Dachi
Horse riding stance,
preparing with arms for
the strike

3.e) Kosa Fumi
Komi Geri (r)
Cross stomp
kick, the knee is
raised up high
and the foot is
aimed at the
back of the knee
joint, striking
with the Sokuto
(blade edge)

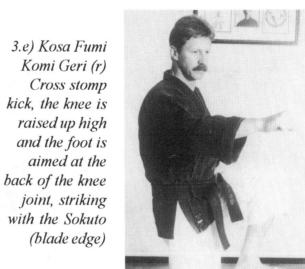

3.d) Ura Ken Uchi (l)
Back knuckle strike aimed at
the Komekami (temple)

4a.) Hachiji Dachi

*4.b) Gyaku Tate Tsuki
Reverse vertical punch,
stepping slightly to the side
into Zen Kutsu Dachi*

*4.c) Fumi Dachi Tate Tsuki
Lunging vertical punch*

*4.d) Lunge forward (far
left), look over the shoulder,
prepare for Ushiro Geri
(back kick)*

*4.e) To execute the Ushiro Geri, the front knee is
lifted and the heel is pulling up (above middle).
The leg is then extended fully (above right),
striking with the Kokato (heel)*

5.a) Hachiji Dachi

5.b) Uchi Negashi Uchi
Palm heel block

5.c) Furi Ouchi
Swing strike

5.d) Furi Ouchi

5.e) Hand is held out to stabilize the
target of the Hiza Geri

5.f) Hiza Geri
Knee kick

*6.a) Kakete Uke
Hook hand block*

*6.b) Yoi position for Otoshi
Geri (squat kick), knee is
up, heel is in*

*6.c) Otoshi Geri
Squat kick (also known as
Mawashi Otoshi–short
roundhouse kick*

*6.d) Leg is retracted and
lifted to execute the Yoko
Konate (side angle kick)*

*6.e) Yoko Konate
Side angle stomp kick
to the Hiza Kansetsu (knee joint)*

*6.f) Hiji Ate
Elbow smash*

7.a) Hachiji Dachi

7.b) Tegatana Uke
Sword hand block, also called
Tegata Barai (sweeping sword
hand block)

7.c) Tegatana Uchi
Sword hand strike

7.d) Hiji Ate
Elbow Smash

*8.a) Uchi Uke
Inside block*

*8.b) Pulling the hand back
to prepare for the strike*

*8.c) Ura Ken Uchi
Back knuckle strike*

*8.d) Gyaku Tate Tsuki
Reverse vertical punch*

*8.e) Preparing for the Hiza Geri
Knee kick*

*8.f) Hiza Geri
Knee kick*

9.a)   9.b)   9.c)   9.d)

9.a) Responding to an opponent to the rear the Uke drops into Nekko Ashi Dachi

9.b) Hiji Ate
Elbow smash

9.c) Tegatana Uchi
Sword hand strike

9.d) Ura Ken Uchi
Back knuckle strike

9.e) Pivot 180° taking hold of the opponent

9.f) Raise the knee up high in preparation for Mae Konate

9.g) Mae Konate
Heel thrust kick

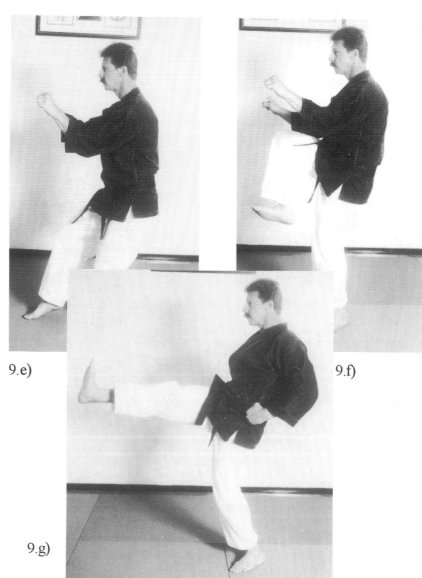

9.e)   9.f)

9.g)

10.a) Hachiji Dachi

*10.b) Kosa Dachi
Pivot to the rear to face an
opponent*

*10.c) Naihanchin Dachi,
Jodan Tegatana Uke
Horse riding stance with
rising sword hand block*

*10.d) Ura Tsuki
Inverted punch (l)
Tenohida Uchi
Palm heel strike (r)*

11.a) Hachiji Dachi

11.b) Yoi Kamae
Seisan stance with the hands
stacked at the hip

11.c) Soto Uke
Outside block

11.d) Gyaku Tate Tsuki
Reverse vertical punch

11.e) Tate Tsuki
Vertical punch

11.f) Gyaku Tate Tsuki
Reverse vertical time

11.g) Mae Geri
Front kick with the Ashi
No Ko (instep)

11.h) Kosa Dachi, Ura Ken Uchi
Cross leg stance, back knuckle strike

12.a) Hachiji Dachi

12.b) Ashi Uke, Ensho Uke
Leg block, Zen circle block

12.c) Gedan Uke
Lower block

12.d) Gyaku Tate Tsuki
Reverse vertical punch (l)

12.e) Tate Tsuki
Vertical punch (r)

*12.f) Yoi Kamae, Haeko Dachi
Ready stance, feet paralell*

*12.g) Knee up in, heel inbefore
the Yoko Geri Keage (side kick)*

*12.h) Yoko Geri Keage
Side snap kick with the
Sokuto (blade edge)*

*12.i) Gyaku Tate Tsuki
Reverse vertical punch*

13.a) Hachiji Dachi

13.b) Jodan Uke
Upper block

13.c) Gyaku Tate Tsuki
Reverse vertical punch

13.d) Tate Tsuki
Vertical punch

13.e) Gyaku Tate Tsuki, Zen Kutsu Dachi
Reverse vertical punch, forward weighted stance

13.f) Yoi Kamae, Zen Kutsu Dachi
Hands stacked at the side, forward
weighted stance

13.g) The knee is raised and the foot
pulled in before the kick

13.h) Otoshi Geri
Squat kick

14.a) Hachiji Dachi

14.b) Nekko Ashi Dachi,
Juji Uke
Cat stance, cross arm block

14.c) Hands are opened

14.d) Hands are reversed

14.e) Hands are "hugged" to the body

14.f) Hands are in Seiken
Normal fist

14.g) Ura Ken Uchi
Back knuckle strike

14.h) Haito Uchi
Ridge hand strike

14.i) Hiki Te, palm up on the hip

14.j) Tenohida Uchi
Palm heel strike

15.a) Hachiji Dachi

15.b) Kakate Uki
Hook block

15.c) Nukite Uchi
Spear hand strike

15.d) Hand retracted back

15.e) Uchi Uke
Inside block

Bunkai: Goshin Jutsu

    Goshin Jutsu are the bunkai (practical applications of technique) for the fifteen Isshin Ryu Te Waza (hand techniques). These are practiced as groups of technique to facilitate the learning of sequential movements. In this way, the student can practice and become adept at more than just single techniques, but groupings of moves which are smaller than Kata (forms).

    In self–defense situations the gravity of the circumstances always determines the responses of the defender. In mild encounters little or no force is necessary. In more serious situations the response must be escalated to a higher level of defense. These training techniques, although they are to be memorized as groups, are in no way substitutes for good judgement. These must always be used appropriately and responsibly. Without this crucial decision making process about the level of defense, the Goshin Jutsu become no more than blind thrashing at a perceived enemy.

    Proper Reigisaho (etiquette) must always be followed before training with a partner. Always show respect for another's efforts, sincerity and desire to learn. Bowing, the Rei, with the proper verbalizations is the manner in which Karate Ka begin and end training sessions.

1. Ritsu Rei (standing bow), is executed before training with a partner

2. Rei is done from the waist, facing each other, in Mesubi Dachi

*3. Seme takes a Seiken No Kamae
Normal fist guard
Uke remains in Soto Hachiji Dachi
Outside eight stance*

1. Seme (r) grabs the shoulder of Uke

1

2. Fumi Dachi Tate Tsuki

3. Jodan Age Ura Tsuki to the jaw of Seme

4. Gyaku Tate Tsuki to the floating ribs

5. Prepare for the Nage (throwing)

1

1.

2.

3.

Nage (throwing) is more than simply muscling the Seme to the ground. These are exact movements that require a working knowledge of physics and the laws of motion and gravity. A strong foundation of Taore (falls) and Ten (rolls) is necessary for both Seme (who is thrown) and Uke (who throws). Once the opponent is down, there is always a follow–up technique. 1.) Begin by swinging the leg behind the leg of the Seme. 2.) Push on the opposite shoulder while continuing the leg sweep. 3.) Shiko Dachi or Seiuchin Dachi is maintained when dealing with an opponent on the ground, while controling Seme with Gyaku Te (joint reversal). 4.) A Hineri Tsuki (full twising punch to the face)

4.

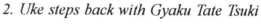

2

1. Seme (r) grabs the shoulders of Uke with two hands

2. Uke steps back with Gyaku Tate Tsuki

3. Jodan Gyaku Age Ura Tsuki to the jaw of Seme

4. Tate Tsuki to the floating ribs

5. Prepare for the Nage by swinging the leg behind the Seme's

2

1. Push the opposite shoulder while continuing the sweep

2. Yoko Taore (side fall) Uke does not release the arm of Seme

3. Hold the arm over the leg to control the Seme

4. Hineri Tsuki to the face of Seme

5. The Gyaku Te (reversal joint technique), seen from the opposite direction

2. As Seme attacks with Fumi Dachi Otsuki, Uke steps behind with Kosa Dachi, Tate Tsuki

3

3. Holding the Seme's attacking arm, Uke retracts arm in preparation for striking

4. Ura Ken Uchi to the Komekami (temple)

5. Raising the knee high for a Kosa Fumi Komi Geri

1. Kosa Fumi Komi Geri Aimed into the Hiza Kensetsu (knee joint)

2. Drive the Seme to the floor, retaining pressure on leg and holding the arm

3. Pull the Seme backwards to the floor, Ko Ten (backward roll)

5. Hineri Tsuki to the face

209

4

1. Seme prepares to attack Uke from Seiken No Kamae

2. As Seme lunges in with Tsuki, Uke steps to the side with Tsuri Ashi (sliding of the feet) and delivers Gyaku Tate Tsuki to the floating rib cage

3. A second Tsuki is then placed in the same position

4. Uke uses Fumi Dachi to create more distance

5. Ushiro Geri to the back, the spinal column or kidney area

4

Seme is forced to either fall forward or Zen Ten (forward roll—above, right and far right)

Taore and Ten are not often practiced by Karate Ka and yet they are so necessary to Martial Arts training

The Seme, after completing the roll, returns to Kamae, facing the Uke. To do this a Tenshin Waza (body shifting pattern) is used called Furi Muki (body turning)

1. Seme (r) in Seiken No Kamae
Uke in Hachiji Dachi

2. Fumi Dachi Otsuki
Uke steps outside the punch with Uchi Negashi Uchi

3. Furi Ouchi to the Danchu

4. Uke holds head to stabilize the
for the Hiza Geri

5. Thrusting Seme's head
toward the floor

1. Seme begins the Zen Ten

5

2. The velocity and force of the body will be dissipated by slapping the hands on the floor upon impact

3. The Seme is not released until after the final technique has been executed

4) Tsuki to the Tento (crown of the head)

6

1. Seme begins in Seiken No Kamae

2. Uke side–steps the punch, with Kakete Uke, grasping the arm

3. Otoshi Geri to the Mizouchi

4. Knee is raised and foot is placed into the Hiza Kensetsu

5. Kosa Fumi Komi Geri, driving the knee to the floor

214

1. Switching hands, the Uke prepares for the strike

6

2. Remaining in control of the arm and the leg before the strike

3. Hiji Ate to the back of the head or neck

4. Zen Taore (forward break fall) is performed by Seme, in Iagoshi Dachi (kneeling stance)Uke retains control with the arm and hair

1. *Seme begins in Migi Kamae (right sided guard stance)*

2. *Uke blocks Fumi Dachi Otsuki with Tegatana Uke to the Kote (forearm), raising the opposite hand to prepare for the strike*

3. *Tegatana Shuto (chop) to the Kubi (kneck)*

4. *Hiji Ate to the side of the head*

7

1. Pushing the head and pulling the arm while stepping towards the Seme, Uke performs the Nage

2. Seme lands with Yoko Taore (side fall)

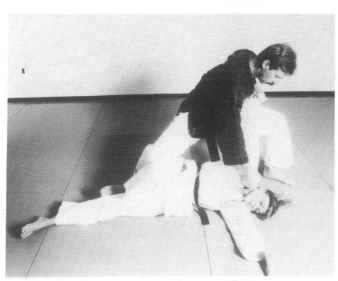

3. Holding the hand with Gyaku Te, the Uke performs Tate Tsuki to the face

8

1. Seme begins in Migi Kamae (right sided guard stance)

2. Uke blocks the Fumi Dachi Otsuki with Uchi Uke (inside block)

3. Ura Ken Uchi to the Komekami (temple)

4. Gyaku Tate Tsuki Reverse punch to the Mizouchi

5. Hiza Geri to the face, while holding the arm and head

1. Pushing down on the head, pulling up on the arm (above) the Seme is thrown to the floor (right and far right)

2. Holding the arm, Kosa Fumi Komi Geri to the Hichu (windpipe), then turning to use Gyaku Te (joint reversal) on the Tekubi (wrist), arm and shoulder to control the Seme

9

1.) Seme and Uke Rei (bow)

2.) Seme attacks from behind (top right) in a "bear hug"

3. Hiji Ate
Elbow smash (above)

4. Tegatana Uchi to the groin (above)

5. Ura Ken Uchi
Back knuckle strike to the face (r)

9

1. Uke grabs the arms and pivots to face Seme, raising the knee for Mae Geri

2. Mae Geri to the Mizouchi

3. Dropping down (l), Uke performs Ko Ten (backward roll) pushing Seme over with extended leg (bottom right and left)

9

As Seme lands (above), Uke uses Ko Ten to land on top of Seme (below left)

Uke prepares for the Tsuki (center)

Tate Tsuki to the face (right)

1. Seme take a Kamae from the rear (above) grabbing Uke's shoulder (center), Uke steps behind with Kosa Dachi and Jodan Tegatana Uke, pivoting towards the Seme (right)

2. Uke encircles the Seme's arms and prepares for the strike (far left), Ura Tsuki (inverted punch) into the floating ribs (right), several inches above the belt line.

3. Tenohida Uchi to the side of the head or ear (above left), Uke pushes while sweeping the legs (center) and completing the Nage. This is immediately followed by a Tate Tsuki to the face.

1. Seme faces Uke with Migi Kamae

11

2. Seme's Fumi Dachi Otsuki is met with Soto Uke (outside block)

3. Gyaku Tate Tsuki Reverse vertical punch

4. Tate Tsuki, aimed at the same target, Danchu or Mizouchi

5. The third Tate Tsuki is again aimed at the same target area

11

1. Mae Geri with the Ashi No Ko to the groin of the Seme (top, far left) followed by Kosa Dachi, Ura Ken Uchi (top right)

2. Uke entwines the legs of the Seme(above left and center) and performs Yoko Taore (side fall). Seme performs Zen Taore (forward breakfall) Using Gyaku Te, Uke does not release the arm of Seme, Tegatana to the back of the neck (both far right)

1. Seme faces Uke in Seiken No Kamae

2. Ashi Uke, blocking the Mae Geri

12

3. Gedan Uke, blocking the Fumi Dachi Otsuki

4. Gyaku Tate Tsuki to the Danchu

5. Tate Tsuki to the same target area

1. *Uke takes hold of the attacking arm and raises knee to kick*

2. *Yoko Keage to the floating ribs of Seme*

12

3. *Gyaku Tate Tsuki to the head*

4. *Uke prepares for the Nage, not releasing the hand*

227

12

Scissoring Seme's body with the legs (above), Uke performs Yoko Taore to take the Seme to the floor (right)

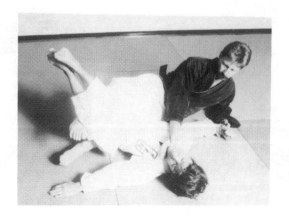

Uke controls the legs, rolling up to Tegatana Uchi into the throat of the Seme (left, as seen from the opposite side and above far right)

1. Seme faces Uke in Seiken No Kamae

13

2. Fumi Dachi Otsuki is blocked with Jodan Uke

3. Gyaku Tate Tsuki

4. Tate Tsuki to the floating ribs

5. Tate Tsuki to the same target area, Uke leans in deeply into Zen Kutsu Dachi

1. Uke positions the hands at the hip

2. Otoshi Geri to the abdomen

13

3.Stepping behind the Seme, Uke takes the arm and begins the Nage

4. Pulling the arm behind the Seme and sweeping the leg

1. Seme uses Ko Ten to break fall

13

*2. Uke controls the hand
and arm with Gyaku Te*

*3. Uke positions for
the punch*

4. Tate Tsuki to the face

1. Seme faces Uke in Migi Kamae

2. Seme's Fumi Dachi Otsuki is met with Kosa Uke (cross arm block) with Uke in Nekko Ashi Dachi

14

3. Uke reverses hands and grabbing the punching arm performs Ura Ken Uchi to the Danchu (sternum)

4. Uke releases the arm and follows with a Haito Uchi to the Komekami

5. With Toho Uchi (Y of the hand strike) Uke prepares to Nage the Seme

14

Uke steps beyond the Seme to perform the Nage (top left). Seme performs Ko Ten (center 2 photos). Uke performs Tate Tsuki to the face while still holding the throat (far right)

Viewed from the opposite side, Tate Tsuki to the face, controlling the arm

1. Seme faces the Uke in Seiken No Kamae

2. Kakete Uke blocks the Fumi Dachi Otsuki

15

3. Uke performs Nukite Uchi to the floating ribs while controlling the punching arm

4. Uchi Uke serves as a strike here to break the elbow, and begin the Nage

5. Prepare for the Nage by pivoting and turning the Seme, controlling with the arm

15

The Seme uses Zen Taore to break fall (above) while Uke remains in control of the arm (r) and uses Tuite (pressure points)

Seme and Uke always perform the Ritsu Rei (standing bow–above) while saying Domo Arigato Gozaimashita, thanking each other for the opportunity to train together and learn from each other.

Section III

The Heiho of Kata

Chapter 1

Bushi No Kata

The Shito Kan Kata: Bushi No Kata

Bushi No Kata is one of the five Kata created in the 1970's by Dr. Aiello in a series of eight Shito Kan Karate Kata. The Kata that are currently taught are Tachi Kata, Ukemi No Kata, Yon Ju Shichi Kata, Zensho Kata, Bushi No Kata and San Kaishu Kokyu Kata. Bushi No Kata, The Warrior Kata, reflects some of the more profound concepts and personal insights that are to be gained by a Martial Artist in the pursuit of personal excellence through the practice of the Budo Arts.

Bushi No Kata contains elements necessary for the study of self defense, street combat, Kumite and all of the strengthening and conditioning aspects of most traditional Kata. It also contains the key to the timeless codes found in all great Kata, the code inherent in what all creative thinkers have discovered, the essence of life and universal truth; reality. Bushi No Kata was designed to develop a sense of single–minded purpose in the practitioner. One of the primary weaknesses found in Martial Artists is their lack of focus over a long period of time. They are unable to hold a "present time consciousness" for more than a few moments. In doing the Kata the practitioner develops a trait necessary for success in combat, Kumite (sparring) or in achievement of personal goals on any level. The relentless pursuit of a goal is the characteristic that this Kata forges within the thought process. Bushi No Kata could be referred to as "the pursuing Kata." Through this vehicle (Kata) and via the central nervous system the martial skills are translated into mental skills, including the undaunted drive for a goal.

Most people who begin the Martial Arts stay through only the initial stages where there is still great excitement and short term goal achievement. When the newness wears off and the difficulty begins, many drop out. This reflects not a flaw in the Martial Arts but the weakness in the individual whose short attention span and lack of follow–through prohibits even the development of a "pursuit" oriented consciousness. Rather than stress what the students need and should be getting from the practice of austere Martial forms and ways, it seems that many instructors and clubs would rather cater to the desires of the public and "give them what they want." Many people would rather take the easy road than the difficult one, even at the cost learning a new skill or becoming a better, more fulfilled and self–confident person. The confrontation of difficulties, obstacles or adversaries are essentially the same whether in the training or in personal life, they require the characteristic of perseverance to succeed. On the street or in combat, failure to persevere and pursue will result in immediate and often permanent consequences. This attention deficit disorder is the character flaw of so great a number of adults today and is at the root of much of society's troubles. Failure to pursue, first and foremost, the perfection of character and with single–minded purpose to express personal excellence in all activities can be seen everywhere. Multiply by 260 million people in the United States alone the problems of one lazy, unmotivated and less than excellent person and one have the chaos of crime, machinery failures, poor education, bad habits and manners and general societal discord.

This is all easily correctable; with hard work. Yes, the bane of the new generation, work. The four letter word that leads to health, success, fulfillment and self–realization when the vehicle is Kata practice is *work*. Diligent, persistent and hard work are the best types. The current unhealthy trend is to excuse people from being personally responsible for themselves. It is a cooperative effort to "cop–out" of living fully and is the hallmark of those who prefer rationalizing failure by blaming society, the Dojo, the family or lack thereof.

The practice of Bushi No Kata will help in the forging of physical skills and mental fortitude through thousands of repetitions and the correct mindset. All practitioners of Budo arts experience the moments of despair, when all seems futile. However, the difference between those who go on and those who quit and become part of the floundering masses of "attention deficit disorder" adults is that the practitioner makes a conscious decision when faced with *any* obstacle or crisis to continue to pursue the objective—personal excellence. It is this character trait of pursuit gained through Kata practice, such as

Bushi No Kata, is just what most people need more of and is also the reason many drop out of training. Success in most things is determined by the perfection gained through practice. Often this success is what determines life or death and certainly it is what determines happiness.

Bushi No Kata proceeds through a series of movements that allow the practitioner to pursue one opponent to the finish, complete the job at hand. With the correct concepts in mind and a comprehensive understanding of the importance of this dogged pursuit all that remains is to train. What!? You're not training yet?

Today, there are a glut of Martial Arts books, tapes and magazines available for the student or potential student to read and unfortunately to mistakenly believe that since it is read, it is understood and physical training is unnecessary. Nothing could be farther from the truth. Reading and knowing are two separate things, one must train to get *all* of the results. Climbing the "Warrior Mountain" and seeing the view firsthand can never be replaced by talking, reading, watching or thinking about training. Some things must be experienced to be understood. This is the way of all Kata, especially Bushi No Kata.

The saying "Shut up and train" no doubt came from a Martial Artist in pursuit of the elusive Budo and was being bothered by someone who lacked the character trait of pursuit. The true commitment to personal excellence is one that one makes to one's self, for oneself. Therefore, it is not necessary to discuss it at length with others, contrary to what many current "pop" psychologists and Martial Arts business consultants may say. If one is at the level of Kodansha (advanced black belt level, low master) in Shito Kan Karate training one is making the commitment and following it through with the practice of Bushi No Kata.

Since the inception of the Dai Nippon Butoku Kai in Japan, established to help transmit the Art internationally as a sport, there always existed the technique called Kata, or forms, within the traditional Ryu. The classical traditional Jutsu, or Do Arts, contain Kata. Kata is the essence of Karate and has been the encyclopedia or textbook by which the Masters have passed on to their students the traditional Art. Kata were taught individually at one time with a great amount of secrecy and protection to the skills and techniques within them. They are the essence and are thereby the heart of Karate Do and the Budo and Bujutsu Arts. Sport karate today, or sport Martial Arts, have eclectic aspects. The modern eclecticism of putting the Kata aside, frequently because of lack of understanding and the lack of discipline required to spend long hours under one Sensei to learn the true Art form, has resulted in the curriculum changing to that of a combat or sport regimented art only. It is the author's hope and contention that the future of Karate Do and of Shito Kan and Isshin Ryu Karate Do in particular will continue on with the traditional concept of Kata, passing these along unchanged.

Studying and perfecting the form and studying the Bunkai (applications within them), as well as the Kakushite (hidden hand moves, also known as Tuite) will always have a place in Karate Do, Budo and Bujutsu. To throw the baby out with the bath water, to eliminate Kata, tradition, the esthetics and also the tool which is used to connect the physical with the intellect, would be a gross injustice and mistake which would eventually destroy Karate Do. At that point, we would see the end of the brilliant Art that came to us from Okinawa, first to Japan and then overseas to America, Europe, South America and worldwide.

Chapter 2

Bushi No Kata: A Pictoral View

1.) Hachiji Dachi

2.) Mesubi Dachi

3.) Ritsu Rei

4.) Yoi with Kakushi Tsuki
Ready guard with hidden fist

5.) Seiuchin Dachi

6.) Hachiji Dachi

7.) *Beginning Hazushi Uke*
Releasing block

8.) *Hazushi Uke*

9.) *Nekko Ashi Dachi*
Tegatana No Kamae

10.) *Gyaku Tate Tsuki*

11.) *Nekko Ashi Dachi*
Tegatana No Kamae

12.) *Gyaku Tate Tsuki*

13.) *Tegatana No Kamae*

14.) *Koshi Hineri*
Hip stwist

15.) *Gyaku Tate Tsuki*

16.) *Knee up for kick*

17.) *Mae Geri*

18.) *Gyaku Tate Tsuki*

19.) *Tegatana No Kamae*

20.) *Tegatana No Kamae*

21.) *Koshi Hineri*

22.) *Gyaku Tate Tsuki*

23.) *Knee raised for Mae Geri*

24.) *Mae Geri*

25.) Knee raised for kick

26.) Gyaku Tate Tsuki

27.) Tegatana No Kamae

28.) Tegatana No Kamae

29.) Koshi Hineri

30.) Gyaku Tate Tsuki

31.) Knee raised for kick

32.) Mae Geri

33.) Gyaku Tate Tsuki

34.) Tate Tsuki

35.) Tate Tsuki

36.) Tate Tsuki

37.) *Tate Tsuki*

38.) *Tate Tsuki*

39.) *Tegatana No Kamae*

40.) *Koshi Hineri*

41.) Ura Ken Uchi

42.) Gyaku Tate Tsuki

43.) Knee raised for kick

44.) Mae Geri

45.) *Gyaku Tate Tsuki*

46.) *Tate Tsuki*

47.) *Furi Muki*
Body turning

48.) *Tegatana No Kamae*

49.) *Koshi Hineri*

50.) *Ura Ken Uchi*

51.) Gyaku Tate Tsuki

52.) Knee raised up for kick

53.) Mae Geri

54.) Gyaku Tate Tsuki

55.) Tate Tsuki

56.) Furi Muki

57.) Tegatana No Kamae

58.) Koshi Hineri

59.) Gyaku Tate Tsuki (left)

60.) Knee raised up for kick (right)

62.) Tate Tsuki (below)

61.) Mae Geri

63.) Gyaku Tate Tsuki

64.) Tate Tsuki

65.) Gyaku Tate Tsuki

66.) Tate Tsuki

67.) Gyaku Tate Tsuki

68.) Tate Tsuki

69.) *Furi Muki*

70.) *Tegatana No Kamae*

71.) *Koshi Hineri*

72.) *Ura Ken Uchi*

73.) *Gyaku Tate Tsuki*

74.) *Knee raised for kick*

75.) *Mae Geri*

76.) *Gyaku Tate Tsuki*

77.) *Tate Tsuki*

78.) *Furi Muki*
Tegatana No Kamae

79.) *Koshi Hineri*

80.) *Ura Ken Uchi*

81.) *Gyaku Tate Tsuki*

82.) *Knee raised for kick*

83.) *Mae Geri*

84.) *Gyaku Tate Tsuki*

85.) *Tate Tsuki*

86.) *Tegatana No Kamae*

87.) *Tegatana No Kamae*

88.) *Tegatana No Kamae*

89.) *Koshi Hineri*

90.) *Kosa Dachi*
Wadi Uke

91.) Yoi Kamae   *92.) Knee raised for kick*   *93.) Mae Geri*

94.) Knee is retracted after the kick   *95.) Yoi Kamae*   *96.) Gyaku Tate Tsuki*

97.) Hiji Uke, Elbow block   *98.) Knee is raised for kick*   *99.) Yoko Konate*

100.) Knee is retracted   *101.) Zen Kutsu Dachi*   *102.) Yoi Kamae*
                                    Gyaku Tate Tsuki

103.) Knee raised for kick

104.) Otoshi Geri Squat kick

105.) Heel is retracted after the kick

106.) Zensho Dachi,Ensho Uke Remaining spirit stance, Zen circle block

107.) Turn to look

108.) Furi Muki

109.) Koshi Hineri

110.) Kosa Dachi
Wadi Uke

111.) Yoi Kamae

112.) Knee raised for kick

113.) Mae Geri

114.) Heel is retracted after the kick

115.) Gyaku Tate Tsuki

116.) Hiji Uke

117.) Knee is raised for kick

118.) Yoko Konate

119.) Gyaku Tate Tsuki

120.) Yoi Kamae

121.) Knee is raised for kick

122.) Otoshi Geri

123.) Heel is retracted after the kick

124.) Zensho Dachi

125.) Naihanchin Dachi
Hazushi Uke

126.) Mesubi Dachi
Kakushi Tsuki

127.) Hachiji Dachi

Section IV

Addendum

Addendum

Interview with a Master

Author's Note: Featured in the following addendum is an exclusive conversation with the current second generation Patriarch of Isshin Ryu Karate Do, Master Harold Long. This interview was transcribed out of eighteen hours of conversations, questions and answers and teaching during a 1997 visit to Detroit, Michigan and the Shito Kan Warrior Training Centers.

The purpose of here is for historical documentation of the facts, past and present, in the world of Isshin Ryu by the most credible living resource on the subject. Master Long has dedicated the 43 years of his life in teaching and promoting the art of Isshin Ryu throughout the United States and the world. He is considered a Martial Arts pioneer and is recognized by Councils of Masters and Halls of fame from around the world.

The original tapes and transcriptions have been maintained for historical purposes, however, for this publication some of the material has been edited out due to space considerations. Some of the names have been removed to avoid any misunderstandings or embarrassment. It is not the authors nor was it Master Long's intention to incriminate or harm anyone involved in Martial Arts or Isshin Ryu. The purpose does not include name calling or focusing blame on any individual or organization. Master Long has given here what is most probably the most extensive and thorough interview ever granted by a legitimate 10th Dan Hanshi–Sei of a Ryu Ha from Okinawa.

Having interviewed over 100 Martial Arts Masters over the years of hosting the radio program Warrior Talk, it can be said without hesitation that Master Long has given a truly cogent and valuable historical overview of Isshin Ryu, Grandmaster Tatsuo Shimabuku and a thorough and honest overview of the current state of the Art. As you will read, Master Long is a Karate Ka of action and also of integrity. He pulls no punches and can be brutally forthright at times.

Editor's Note: The following is a speech given by Grandmaster Harold Long to the students of Shito Kan Karate Do in March of 1997 in Canton, Michigan. This is followed by excerpts from interviews done with Dr. Aiello over the course of that weekend.

"Grandmaster Tatsuo Shimabuku went to a specialized instructor all the time. It is an accepted fact that the greatest Karate fighter of all time on Okinawa was Choki Motobu. Motobu Sensei had no refinement at all. He did not know a lot about protocol. He was a very aggressive person and he would actually go out on the street and whip people to check his techniques out. He was a very crude individual, but this is where Grandmaster Shimabuku went to get his fighting ability. He learned the concept of how to deliver these techniques. What would happen to your opponent if you use a certain technique on a specific part of the body? You do not get that in the Kata, you have to get that by separating the parts of Kata and then bringing these things out and working on the charts. This is very poignant way of doing it, to prove the techniques by going out and fighting people. Fortunately, we do not do those things today. We have to humble ourselves and come back to the very basics. The basics techniques are what are going to win for you. All of these things we see on television and in the movies, this is a fantasy world. These are exciting things to see but, how many times do you expect to hit an opponent before you render him completely harmless on the street? I have seen them kick a guy five or six times, he goes down spiraling and then gets up. I do not relate to anything like this at all. People like Choki Motobu, he hits or blocks you one time. That is where the concept as Grandmaster Shimabuku says, "Your defense is your offense. A person throws a punch, you block a punch, you have a good, quick, strong snap block. The quickness is what gives you your breaking power." He says, "This person is no longer a threat. You do not have to block a punch because there is not going to be another punch coming because just as soon as his arm breaks, the guy immediately is going to react, because he is going to show favoritism to that arm." This comes from the legacy that he left. Grandmaster Shimabuku passed the legacy of six different people. Goju Ryu, Shorin Ryu, the fighting techniques, the two Bo Kata, the Sai Kata and the Tonfa Kata. That came from six different instructors. The only reason that we learn the weapons Kata in the Dojo today is to keep history and tradition alive and maintain this contact with history.

We really do not have a history in this country. If you cannot trace your history back to the established Masters, back to the people that dedicated their lives to the Martial Arts, then you will never have a history. You will never have a background or a solid foundation. Here in this Dojo, you trace your history all the way back to the beginning of the Martial Arts.

The Okinawans were the people that refined the Karate and Kobudo (ancient weapons). When Master Chinto showed up on Okinawa, he had no refinement to his Kata and this Kata was named after him. It was for uneven terrain, like you have so much of in the Orient. A whole system of Karate was incorporated from this one Kata. The Okinawans are very intelligent and innovative. They took this rough Kata and they sanded it down, polished and refined it. Now it is a Kata that is recognized and has proven self defense techniques. Information they got from China, India and other places throughout the world. It seemed like Okinawa was a point where everything finally focused. I do not know whether the word got around that the Okinawans were brilliant on the Art of self defense. They could take your ideas and concepts and really refine it. Take a rough product and make a beautiful, finished product.

It was destiny that took me to Grandmaster Shimabuku because he was hard to find. He did not have a big Dojo like we have here today. His front yard was his Dojo and he had a big concrete wall, that was your Makiwara board. That is what you kicked. He was afraid that Kinjo was going to kick the wall down, so he started making Kinjo kick a tree. Kinjo was so powerful that every time that he would hit the wall, it would shake.

We take these people lightly, but they are our whole foundation. They are our grandfathers, our godfathers so to speak. Without the knowledge and the dedication that these people were willing to pass on to us, we would not be where we are today. Grandmaster Tatsuo Shimabuku, my Sensei, has always been the most influential person in my entire life. God, naturally, has more influence, but that is a different life. Consequently, you reach a point in your life which we call the final phase of Karate as being, Gokei. This is just a very elementary explanation. I think that the true meaning of Gokei is when your Martial Arts life and your spiritual life meshes. I feel that is when you recognize the true meaning of your purpose in life. The things that you have not done, I think that is the time to make the preparation, make sure they are done. If I were a selfish person, I would want to keep everything to myself. I would have never taught anybody, I would not want anybody else to have this knowledge. That is not what my promise to my Sensei was. I promised my Sensei that I would come back to America, I would do everything within my power to teach and promote Isshin Ryu Karate and to represent Isshin Ryu at other events of the other Martial Arts and I would do it to the best of my ability.

At that time, the Martial Arts in this country was not well known. We really had a captive audience. We all worked together because to be honest with you, none of us had the depth of knowledge that we should have had. Grandmaster Shimabuku taught me enough to be an instructor. He took me at my word, I promised him that I would be an instructor and carry on his work in this country, the way he had carried on his work on Okinawa. Without me, Don Nagle, Steve Armstrong, Harold Mitchum and all the people that trained at that time that decided to be instructors after we got back and fulfill their obligation to Grandmaster Shimabuku, the Isshin Ryu System would never be known. It would have never gotten off the island of Okinawa. It would have been a tremendous fighting Art that no one knew about. When we brought it back into the western world, in the United States, Canada, Mexico and some of the European Nations, it is just amazing, in this short period of time, since January, 1954, the growth of Isshin Ryu Karate. It is a tribute. Everything that I have done, I have done because I wanted my Sensei, who was my Master, to make sure that his life's work was continued. I wanted to make sure that it was presented in the proper light. I have never, ever pointed at myself. I have always had a big picture of my Sensei in the Dojo and the Mizu Gami. I tell my students time and time again, "Every time you talk about Karate and the Martial Arts, every time you come into this Dojo, always think first about where your heritage is. Without Grandmaster Shimabuku, you would not be in the Martial Arts and an important part of your life that you now have, would never be realized." The most important part of my life has been the Martial Arts. If I had not obligated myself, I probably would not have ever been a teacher.

I knew that I was fascinated by it. Grandmaster Shimabuku always cautioned me, "You have to be humble." He was telling me, a good teacher is not a good performer. There has to be a distinct line drawn between the two. "If you want to be a performer, that is fine, but than you cannot be a teacher. You cannot do both at the same time. I have seen people try time and time again. How many times have you seen a Sensei get beat at a tournament and one of his students win the championship? The student trains, the Sensei trains part time and tries to teach part time. You cannot be a part time Sensei. If you are going to be a competitor, quit trying to teach. Grandmaster Shimabuku told us well in advance that we did not have those capabilities and I have seen throughout the years, everything my Sensei told me has been true and accurate.

Grandmaster Shimabuku was also a famous fortune teller on Okinawa. When he retired from the Dojo, he spent his entire time telling fortunes. I can testify that he had the ability to foresee into the future. I feel that God led me there. Being in the Martial Arts world, I can be a better person. This gives me a means to be able to talk to some of the young people about Christianity and that is the ultimate goal. When a new student begins in the Dojo, he needs to envision himself being in a high position to develop into a Karate Ka. Set your sights high, but maintain a humble attitude.

I think it does us good to occasionally lose our temper. If we see someone doing something so drastically wrong that really offends us, we have a right to lose our temper. It may be the only language that some people understand. It does not mean to start yelling and carrying on. There have been times when I did not even try to control my temper. That is when people have actually disgraced you. That is when people are casting the Martial Arts in a bad light. I am not nice to them, never have been, never will be because they are stepping on something I love with dirty feet and I cannot stand back and see this occur. Our obligation is to present the Martial Arts in the true light.

If you do care, you believe in tradition, in proper protocol, in your teacher, as he believes in his teachers. Grandmaster Shimabuku shaped my life and that is the most wonderful thing he could have ever done for me. The first time I showed up at Grandmaster Shimabuku's Dojo he did not even acknowledge the fact that I was there. He did not care who I was, or what I wanted. He did not have time for a fellow he did not even know. My house girl was trying to tell him who I was, but he did not seem to care. The second time I came back, he let me watch and he nodded to me, but he was busy working students. The third time I went back, he told me that he would take me on a trial basis. His original concept was to convince you that this was not for you. He did not want to waste his time unless you were going to be a serious student. That was his way of weeding people out.

He charged the Americans $5.00 a month, he charged the Okinawans $1.00 a month because that is all they could afford. There were several marines working out at Grandmaster Shimabuku's Dojo when I was there. We took Grandmaster Shimabuku to the special services officer and we explained to him, if he would agree to teach as many as thirty marines, the Marine Corps. would give him $200.00 a month. I have never seen a more stunned expression. We had an interpreter there to make sure that he understood fully what was going on. The interpreter was so awed, it took him a little bit before he could tell Grandmaster Shimabuku. Grandmaster Shimabuku shook my hand for ten minutes saying, "Thank you very much." He was so thrilled. At that time a skilled worker on Okinawa made approximately eight cents an hour. Grandmaster Shimabuku was going to be the highest paid man on Okinawa. That was our way of saying, "Thank you Sensei, for accepting us as your students." We had the means of providing our Sensei with a better life. That strengthened the bond between Grandmaster Shimabuku and I. He knew that I looked at him as being something other than a Sensei. Although we did not understand each other's language, we automatically understood the communication."

Author's Note: Grandmaster Shimabuku was following an unwritten tradition in the ancient Okinawan Martial Arts by not acknowledging students on their first few trips to the Dojo. At the age of 8 Shinkichi, as Grandmaster Shimabuku was called as a child, walked several miles to his Uncle Urshu Matsumura's home and Dojo. Until he felt that Shinkichi was determined enough to become a student, Matsumura Sensei, of the Kamasu Clan, turned him away. Even today, the most traditional of Okinawan Dojo do not solicit students, rather they use referrals or diligent research on the part of potential students. In the United States and throughout the rest of the Martial Arts world the trend is toward accepting anyone regardless of their intentions, character or lack of will. The commercial aspect has overcome the traditions of the Dojo. Payment arrangements and contracts are the topic of most conversations with new or potential students, not what they will do or are to expect in the training.

Many training centers use a sales pitch to potential students, they are signed up on a contract or a trial membership with a week or month free training and a free uniform just for joining. Many Senior Masters feel that this encourages the wrong attitude in the student from the beginning of their training. This type of arrangement reverses the role of Giri (debt of obligation) to having the Sensei owe the student rather than having the student enter into training desirous of personal development through hard work on their part via the guidance of the Sensei. The Sensei in the commercial Dojo of today finds that he must then use the carrot–and–stick method of belt ranking to keep the student training. Eventually, the Dojo closes, being unable to keep up the pretense of the health spa, party time atmosphere.

Unless the student is looking for a sport to compete in or just another gimmick, we suggest bypassing the training center that displays all of their trophies in the window and has great incentive plans to lure in students. Great Martial Arts training is incentive enough for anyone to become involved. It needs no freebies to sell it to people and it is not something that one can buy or even give away with a contract. Nor can the Sensei achieve the result of personal excellence in a student's life by using the tournament circuit as a path and a gage of progress. Long term, serious Karate students incorporate their training into their lives. These are the people who move away from fads and trends rather than towards them.

"Grandmaster Shimabuku knew that I understood the Martial Arts terminology. I was his interpreter when he made some personal appearances in the United States in 1966. I knew exactly what he was saying and he was the most honest, down to earth, honorable, person.

Grandmaster Shimabuku trained some of the students in Bo Sai Gumite and it was being recorded. The students forgot what he had taught them. He stopped them, walked right in front of the camera and you knew he was going to say something really important. The first thing he did was he would wipe his nose on his sleeve, he would scratch his rear, now when he did that, pay attention, he had something really important that he was going to say. He said, "Two days I teach, now no one can do." He bowed out and left. Grandmaster Shimabuku was so honest, he would not cover up for their mistakes. My work was Grandmaster Shimabuku's work. The only thing I knew was what my Sensei taught me. I have never passed myself off as anything else except Grandmaster Shimabuku's student. I still consider Grandmaster Shimabuku my Sensei, although he died in 1975. My obligation to him was to carry on his work in another part of the world and to do it as closely as I possibly could. The way he wanted it done. People say they would have liked to have known Grandmaster Shimabuku. By knowing me, you do know Grandmaster

Shimabuku. My way is Grandmaster Shimabuku's way. That is the only way that I know. That is the way to show loyalty and respect to your Sensei. I had to develop my training program the way my Sensei wanted to do it. I am passing on exactly the same information to you that he gave me.

Grandmaster Shimabuku told me that for every technique that you find in the Kata, there are ten that you did not find. It is a never ending process. He was telling me the human mind cannot comprehend all the different techniques and all the combination techniques found in the Kata. All the basic techniques that we practice in the Charts as separate items are exactly the same techniques that come from the Kata. The Kata is Karate. Fighting techniques come from the Kata, breaking techniques come from the Kata. Everything you do comes from the Kata.

Make sure you understand where your position is in the lineage. Make sure you know where your position is in the Dojo and make sure that all of your students are well aware of the same concepts. It is similar to a military chain of command. The senior is never junior and the junior is never senior. If we had big egos you would be teaching what you see now on the commercial market. American Karate. There is not an American Karate. There is no Karate that originated in America. It originated in India in 525 A.D. These people that wear flags and wave flags and want to do all these strange things, they are someone's drop out. They originally were in a Martial Arts Dojo, but for some reason they could not hack it. Maybe they quit, or maybe they got run off, or were disillusioned. Whatever the case, how can a drop out teach anyone? If a person has been wronged at a Dojo and he comes to you and asks you to let him be a member of your Dojo and he knows that he is going to get good, legitimate training, then you take this person and make a Karate Ka out of him.

You have to overcome the general public's view that all Karate is the same. They will shop in the yellow pages for a Karate School. They will see all the trophies lined up at the school. They think that represents the Martial Arts. Up until recent years the Orientals did not even have a name for trophy. They did not give trophies. You competed because you were representing your Dojo. It was a learning process and an honor to be chosen to represent your Dojo because that meant your instructor was proud of you. You had really worked hard and you had accomplished something.

Dr. Aiello and I do the same thing. We are proud of every one of the members of our Dojo that do something good. We want to focus on you and put the spotlight on you, because you are deserving. One thing that most of us forget, when that light goes off that period of time is over. Put the Gi on, go back to the Dojo, because you have got some hard work to do.

We have stories to tell, this is part of learning, this is a part of history and these are the things that will lead you to be a better Karate Ka. What I have told you today, is no different than reading a history book. I cannot say how many Martial Arts books that I have read throughout the years and once I start a Martial Arts book, I do not put it down until I have read it through. I can learn from every black belt in the world. The day that we quit learning is the day we have served our purpose and our usefulness is no longer needed in the Martial Arts. The person that thinks he is too big to learn, or too intelligent to learn, they are not thinking clearly at all. Every time I go into the Dojo, I learn. When I am teaching, I am learning. That is the way it should be. Anytime that you did not learn in the Dojo that means that your mind is somewhere else. Dr. Aiello is one of the few people that can teach two systems of Karate effectively. This gives you an edge over everyone else. Some people only have one person to go to, other people have no one but themselves. They do not put a Gi on, because they do not even have a Dojo anymore. Unfortunately, these people will criticize you and I. The day you quit training, you should take off your Gi, take off your belt because you are no longer in the Martial Arts. We do not have a place for people to stand around with their arms folded, looking at you with contempt. They expect someone to pay homage to them because they may have done something a few years ago.

My personal certificate which I presented to Dr. Aiello, which is irrevocable, means that he has met, in fact, exceeded the qualifications that Grandmaster Shimabuku set down. No one can ever dispute it. If Dr. Aiello gives you a rank certificate, I will honor that certificate, because there is no doubt in my mind that any certificate he awards you will be well earned. With Dr. Aiello as your Sensei, you automatically have whatever strength I can lend to your Dojo and your organization. Your lineage goes back to Choki Motobu, the greatest Karate fighter of all time. It goes back to Chotoku Kyan, to Tatsuo Shimabuku, to Harold Long, to Dr. Aiello. You can trace your lineage and it is so strong, it is undisputable. No one can dispute your position in the Martial Arts world, because they cannot dispute the great Karate masters who Grandmaster Shimabuku trained under.

Grandmaster Gichin Funakoshi was selected to go to Japan to introduce Karate there because of protocol. That was so important back then. There were only two classes of people on Okinawa. The ruling class and the peasants, the working class. There was no middle class in the Orient. They had to send a person that had knowledge of protocol. Master Funakoshi was a school teacher. He was the only instructor on Okinawa that could fit in with the society in Japan. Master Choki Motobu certainly could not have. The other senior instructors of note could not have. The Okinawans did not want to send their own masters anyway. Conferences were held and the decision was made. Master Gichin Funakoshi was the ideal instructor to send to Japan because he was an educated man, he was a learned man, he knew protocol, he knew how to conduct himself. That is how Japan got Karate.

Everything that I have told you has been recorded, so it cannot be disputed. Someone will come along some day and say, "I knew Harold Long very well and I never heard him say anything like that." I have heard the same thing concerning Grandmaster Shimabuku. I say, "Well, I really do not care how well you knew him, it is not important to me what he told you, what is important to me is what he told me." Sharing knowledge is the only way you can have a successful operation. You do not know how good I feel about being here and being a part of this organization. This is my top Dojo, you are my top people and I am thrilled to be a part of the program."

Author's Note: Master Gichin Funakoshi was selected to represent Okinawan Karate to the Japanese upper social class. Crude ruffians were passed by for this honored duty, as well as those who lacked social refinement and etiquette. A true Master always complies with proper hierarchial process and respects authority and seniority. Master Funakoshi strove to elevate the art of Karate and worked and trained to his fullest ability towards this end. Focus on the constructive values and qualities of the Martial Arts, not the negative and egotistical or violent potential should be foremost in the hearts and minds of all Martial Artists.

And Now for the Rest of the Story...Who's Who in the World of Isshin Ryu

Author's Note: We start with some information about organizations and people who have been involved in Isshin Ryu Karate Do over the years.

Dr. A: Once the A.O.K.A. [American Okinawan Karate Association] was no longer recognized by Okinawa...

ML: ...because the name was reversed, Grandmaster Shimabuku refused to recognize it...

Dr. A: ...then in 1974, Kichiro started the World Isshin Ryu Karate Association.

ML: I'm not really sure what year it was. Somewhere in that area.

Dr. A: Was that sanctioned by Tatsuo Shimabuku?

ML: No.

Dr. A: This was his own.

ML: That was Kichiro only.

ML: When I was there in [on Okinawa] 1974, they had a grand opening of an Isshin Ryu Dojo. All the local dignitaries were there. I had about 14 or 15 people with me. We had been through Japan and came over to Okinawa to visit Grandmaster Shimabuku. At this formal opening of the Dojo, they asked the mayor to give a speech. Everyone was very respectful. Then the chief of police was called on to give a speech and you could hear a pin drop while these people were talking. I was the third one called on to give a speech. Grandmaster Shimabuku explained to them that I was his student in America and some of the things I had accomplished. So I gave the speech and everyone was very respectful, although they didn't know what I was saying. Then, Kichiro got up to give a speech. Nobody had called on him, but when he got up, everyone got up to get their refreshments. His father and I were sitting there talking. He came and tried to make enough room so he could sit between us. Obviously there was some type of a problem.

Dr. A: There have been other problems with him.

ML: It's mostly a recognition problem. Kichiro was always trying to run his brother down. What he doesn't understand is that he can't berate his brother, who was a much better Karate Ka than Kichiro would ever be. His brother didn't try to sell himself or prove himself. It wasn't a personality conflict because Kichiro didn't have a personality. He didn't know anything about Isshin Ryu Karate either. His father used to joke about it, he said, "Kichiro doesn't understand Karate."

Dr. A: What happened with Ciso? Did he stop training at some point along the way?

Author's Note: Ciso was the nickname of Shinso Shimabuku, Kichiro Shimabuku's brother.

ML: He quit after his father retired because he and his brother couldn't get along. He refused to be under his brother. We had a big party at the Grand Castle Hotel in Naha. Kichiro was telling people not to invite Shinso, that was the name he went by then. I came in and said, "Kichiro, just who the hell do you think you are to be inviting people to a party that I'm giving? Certainly your brother is invited. I'm going to go by his house and invite him myself." Then Kichiro told his father that he shouldn't go in such a tall building because it may collapse. He tried to talk his father out of going to the party. His father said, "These are my students from America. Sure I'm going to go the party."

Dr. A: Shinso (Ciso) stopped training. I've seen pictures, just recently, of him wearing a red belt.

ML: I've heard that he started working out again, but I don't know where I got the information from. Somebody I talked to recently said he was working out again.

Dr. A: There are still some of the Isshin Ryu people in this country who consider him the true successor of the system. I have actual photographs or copies of the photographs with Shinso wearing a red belt and they are recognizing him that way. But I've heard that he was inactive over the years.

ML: He was inactive for a long period of time, so he doesn't rate a red belt by any means.

Dr. A: This will just create more problems. Kichiro has been involved since before 1974, so he would have at least 23 years or more of consistent training invested. He is in his sixties now. Should he still have a credibility problem after all these years? Obviously he knows what he's doing now. He should be somewhat of a serious practitioner, wouldn't you say?

ML: In Kichiro's case, he can work with you on Seisan Kata today, but he'll show you a different Seisan Kata tomorrow. He's not consistent with the techniques at all.

Dr. A: His highest ranking student anywhere, Okinawa or the United States, is an American, William Duessel, who I've had on the show. He is a 9th Dan, very knowledgeable, very honest and does nice work. But he doesn't know much about Kichiro and has not seen Kichiro do all of the technique at this point.

ML: When I was there, Kichiro told me about all the students he had at Camp Hanson, which is a Marine base. I told him that was fine and I wanted to go up there and meet those students. He said no. I told him, "Well Kichiro, I don't know if you can get on the Marine base, but I can get on any Marine base in the world. You don't mean anything to those people out there, I do." So he decided that since I was going to go out there and observe his class anyway, he better go with me. He told me he had some fantastic number of students. When I got out there, an American black belter who had just arrived, had seven people in the Dojo.

He did a couple of techniques, something that you would expect a four–year–old child to do. Then he told everyone he had important visitors from America and had to leave. I've never looked at Kichiro Shimabuku as any Karate Ka.

Dr. A: And most contemporary leaders today don't either. Even today he has a credibility problem, however, he does carry the family name and he is the oldest son.

ML: He would wear a red belt in his class in Okinawa, on a Marine base. But, when he came out and got in his car, he would take the belt off and lay it on the back seat. If he had to go to the grocery store or somewhere, he didn't have a belt on.

Dr. A: Today, he doesn't wear a red belt, he just wears a black belt. And he doesn't recognize the colored belt systems. He wears only a white Gi, which is somewhat formal in its use. But, his father wore a red and white belt and then eventually a red belt.

ML: Kichiro went as far, at one time, to tell people that his father never awarded anyone a red and white belt. But, in 1966, there is a picture of me wearing a red and white belt and his father wearing a red belt in my Dojo in Knoxville, TN. If he didn't award it to me, where did I get it? He is there. If I didn't award you anything, I'm certainly not going to have a picture taken with you wearing it. Kichiro has never been an asset to Isshin Ryu Karate, or anything else as far as I'm concerned.

Dr. A: Now, Angi Uezu broke off and formed his own organization. However, he was junior to many of the marines.

ML: Yes.

Dr. A: Angi started training in the sixties and although he was important, representing Tatsuo Shimabuku as his emissary over here, he still is junior to a lot of people. Is that why they didn't follow him when he came over?

ML: This is true. Grandmaster Shimabuku wanted to give his son–in–law some exposure and he asked us if we would sponsor him over here. I believe he was a Nidan at that time.

Dr. A: A Nidan. So, he was junior and had a seniority problem. Is that why everyone didn't fall in line with him? He was literally here to get exposure more than to teach everyone?

ML: He didn't teach the way Grandmaster Shimabuku taught. Kichiro was more or less Angi's teacher. That created a problem. It was a family problem. But, Angi had the potential to be a first rate Karate Ka. Of course, Kichiro didn't have the potential to do anything, really, other than muddy the water and try to be a problem child.

Dr. A: Later, Angi would make 18 trips over here, had quite a good following and did a lot to promote Isshin Ryu. He did a fine job right up until the time he was sick. Now, he's turned his organization over to Sensei Uechi. Uechi Sensei was a Godan at the same time I was and, then of course was promoted to Shichi Dan and is the president of the association.

ML: But see, the strange thing is these people kept bringing Kichiro over, they kept bringing Angi Uezu over, but they had no part in building Isshin Ryu Karate in America. It was the Americans who built it here. These people who they were coming to visit weren't their students. Never had been. They were training with someone else, they were someone else's students.

Dr. A: They were promoting themselves for the obvious commercial purpose.

ML: This is true.

Dr. A: You and Don Nagle trained together in Okinawa, came back and Steve Armstrong was a junior to you two.

ML: Yes.

Dr. A: Did he get an eighth Dan also, even though he started training later on as did Harold Mitchum?

ML: Yes.

Dr. A: Harold Mitchum did not start his organization until much later, because he stayed in the service which put him ten years behind as far as building an organization.

ML: His organization really wasn't an organization at all. It was just four or five Dojo of people who came under him.

Dr. A: But he seemed to be highly respected.

ML: He was. He was a real good Karate Ka. Mitchum was a real fine person, I really enjoyed him.

Dr. A: He is retired now and dropped off the scene a few years ago.

ML: Mitchum developed personal problems, gave his Dojo to his son and moved. I had a post office box number for him and wrote a couple of times sending information, but I never heard anything in response.

Dr. A: His son is still active?

ML: Yes.

Dr. A: What is his son's name?

ML: I don't even know his son's name.

Dr. A: No one seems to know his son's name. I understand he is a 7th Dan under Mitchum, under his father and took over whatever was left of it. We don't hear much of Sensei Mitchum, he's still not that active anymore. At one time Mitchum and Advincula were linked together in some type of organization or was Advincula training under Mitchum?

ML: Mitchum hated Advincula. At one time, they were fairly close, but when I came back from California about ten years ago, Mitchum called me at home. He asked me if I had just returned from California. I had. He asked if I saw Advincula and I said I did. Then he went on, "What does he say about him changing the Mae Gami to the Mizu Gami?" I told him just what he told me, he says, "He is a lying son of a bitch." He gave me more background saying Advincula is telling everyone that his wife interpreted all of this information for him. But, what he forgot to tell people was that Mitchum's wife is the one who taught Advincula's wife the Karate terminology.

Dr. A: Did Advincula design the original patch?

ML: I don't really know who designed it. But the Mizu Gami came about as a dream to Grandmaster Shimabuku. I hear people saying, so and so said this represents this, this represents that. It's not up for everyone's own interpretation. This is a dream. If I have a dream and I interpret this dream to you, you can't interpret it as being something else because it wasn't your dream. Consequently, everyone's got their own explanation, just like the Karate code. If you've got fifty black belters who interpret the Karate code for you, you're going to get fifty different explanations. That causes some confusion. Sometimes how things are and how they are related, have no connection.

Author's Note: The Mizu Gami was drawn by Shosu Nakamine, Eiko Kaneshi's uncle. This was chosen then for the symbol of Isshin Ryu.

Dr. A: So, did Sensei Mitchum and Advincula, at one time, have an association?

ML: I don't think so. I think they were in the Marine Corps together and they went to Grandmaster Shimabuku's Dojo together, but Advincula has never been a Karate Ka like Mitchum. In fact, Armstrong didn't have anything to do with Advincula after a short period of time.

Dr. A: You worked out with Don Nagle over there, what was the caliber of his Karate?

ML: Don Nagle has always been a first rate Karate Ka.

Dr. A: In this country, yourself and Don Nagle are considered the top two Isshin Ryu pioneers, the true patriarchs of the system. There is some dispute between the intermediate rank people, but, when all is said and done, you look at the record of what you've done and what Don Nagle has done, you two have been consistent over the years.

ML: There is another thing that is ironic, Don Nagle and I never fought each other, even back in our young days. We felt that since we trained together, we knew one another too well and had enough respect for one another, we really wouldn't have been able to give it our best shot. It wasn't one of those "I know I'm better than Don Nagle" things. There wasn't any reason to challenge one another because we were trying to teach good Isshin Ryu Karate to challenge the other people. It's ironic how some of the things work out. Don Nagle and a Goju Ryu Karate Ka had a couple of public matches in New York. But the most talked about one was the match between Don Nagle and Harry Smith. I wasn't a witness to it, but I understood that it was at Smith's Dojo, using his students as the judges. He out–pointed Nagle and wouldn't give Nagle an opportunity to redeem himself. Of course, I've heard several conflicting stories, because it was obviously all Harry Smith's students. But the match you've never heard of took place when Grandmaster Shimabuku was there and I beat Harry Smith 22 to nothing in a match, using his students as judges.

Dr. A: There is a trend today to undermine the seniors at sixth, seventh and eighth Dan level, instead of giving credit where it is due and let them gracefully retire.

ML: These are the same people we've discussed before. If they do not respect their elders and their seniors, how do they expect their followers to respect them? You can't earn respect unless you're a respectful person. If you're not willing to give the proper respect to your seniors and your elders, well then, I think these people will change the philosophy of Karate so bad, that there won't be any courtesy or protocol. It's going to be a conglomeration of whatever a person's personality will dictate.

Dr. A: Part of that, which we're starting to see today, is lack of respect for the rank. You meet someone, who is a well ranked individual or leader of several Dojo and they don't go by "Sensei." They will say, "Just call me Fred. Just call me Joe." Their students call them by their given name. If you ask them about their rank they deny that it means that much to them. There isn't anywhere in the world of martial artists where sensei aren't called as such by their students. Though rank isn't the priority, it is a very important issue.

ML: If you're in a leadership position, you have to establish its parameters. You can't be good time Charley over here and command respect. To me, when you walk into the Dojo, that's another world. Any person who has ever walked into my Dojo, either pays proper respect or I show them the door.

Dr. A: People who were taught by Grandmaster Shimabuku, you, Don Nagle, or Harold Mitchum, were taught proper protocol. They addressed their teachers properly, such as Sensei, Shihan or Hanshi and were taught that ranking and seniority, just like in the military, stands at all times.

ML: Most people who don't measure up to standards have to justify themselves and I think this is what we're seeing now. For example, people say, "I don't belong to an organization, but I'm doing this." If he doesn't belong to an organization, he doesn't really exist. He's not helping the image of the system and what it means. He's not willing to come under the proper authority to grow and prosper within an organization.

Dr. A: There are several intermediate Dan in Isshin Ryu around who have gathered some followers because of their prior reputations. They go right down this path of informality and lack of hierarchy because they're not in an organization. I've confronted several of them on the radio show about promotion and how they are going to go up in rank.

ML: They can't go up in rank. There is nobody to verify that they have the knowledge, the background, or the efficiency to go up in rank. Why should a person like that ever expect to go up in rank? If he's not willing to work within the framework of a system, well then, he shouldn't ever be able to go up in rank.

Dr. A: Where does this leave their students, the followers of these people?

ML: They are doing their students a real disservice–service because their students don't know any different. They don't know about a framework or an organization so they get hooked. Then, all of a sudden, they find out that no one really cares. No one recognizes them because they don't go anywhere, they don't do anything.

Dr. A: And that has never been taught by Grandmaster Shimabuku or Chotoku Kyan or Chojun Miyagi or Choki Motobu. No major master has ever taught without formality, without structure of rank, without hierarchy. That has never been the way, yet they say they're the real traditional way.

ML: They are living in their own little world, their own little mind. They don't know what history has dictated. They don't know the proper protocol. They really don't have the knowledge. They claim they are independent or don't want to work within an organization or don't like Harold Long or Don Nagle. You know, likes and dislikes have nothing to do with building a system of Karate and maintaining it.

Dr. A: I've confronted a few of these individuals by asking who they train under. They answer by telling me who they know. I ask again who they train under because there is rank above them, therefore, they fall under someone, whether they like them or not. If you don't train under Harold Long or Don Nagle in this country, that means you're under Kichiro Shimabuku because he is the senior on Okinawa. But, no, they don't train under Kichiro and they don't train under you or Sensei Nagle. They claim to be an independent, but they're really creating a problem for their followers who support them strongly, but don't realize it's a dead end. I've been there myself, so I know what that's about. How did this occur in Isshin Ryu?

ML: The fact is those people are not Isshin Ryu Karate Ka. They're claiming to be Isshin Ryu Karate Ka. They've had a certain amount of training, but they didn't fulfill their obligation to the system or to their instructor, their teacher, their sensei. As far as I'm concerned, they're dropouts. But they want to tag along and be recognized. I'm not willing to recognize these people if they're not willing to uphold the obligation to their systems.

Dr. A: One problem that I'm seeing frequently in Isshin Ryu and other styles as well, they're promoting a lot of people. They are only seventh Dans themselves at this point, but they're promoting people up to fifth and sixth degree black belt. They're not in organizations, they're not working within a framework, therefore, their students are not recognized by anyone except them. Yet, at the same time, it's having negative repercussions on being a fifth, sixth, or seventh degree black belt.

ML: I'll give you a good example that I've come across recently. There is a Dojo in Ocean Springs, Mississippi under Sensei Advincula. I've been down there a couple of times and I was shocked at just how little knowledge they had though he claimed to be a fifth Dan.

Dr. A: By promoting to these ranks without being in an organization, they are not contributing to the art in a general sense the way Grandmaster Shimabuku envisioned it. A lot of these guys don't value knowledge. They think if someone is tough or a buddy, they get the promotions. This undermines the tradition of Isshin Ryu Karate Do.

ML: But one of these days, it's going to be embarrassing for a lot of people. Somewhere down the road, The World Head of Family Sokeship Council will have enough authority and enough power to impose rules and regulations for everyone. If you don't work within a framework or don't have the knowledge your rank requires, then we're going to strip you of your ranks.

Dr. A: How did you get involved in the Sokeship Council?

ML: I had the information on the Council and felt that Master Sanchez had a good idea and a good way of presenting it. He wanted to get as many senior Dan together because you have to have power in order to have rules and regulations and enforce them. That's what he set out to do, to get the senior Dan of every system to be on the council, working together to put those things in place.

Dr. A: You already had the International Isshin Ryu Karate Association. You went into the World Head of Sokeship Council because it includes all styles versus one individual system.

ML: I felt that if I didn't represent Isshin Ryu on this council, we may have someone not as well qualified. That was the reason I felt I should represent Isshin Ryu.

Dr. A: In fact, you retired from the International Isshin Ryu Karate Association. That's now run by J.C. Burris who is the formal president of that association.

ML: Yes.

Dr. A: You recently gave him advice to continue to build that organization?

ML: At one time the I.I.K.A. was the strongest Isshin Ryu Organization in the world. Then people started breaking off because they had differing ideas of what they wanted to do and should accomplish. When Master Nagle and I put Toby Cooling and J.C. Burris in charge of the system, we felt that the United Isshin Ryu Council would be an umbrella organization to get everybody to come together to work and support one another.

Dr. A: Now, you and Don Nagle promoted Toby Cooling and J.C. Burris to ninth Dan.

ML: Yes, we did.

Dr. A: What was the purpose and intention of that promotion and what were your expectations then?

ML: Mr. Nagle felt that Mr. Cooling was the quality of his lineage and I felt that Mr. Burris was the most qualified from my lineage. We expected both organizations to come together but remain independent and invite the other organizations under this one umbrella of the United Isshin Ryu Council. We didn't want to destroy anyone's organization, we wanted different organizations, because that instills good competition and sets standards. It gives an incentive to do better for all. We wanted everyone to work together and it would have worked very well, except everyone wanted to be the head. When they can't be the head, they want to be the person who sits and criticizes those who are. I'm real disappointed, [enough hasn't been done to] promote the United Isshin Ryu Council. I recently told Mr. Burris to forget about the United Isshin Ryu Council and build the I.I.K.A. to the strength that it was at one time. Consequently, he's doing this. He's brought in a lot of new members in just the last three months.

Dr. A: Where is The United Isshin Ryu Council right now?

ML: Until Mr. Cooling does something, there will be no United Isshin Ryu Council, because he was the chairman of it. Mr. Burris was the Vice Chairman. All of the great plans that Mr. Cooling had were never put in writing or in a text, so, as far as I'm concerned, The United Isshin Ryu Council doesn't exist, except on paper.

Dr. A: Toby Cooling was a student of Don Nagle. Did he visit Tatsuo Shimabuku and spend a month with him?

ML: Yes.

Dr. A: What is the background of J.C. Burris and how did he become so prominent a student of yours?

ML: J.C. was one of my first students who wanted to have his own Dojo. He was a student at the University of Tennessee at that time. I let him have his own class at Maryville College. That Dojo is still operating under Sensei Bruce Gilliam. After J.C. left Maryville, he went to Athens, his hometown.

Dr. A: So, Mr. Burris did not train with Tatsuo Shimabuku?

ML: No. I was the only instructor that Burris ever had.

Dr. A: How many years was he with you?

ML: He's been with me now for 33 years.

Dr. A: Tommy True is also one of your original students.

ML: Tommy True has been with me for 34 years.

Dr. A: Those guys go way back. When you and Don Nagle promoted J.C. Burris and Toby Cooling, did you promote jointly or each individually?

ML: They were individual promotions.

Dr. A: So, you promoted J.C. Burris and he, in turn, promoted Toby Cooling.

ML: Right.

Dr. A: You didn't promote Toby Cooling and he didn't promote J.C. Burris.

ML: Toby Cooling was already promoted by Don Nagle. He requested a rank certificate from me for the same rank, which I granted.

Dr. A: Did you and Don Nagle make any gentlemen's agreement of any type on cooperation between you, or did you have a formal agreement covering what you wanted in the future? You were both retiring and turning things over to whom?

ML: We didn't give any guidelines at all. We told them that we brought the Isshin Ryu system this far and saw so many disasters happen in the martial arts. Bob Trias of The United States Karate Association, had a tremendous following at one time. He died and left no instructions as to who should assume the responsibilities of running the organization. So, The U.S.K.A. no longer exists. It splintered into 15 little groups here and there. That organization was destroyed because there was no planning. The same thing occurred when Ed Parker died. He hadn't designated anyone during his lifetime. He made no provisions for an emergency or his death. Don Nagle and I did not want this to happen to the Isshin Ryu system. We wanted to put everything in place while we were still here to support and advise them and offer whatever assistance we could to them.

Dr. A: Is that panning out the way you wanted it to?

ML: Really, no. I guess I was expecting people to put in the same amount of effort and time that I did. I see this is not going to happen.

Dr. A: For people to put in that kind of effort and time, Master Long, requires the same type of commitment to the art. The commitment you had to Tatsuo Shimabuku seemed to be destined, that it had the powerful hand of God in it, rather than just someone committed to an art or a sport.

ML: I've looked at it in the same manner. I don't want to go too far, but, Christ himself, when he was on Earth, picked some trusted lieutenants, they were his disciples. We found out that some of them weren't all that loyal. In fact, one was most evil. Even Christ had problems with his followers. Basically, we're having the same problem. Some will fulfill their obligation to you, some will only do it as far as talking about it and some won't do it at all. Then you will have a couple who will get in there and try to do it enough to make everybody look good. It just doesn't work that way. Everyone has to uphold their end of the bargain for it to be a successful operation.

Dr. A: I hear it repeatedly from people who trained under Tatsuo Shimabuku, whatever their rank is, that they were his best friend, the one who made the commitment to promote Isshin Ryu in the United States.

ML: I guess I've had ten people say their teacher was Grandmaster Shimabuku's best student ever. There is no such thing as a best student ever.

Dr. A: What was the commitment you made to Grandmaster Shimabuku?

ML: My commitment to him was to do everything within my power to teach Isshin Ryu Karate, promote Isshin Ryu Karate and present Isshin Ryu Karate to the public in a good light when I returned to The United States.

Dr. A: Even if it took 43 years?

ML: Yes. But, time wasn't important to me because I gave a commitment to my sensei. There was not anything that would deter me from fulfilling my commitment.

Dr. A: You've dedicated your life to it whether there is pay or no pay, whether there are rewards, whether there is a kick in the seat of your pants, whether or not you're given recognition. What was different about your commitment that made you follow through for 43 years that we're not seeing today in the people we expect it from?

ML: I was serious when I made this commitment. Grandmaster Shimabuku could never have been recognized in the martial arts world the way he is now if we had not. If he had kept Isshin Ryu on Okinawa, he would have been known on Okinawa, but that would have been the extent. By coming to America and exposing it to a vast number of people, such as we did, his students gave him the recognition he rightly deserved. This is what we expected of our students, to give us the recognition we feel we deserve. In my case, I wasn't seeking recognition, I was seeking to fulfill my obligation to my sensei and to make sure he has the proper recognition.

Dr. A: Which is the traditional way. Not to confuse humility with it. In reality, the way of being humble is to give recognition to your teacher.

ML: That's how his teachers got their recognition. Grandmaster Shimabuku's teachers were the greatest instructors in the world and I felt that he belonged in that same category for his generation and I still do. As far as I'm concerned, Grandmaster Shimabuku is the most brilliant Karate Ka of all times.

Dr. A: He is more famous today than when he died. His recognition continues to grow with the radio show. We reach more people in two hours now than most teachers reach in a lifetime. With technology and the books you've written and tapes you've produced, the books I've written and tapes we've produced, we're dispensing knowledge to thousands and thousands of people. Grandmaster Shimabuku is getting his recognition. He would be amazed, wouldn't he, if he knew how famous he was?

ML: He would be awed by it. You know, even having the Hall of Fame Banquet and Tournament, he wouldn't be able to visualize how many people hold him in such high esteem.

Dr. A: Do you think you've fulfilled your pledge to him?

ML: You never really fulfill a mission. I felt like that when Grandmaster Shimabuku died in 1975, he knew who made the obligations and who carried through. Like I said, the man was brilliant. He knows these things didn't just happen, someone had to do them. I felt good, even after he retired and I went to visit him, because he knew who was doing it and who wasn't.

Dr. A: He trained hundreds of students from America on Okinawa. They came, they went. There was a dozen, or so, main people who trained over there and made big commitments. How were you able to carry on the mission like you have while others have fallen by the wayside? What is it that makes a difference?

ML: It was a total commitment. There is a difference between a commitment and a total commitment. My life has been built within the Isshin Ryu System. I wasn't just a teacher at the Dojo, I was an Isshin Ryu Karate Ka 24 hours a day for all of these years. That was really important to me, to insure that we have the proper growth and teach good, solid Isshin Ryu Karate such as my sensei taught me.

Dr. A: One of the things that has forged a solid bond between you and I, is that commitment. That's the type of commitment I require from my black belts. That's the kind of commitment I felt in my heart when I put a black belt on for the first time. I had not met anybody with that kind of dedication. But, I've also felt, in some respect, that it was destined to happen. You could have dragged your feet; kicked, scratched and fought to avoid it, but God had you by the scruff of the neck dragging you along saying, "Mr. Long, you're going in this direction. Whether you like it or not, you're going here. This is your purpose in life."

ML: Looking back throughout the years, I feel I was probably destined to do this. Otherwise, I wouldn't have been around all these years.

Dr. A: Now, what happens? You thought ahead, you knew these other organizations had collapsed. You laid the foundation and, in some respect, turning the organizations over to J.C. Burris and Toby Cooling, served a great purpose for you. It freed you from the political and commercial pressures so you could really begin to fulfill that mission. It is at this point, what you call retirement, you looked seriously at the transmission of Tatsuo Shimabuku–Harold Long version of Isshin Ryu. Not the Don Nagle version, not the Steve Armstrong version, not the Harold Mitchum version. Not the view of all the people, but the way you saw it. The way you received it from Shimabuku, so it was presented in the purest form. I can tell, from knowing you that over the last few years you are getting very clear about it and starting to transmit that message.

ML: It's really hard to put into words, but every era comes to an end. It doesn't have to come to an end with death. Grandmaster Shimabuku lived in retirement for three years before he died and then the transition took place worldwide in Isshin Ryu Karate. It didn't change my attitude at all, because Grandmaster Shimabuku didn't have to be alive for me to fulfill an obligation I made to him. It felt like a marriage, to death till we part. Every decision I ever made, always had Grandmaster Shimabuku's hand in it. I tried to pattern myself after him in that respect. I felt he was so brilliant in the world of martial arts, that I wanted to be able to make the same type decision he would make under the same circumstances.

Dr. A: He was also destined. It was not just some coincidence, there were hundreds who said they trained with Choki Motobu. Chojun Miyagi had dozens of serious students. Tatsuo Shimabuku was destined to be who he was. He had his dream, his vision and, he realized, he had a destiny. But what are the chances of an American G.I., a young kid like you were at the time, meeting this oriental fellow? Then after training with him for 19 months, committing 43 years to his art and to yourself, because his art is you, you're his art.

ML: They are astronomical.

Dr. A: And it hasn't been that others haven't attempted to do it. Yet, they fall by the wayside, go off track, flounder, drop out, stop. Things go on and you retire and, upon your retirement, I feel you're on the verge of the biggest contribution to your art in all these years. That is astounding.

ML: I feel my biggest contribution was not teaching and promoting Isshin Ryu Karate, but making sure I carried on the portion of the work my teacher gave me the authority and permission to do.

Dr. A: I asked you once, if you could you absorb everything there was to learn about Isshin Ryu in nineteen months?

ML: No one in a lifetime can learn everything there is to know. Grandmaster Shimabuku always cautioned me. He felt, with his background, he had only scratched the surface of the potential knowledge in Isshin Ryu Karate. I always pass that on to my black belters, saying that the most brilliant man in the martial arts I've ever met, says he's only scratched the surface of potential knowledge, therefore, don't ever stand around with your arms folded thinking that you know enough. No matter what your knowledge level, it is still not enough. You haven't achieved the knowledge there is for you. You have to dig and you have to learn.

Dr. A: It's a process, isn't it?

ML: Yes. With regards to kata, he said, "For every technique you find, there are ten you didn't." So, the smarter you get, the longer the road is, you see. I don't care how much knowledge you have or how much knowledge you pass on, look at the knowledge you passed up, which is approximately 90%.

Dr. A: Your statement from him that you shared with me was, "I couldn't learn everything there was to know, but I learned everything he wanted me to know."

ML: He taught me everything that was necessary for me to be a teacher when I got back to this country.

Dr. A: Provided you did a lifetime of work with it to explore.

ML: I had to take that knowledge and develop and analyze it. If you'll notice, I never, in my lifetime, ever changed one thing that Grandmaster Shimabuku did. There is nothing to change. This is it. This is the way it should be done.

Dr. A: You have it the way he taught you.

ML: I teach exactly the way he taught me and I teach exactly what he taught me.

Dr. A: Others say they learned it from him exactly the way they teach it, but it's different from what you teach.

ML: That's right. People who view the videos say he taught them differently and I respond saying, "What makes you think he taught you different? He taught everyone exactly the same, you forgot."

Dr. A: You and I have looked over those films. I've been over those films hundreds of times. I've worn those films out. People challenge the accuracy by saying he was sick, he left moves out, they were low quality.

ML: If you compare the film we made in 1964 with the film Steve Armstrong took in 1966, you won't see any differences. He was sick at Armstrong's Dojo, but went ahead and made the film anyway. That wasn't his best, but the same technique was still there.

Dr. A: There are times when I am fed up or have no one around for advice, so I study those tapes in great detail to try and make myself look as close to Shimabuku as I can with my body build and type. You and I are built a lot different, but we are more alike, than we are to him. If someone is following those tapes, are they going wrong?

ML: No. They are correct if they follow the tapes. I've had a thousand people throughout the years who wish they could have known Grandmaster Shimabuku. I tell them that they do. They just don't understand it, they don't realize it.

Dr. A: We call it the direct transmission when it is spirit to spirit. If you do what they did, you start to think what they thought and see what they saw. I watch the Shimabuku tapes hundreds of times in detail and study your tapes. I see you, train with you, know you mentally and observe what you absorb. I am third generation: Shimabuku, yourself, then me. I never trained with Shimabuku. Can a third generation person like myself get the direct transmission through you and get the art identical for the future?

ML: Absolutely. By training with me, you're getting training from Grandmaster Shimabuku because that's all I know. I transmit his knowledge to you, so you should feel the spirit of Grandmaster Shimabuku every time you walk into the Dojo.

Dr. A: You have Shimabuku and yourself on your tape series. I've gone through them in great detail and it's almost frightening that even though the body types are different, you could almost overlay the two of you on those tapes. You took a great risk because if you weren't able to stand up to what you did, it's right there in contrast. You start to feel that you know what he was thinking when he was doing the moves, is that possible?

ML: It is. I've always felt the presence of Grandmaster Shimabuku and that's what I wanted to accomplish on the film that most people don't recognize or even see. I keep emphasizing that it is a three generation film. It's a training film. But, what I'm really saying is "This is my teacher. This is how he performs. This is the way I do the kata. I do the kata exactly the way my teacher did. This is my student. I've trained her. She does the kata exactly the way my teacher and I do the kata."

Dr. A: If someone sees that film, they're seeing him the way he looked when he did those kata so the films are accurate.

ML: This is correct.

Dr. A: That's very important, because people are revising who and what he was. They're living on the fact that they trained with him for one week to one month or they took a trip and met him and make a little notoriety off one short visit.

ML: The fact is these people overlook so many things. They didn't really know Grandmaster Shimabuku. You have to get to know your instructor. If you don't relate to him completely, then you're not going to get a lot of knowledge. Same as your students. If they don't relate to you 100%, they will never, ever be a good student. Take Don Bohan as an example. In 1978 we put out the first book, Dynamics of Isshin Ryu Karate, Volume I. Don called me one night after I was already in bed and wanted me to send him ten free copies of the book. I said, "I don't give these things away." He said, "Well, what I want to do is let my black belters study them and, if they approve of them, we'll require that our students use them." I said, "No. It doesn't make any difference what you or your students think. It's not something I'm sending out for people to grade or correc." He said, "Well, really, Grandmaster Shimabuku taught me different." I said, "I want you to notice that one copy of the book that you have, Mr. Bohan. If you'll notice there is nowhere in that book that I've said anything at all about the knowledge of Don Bohan. I really could care less what your method of training is, or how much you've got. This is my book. This is accurate. This correct. This is Grandmaster Shimabuku's training."

Dr. A: Now that you have retired from the International Isshin Ryu Karate Association and from the Hall of Fame Tournament, you've put politics and commercialism aside. The true message comes through clear and there can be no conflicts with other people. You've stood the test of time. You're still here, passing on your message which has not changed over the years while these people fluctuate. The true lineage of Harold Long is coming to fruition, not Don Bohan, not Don Nagle, not Harold Mitchum, not Steve Armstrong. You've done the work, you've put in the time. You've gained the wisdom of trying this out everyday for 43 years in all different ways, in all different possibilities. Now the difficulty comes, how do you pass it on? What happens now? You've turned the organization over to Toby Cooling and J.C. Burris. They're doing a good job to an extent, but they're involved in the politics and commercial aspects of the associations and the tournaments. Those are historical institutions you started and they need to be there forever, it is their job to insure this. Now you've gone into the World Head of Family Sokeship Council, which has no membership fees, no politics. You registered J.C. Burris. I'm sure this was done to establish him in the organization in the event something happens to you.

Author's Note: The World Head of Family Sokeship Council is the world's largest Grandmaster council. Membership is only granted by induction, inductees being sponsored and their rank and standing verified. Inductees must be 9th or 10th Dan equivalent or the Soke of a system.

ML: That's the reason I wanted him on the council. That's the reason I wanted you on the council. You must have people with a good strong background and people who have made a commitment. Look at your accomplishments, look at your background and you never had the proper recognition for your contributions to the art of Karate.

Dr. A: Master Long, I don't consider my accomplishments noteworthy.

ML: I understand that, because I never really looked at mine. The things I did, were the things I should do, the things I was obligated to do, the things I wanted to do. You've done exactly the same thing. But the people who have really done things, never want to give themselves credit. I relate to that real well because I don't feel I should take a bow, I felt the credit should go to my teacher.

Dr. A: My greatest regret is that I haven't done more, that so much time has lapsed between things when there could have been more accomplishment. When looking forward, it's hard to know where to go and at times, it is confusing. How did I fit into the picture?

ML: You fit in the overall picture real well because you are a member of the Sokeship Council and you fit into the Isshin Ryu System well because you're with me. In the Isshin Ryu System, it doesn't make any difference if I'm retired. To Tommy True, J.C. Burris, Bill McCillroy, Jerry Smith and Joe Laney, I'm still their sensei. They won't ever have another Sensei. They expect me to fulfill that.

Dr. A: For one thing, a very important thing, I'm a direct student with you. I'm not an association student, I'm not a Dojo student. I'm a direct student and a serious student. One of the most serious students you've ever had.

ML: See, you and I are on a mission. How many people actually have a mission? How many people have a plan for tomorrow? How many people have a plan for next week? Next month? Next year? You and I are probably two of the few people who know exactly what we're going to do.

Dr. A: You sent me a letter saying you were pretty ill and didn't know if you could come up here and do anything. I want you up here, even if you can't do anything, because my greatest lessons from you are these discussions. I work on my technique everyday. I understand mechanics and I do need work on Isshin Ryu, everybody does. But the big lessons come from absorbing your wisdom. As I asked you once before, what would you give to be able to talk to Tatsuo Shimabuku for one hour? Your instant answer was everything. No pause, no hesitation. You'd give everything for one hour of discussion.

ML: I would. You have to understand my line of thought regarding that trip. I felt if I was not physically able to lead workouts and train people, I wouldn't be of any benefit to you and should wait until some other time. I look forward to workouts and doing things in the Dojo. It gives me a better relationship with your students.

Dr. A: Master Long, you have evaluated all of my Kata and my technique. I have your tapes, I have Shimabuku on tape, I've studied and I've read. Fortunately, I'm still young enough to perform strong. So we have the physical pretty well locked in. But the real learning comes from our discussions. As we've worked together for the last few years, it really hit me where you are with this, what work you've done, how intense it's been. I also realize what my commitment would have to be to you and that is to make sure the Tatsuo Shimabuku–Harold Long lineage, the heritage, gets passed on and doesn't get changed in the future. It's going to leave me in a very difficult situation if anything happens because there is no where else to go after you.

ML: It puts you in a good situation in one light because you don't have to associate with these other people. You don't have to tolerate their incompetence, because really, that's what it is. Most of the people who are not doing anything, are the people who offer all of the criticism. I know probably 100 different people who challenge what I'm doing. I make no bones about it, I say, "I'm your superior, that's who I am."

Dr. A: And, they're going to know it when this book comes out too. We put out more information, more education, more facts, so they can't run and hide under the rocks. I know you've taken a lot of criticism over the years for your books and tapes. Every time I publish a book, it's like I did a bad thing.

ML: I think your books are outstanding. In fact, I take your books, read them and I understand what you are saying. I understand what you're trying to get across, but most people who read don't try to understand. They want to find things wrong with them. They want to criticize. Every year I get three or four unsigned letters stating things I did wrong and, of course, I throw it in the trash because that's exactly where it belongs. Any person who's not man enough to sign a letter, shouldn't write me anything, because, personally, I don't give a damn about what they think.

Dr. A: You and I have been featured in discussions throughout this year in some of the chat rooms on the world wide web by people we don't even know.

ML: I look at it in this respect, when we were in high school, we were at the age we knew everything there was to know. We always criticized our teachers, but we never criticize them one on one. If a teacher found out we said this about them, we'd deny it. This is exactly what is occurring today, like these kids who get on the internet. I think someone accused you of giving me $5,000.00 for a Rokudan promotion. Anyone who knows me is aware that I never charge a promotion fee. I've had people, in the past, offer me money. We kicked one man out of the association because he offered money for promotion. No one has ever given me a nickel for promotion because I don't charge for promotion. So, no one can ever say that so and so bought a rank certificate. They're not for sale. When you have exceeded my qualifications, then you get promoted.

Author's Note: All those who know Master Long know that there is no asking for promotion. By the same token, one does not refuse a promotion from Master Long, if it is granted it comes with a testing procedure and it will be well deserved.

Dr. A: The odd part is they are not children in elementary school. Some are Kyu (below black belt) level, and some are sixth and seventh degree black belts. They are coming out of little groups who are not working with organizations and not moving forward. The martial arts are in transition. Scholastic and academic world leaders are communicating. I communicate with more tenth degree black belts in a month, than I had in my first 30 years of the martial arts.

ML: What you're doing has never been done before. You are getting these high ranking Dan and masters on your radio program and trying to educate the public to what the true martial arts is all about. Like we say in the country, "you're plowing new ground." You're performing a tremendous service and should be recognized for this, not criticized such as you've received in the past.

Dr. A: The radio show is getting tremendous recognition. It really is amazing that some of the people who have been on will discuss material they haven't shared with their students in the past. They divulge, for the very first time, things that they haven't told people. We're getting tremendous cooperation among the top echelon of instructors, ninth and tenth Dan of almost every system and organization in the United States and Canada. There is very little criticism of one another and other styles. In fact, they talk about the common ground at that point.

ML: This comes back to the World Head of Family Sokeship Council. This is the concept we want to show everyone, that there is no competition between me and Peter Urban. We're friends, we've been friends throughout the years. We respect one another. We're pleased to be associated with a legitimate Karate Master who has accomplished something and is still doing it. To us, when we get together, there is no oneupmanship. We are always discussing what is going on in the world and what we can do to make things better, what we can do to work together and to be available to the proper people who need the information we have. Which brings us back to the positions filled by Toby Cooling and J.C. Burris and what position you're going to have in the future. I expect you, since you are associated directly with me, to grow, where you will eventually be right at the top as one of the policy makers.

Dr. A: My great concern is that we may lose the amount of knowledge you have. No one has been able to relate at the same commitment level you have. They have not been able to get the knowledge from you and understand it, because so often a student doesn't understand something you tell them until twenty years later. Through the Isshin Denshin, or direct transmission spirit to spirit, our relationship is growing strong. I feel I'm able to grasp, a good portion of the teachings you got from Tatsuo Shimabuku. After 43 years of research and development, your ideas are not what they were a year ago. You are more clear about your position. That's my mission, to have an accurate recording of it, so we can pass it on through transcription and books and direct teaching.

ML: These tapes are very important for two different reasons. One, if you don't have the tape, you're going to find people who will have their doubts about whether we even had a conversation like this. Two, by having a tape, there is no doubt about what was said or discussed, because it is recorded, true and accurate.

Dr. A: People will often state that I can't be a direct student of Harold Long because you're in Mississippi. They don't know that we talk on the phone every two weeks, they don't know that you come to my Dojo, and that you regularly work with my students. They've never been in my Dojo, yet they criticize what they *think* we do.

ML: The fact is, I can do anything that needs to be done, as long as it's legitimate. When I check you out for promotion I didn't tell you ahead of time that I was testing you. I have made a point of this throughout the years. I don't have formal promotion exams as such. When I was checking you out last year, I have the plus and minus system and I felt you did a fantastic job. All of your students were doing traditional Karate, outstanding. I was so impressed with it, I told you then I felt you had one of the top five Dojo. I still feel the same way. You're the guy who sets the tempo, you're the guy who has the training program, you're the guy who runs the show. I observed you working at a certain level, when you were actually at a higher level. I wouldn't be doing my duty and I fulfilling my obligation if I didn't recognize you at the higher rank.

Dr. A: Thank you. I feel the same way with my students as well. So many sensei today set standards for their students that they can't live up to. The more books you write, the more tapes you put out, the less these people want you to have any recognition. Frequently, they want the opposite. They want to hold you down.

ML: You have to look at it from their point of view too. The only thing left for them to do is criticize us, because these people have never done anything. They really have no backgrounds. They don't have any accomplishments. They have a lot of hot air, but, as far as earning a position in any lineage, they haven't earned anything. They may have at one time, but they haven't progressed. They still want to be given rank and recognized as something they're not. I'm not willing to do that.

Dr. A: By fifth Dan, a person is at their peak physical performance. At that point in rank, the physical is accomplished and they are competent. What goes into rank at sixth, seventh and the higher levels?

ML: Let's go back to the rank of Shodan first. Shodan, Nidan, Sandan, Yondan and Godan are ranks of proficiency. Then, when you advance to Rokudan, you achieve your first instructor rank. From then on, what counts is your teaching, promotion of the art and the manner in which you're doing both. You're being prepared for a higher leadership position with every rank you advance. You see, during the first five ranks, you're taking knowledge. In the next five ranks, you're returning this knowledge. You're giving it to other people so they can work and go up the same ladder you've climbed.

Dr. A: In a recent conversation with prominent Isshin Ryu people in this country, I asked what accomplishments they achieved with the rank they are carrying? They stumbled, because they try and keep the hierarchy on a physical or performance level. It is not a performance rank at sixth, seventh, eighth, or ninth Dan.

ML: Those are honorary ranks. No performance at all, while that may not be the right terminology. You have to maintain your physical and mental capabilities, but the criteria is different. You're graded as a teacher, not as a student. The first five ranks are taking knowledge. In the next five ranks you're returning this knowledge. So, you're putting back what you've taken out. This has always been the case. Because you're a big, strong fellow and real intelligent doesn't count for anything. It's what you're doing with this intelligence, it's what you're doing with this knowledge. That's what you're graded on.

Dr. A: Why do we have seventh and eighth degree black belts around this country today who can't show much in the way of accomplishment?

ML: They should not hold those ranks if they can't show any accomplishments.

Dr. A: Do you agree that many are making it on their physical ability and do not have the appropriate accomplishments?

ML: If you gave all the senior Dan, the people who have earned it and those who haven't, a test on knowledge that rank should have, 90% wouldn't pass it.

Dr. A: Where do you think that will lead in the future?

ML: It's appearing all the time. If we get away from respect and courtesy and obligations, we're losing much in the process. One character wasn't in Isshin Ryu, but what he called the 'American Style'. There is no such thing as the American Style, these are somebody's drop outs. They couldn't hack it in a regular system. Then, all of a sudden, they claim to be the American Style. This guy went further, wanting to salute instead of bow. I told him, "Young man, you come to my tournament, you don't set the standards. You will bow when you are instructed to bow or I will personally throw you out of this building and all of your students will go with you." I instructed him to either be in the martial arts or not. If he didn't want protocol, tradition and standards, then he better leave.

Author's Note: The above mentioned individual did leave, as did his students.

Look at these people who have quit, stay gone for 10 or 15 years, then come back wanting to be promoted. They have no qualifications for promotion. I've been exposed to this in recent years. I can't promote these people because they don't have the knowledge, they don't have the proficiency. And there is no way you can train people like that because they're not going to come and stay with you for any period of time. They get insulted because you tell them they no longer have the proficiency and the qualifications. They are the same people who run around trying to cut current seniors down.

Dr. A: What should we do, from organization to organization? We teach our students to always have respect for any black belt because it is a major accomplishment. I also teach our students, just like in medicine or education, to treat everyone with respect. Treat all who deserve it, with respect. There is a point to recognize when a person doesn't deserve respect, but do you think there is a solution to this? We have to keep decorum and protocol, even with people whose rank and ability are questionable. Someone gave them rank they felt they deserved. They continue to be around. If we grandfather those people in, what is the resolution?

ML: First of all, too many people made rank through the buddy system. He's my buddy and I'm going to promote him. That should never be done. The only way we are going to accomplish what we are talking about right now, is to have an official governing body. They would set rules, regulations and standards. If you do not meet these standards, or if you try to do something other than what you're instructed to do, these people will have the authority to confront you and say, "Look, you have violated our standards. You're not adhering to the guidelines set by this board. Now you've got one of two choices; either straighten up and do what you're told, or we will strip you of your rank." If they can't hack it, get rid of them!

Dr. A: Call it what it is, identify it, label it and don't compromise yourself with it, is what you are saying. In the future, the Tatsuo Shimabuku–Harold Long lineage can grow a brand new organization, the vision will not be to recruit the old, bad wood and rotten apples. There are too many new, healthy, young people who are seeking this now. We want to train them from within, the one way, the right way, no compromise. When the old retreads or the drop outs come back they destroy organizations. When we have brought in "senior" people like this to be around my students and they have left negativity behind and they lower the status of the rank they hold.

ML: They automatically cast some doubt on your Dojo because your students use you as an example. When you bring in someone for your students to see, suppose they hold a higher rank than you, but don't have the same standards, don't conduct themselves in the same manner, your students pick up on that immediately. They think, why did Dr. Aiello bring in this guy, because he certainly doesn't meet our standards.

Dr. A: Yes, the students think a seventh, eighth, or ninth Dan is way up there, but then see that in certain people, it's not. That undermines their life's work, their spirit and their heart. That's the opposite of the One Heart Method.

ML: I never let anyone come into my Dojo who is not a good example for my students. I've had a lot of people want to work with my students. But I always find out what they are going to teach them. One senior Dan wanted to hold a demonstration because he wanted my students to see two sides. Two sides of what? I told him that he didn't have the qualifications to stand out there and teach my students. He didn't have the knowledge, because my students knew more than he.

They would like to be able to say, "Even Master Long had me come in and train his students." There is no way they can train my students or your students either because they don't have the knowledge you have. Unless someone has more knowledge than you, you don't want them in your Dojo. You've tried being a nice person and resurrect these people, but it's been a failure. It hasn't worked out, but you've tried and that's the key to it.

Dr. A. We try to bring them up, try to salvage them. We see a person in trouble, someone we've known for a lot of years and try to give a helping hand. Then they bite the hand that feeds them and once bitten twice shy as they say. I've got clear direction from this conversation, where to stand with people from other organizations who are out there, doing it their way, so they can show people two sides of the coin. For people in the future, black belts don't return. I want people to know that other like minded people think the same.

ML: I've always told people, "You don't have a way and I don't have a way. We're doing Master Shimabuku's Isshin Ryu Karate. You don't have the knowledge to add or take away. You do it the way he wanted it done and you're going to be a success. You're going to be an outstanding Karate Ka. First thing I want you to remember, don't you ever, in your lifetime, change Grandmaster Shimabuku's Isshin Ryu Karate. You don't have the intelligence to do it. You don't know what he had in his mind when he brought this system into being. You don't know him, you don't know me. So, how can you justify that you've changed something?"

Dr. A: There is a difference between changing it and working with it for research and development and to explore the other ten techniques you've overlooked in Bunkai as you stated earlier.

ML: I teach many, many more individual techniques than Grandmaster Shimabuku did, but he was teaching me to be a teacher and he gave me the necessary knowledge. If I had spent 20, 25 years working directly in the Dojo, then he would have taught me the same way I've taught my students throughout the years. He would have developed all the things that put me on the right track.

Dr. A: We don't want to change the charts or the kata at all. That is your alphabet and the alphabet never changes, but you can spell more words.

Author's Note: There should always be room for more "vocabulary" and greater mastery with the "words" that are currently used.

ML: About Grandmaster Shimabuku's religious beliefs. He believed in the same God that you and I believe in. He was not a Buddhist. That's everyone's personal relationship with God. You can't judge people from that aspect. He drank Saki. But he wasn't a drunk or anything of this nature. That relaxed him after a hard day's work. He would have a cup of Saki before he went to bed so he could sleep. When he visited Knoxville, TN, in 1966, my doctor said this was an ideal thing for a person like him to do and it was normal. It certainly wasn't anything detrimental to his health. There are a lot of people who see things in a different light. Even myself, I get credit for the years I've spent in Karate. I'll bet there are not ten people who know, or even care, that I'm also an usher at the parson's chapel services at the naval home in Gulfport, Mississippi. This is something I enjoy doing. I get to meet people and the chaplain told me, since I go to church on a regular basis and consider myself a Christian, I should be an usher and take an active part in the chapel services. Wednesday afternoons I attend one hour of bible study that we have at the chapel. But people, obviously, are not concerned with that part of your life.

Dr. A: We're trying to better people, as well as better martial arts and continue to on self perfection.

ML: This is very important. If we don't offer guidance to these youngsters, who is going to? We have, really, only two elements to society. We have the Christ and we have the anti–Christ. If those who believe in God try to follow God in the manner we do, don't take these young people and offer guidance, then we're not fulfilling our obligation to God. I've heard a lot of different stories about Christianity, but each person has a personal and a special relationship with God. I know myself. Sometime before the day is over, I'm going to show you a medical history you won't believe. If you read this history without knowing who it is about, you would say this person could not live under such circumstances. A few years ago, I was at the hospital and my cardiologist ran two tests. When he had the results, he told me I had a very serious heart disease and needed a heart catheterization to asses the extent of the damage. I agreed and the procedure was set up for 7:00 the next morning. He was taking me first since he was working me in ahead of his regular schedule. That night, I was laying there, commenting and talking to God, which I do on occasion. During that reflection I said, "Lord, if the Holy Spirit dwells in my heart, how can there be a disease? I don't understand that part at all. I can understand heart problems, but not a diseased place." Of course, most people say this is coincidental, but the next day, when they took me down and ran the test, looked around, took pictures and did some more extensive study, they discovered I did not have a heart disease at all. I still feel it was God's way of saying, "OK., you asked a good question, here is your answer."

Dr. A: When did your health problems start?

ML: In 1982. It was something I ignored for quite sometime. It started in my doctor's office when he noticed that my most recent physical was four or five years old. So we scheduled a new one. Two or three days later, he did the electro cardiogram. I knew something was wrong when the technician doing the test had to talk to the doctor. He came back and told me I was being admitted to the hospital because I had heart problems. I didn't understand that because I wasn't sick, hadn't been sick, didn't even feel bad. But he assured me that had nothing to do with the heart. He was the one who discovered it, quite by accident. He asked me if I heard of someone just keeling over, dying, all of a sudden. Hadn't been sick, nothing wrong. I know a dozen people from that category. He told me that's exactly the category I was in.

Dr. A: Then they wanted to do a catheterization?

ML: No. They ran a treadmill test and one other test. That's when the cardiologist said they needed to do a catheterization, because the results, so far, indicated that I had a very serious heart disease.

Dr. A: After they went in and looked around, everything was OK. But you still had health problems. What happened then?

ML: I developed an arrhythmia after that, which is treated with medication. I have arterial sclerosis and diabetes. I can live with those things. If I take the medication and care for myself the way I should, I don't consider it to be a problem at all.

Dr. A: When you lose the health component, you have nothing left. In our program, I stress chiropractic adjustments to keep the nervous system in peak condition, multiple vitamin and mineral supplements, a balanced diet, limited ingestion of alcohol and abstinence of smoking. Back in the sixties, we didn't have guidance so we went to incredible extremes with our training. I worked twelve hours a day teaching from 10:00 am to 10:00 PM. Karate was a big fad. We would have 300 students a day in each club. Then we worked out after that, or before. I saw a lot of my contemporaries going to great extremes. They didn't know the right training method, they didn't have a right perspective and they hurt themselves. Today these men, like myself, are in their late 40's coming on to 50 years old. Most of them have had hip replacements, knee replacements, multiple surgeries, or heart attacks.

ML: They didn't understand their body and they didn't know how to care for it. They envisioned themselves as being superman. This is not a true assessment of themselves.

Dr. A: Yet, the training, itself, makes you so strong, that you feel like it at times. You get so strong, you are oblivious to pain.

ML: I told each of my students, "You are the only person who knows your outer limits. When you discover your limit, withdraw slightly, then you will always do well because you know your limitations."

Dr. A: We teach Karate, not only for self defense and personal development, but as good exercise to balance your health. To be healthy, you have to do a good, serious exercise program. What happens when so many Karate people, yourself, Master Peter Urban, William Duessel, Ed Parker, Robert Trias, still get sick even with hard training? What was missing?

ML: Your genes have a lot to do with it. In the Long family, no male member has lived as long as I. My father died at the age of 62 and only one brother made it into the 60's, he was 61. Here I am 67 and still do everything.

Author's Note: Master Long has provided a complete dossier on his medical history and current health status. In addition he has provided many letters verifying many of his statements pertaining to individuals of concern.

Dr. A: So, you think part of it is the genetic factor, not just the life–styles.

ML: That's part of it, but I think your relationship with God has a lot to do with your length of life and the life–style. Your belief in God and your Christianity helps you over the rough spots. All Christians belong to God. The people who are not Christian, do not belong to Him. He doesn't give the same assistance he gives to us. It's just like the Dojo. Everybody there is a worthy person. They come in and want to do the right thing. I don't care what kind of problems they have, we work with them on these problems. God does the same thing.

Dr. A: Speaking of Grandmaster Shimabuku's spiritual relationship to God. He had a picture of Jesus on his Shomen wall. This was not just for the Gi's who came in to train. This was for him as well?

ML: That was for him. That wasn't for the Gi's at all. Grandmaster Shimabuku was a Christian.

Dr. A: When he had his dream about the Mizu Gami, someone stated that it was a Shinto or Buddhist goddess. He did not say this occurred during his spiritual practice or that he had a spiritual awakening from a Buddhist God.

ML: No. This is not true. I've heard a lot of things like that too. This has nothing to do with religion, this was a dream he had and felt it should be a symbol for Isshin Ryu Karate. If you'll notice the Mizu Gami we wear proudly on our Gi, Grandmaster Shimabuku never used it on his Gi. He never had anything on his Gi. It was just a plain Gi and most of the time the Gi he wore was like cheese cloth. He wanted something cool and comfortable.

Dr. A: The Mizu Gami came not long after you started, maybe in '57 or '58? How was it drawn up for him?

ML: It came later than that, probably '58 or '59. He had an artist come down and related his dream to the artist. The artist drew his dream on paper.

Dr. A: What influence occurred by the American design of the patch?

ML: They took pictures of the Mizu Gami drawn by the artist which hung in Master Shimabuku's Dojo. They came back to the United States and made a commercial patch changing the shape to an oval.

Dr. A: Originally, Arsenio Advincula Sensei told me that he put his fist down, drew around it and that was the shape of the first patch cut out with the Mizu Gami, the dragon, the water and the stars. Then Steve Armstrong returned to the United States and made it into an oval.

ML: This is true, the first patch put out was in the shape of a fist. But it wasn't Master Shimabuku's fist, it belonged to Steve Armstrong.

Dr. A: It was Armstrong's or Advincula's?

ML: Armstrong. Steve is the one who had the first commercial patches. It was not Master Shimabuku's fist because he did not understand why you would wear that on your Gi. He understood the emblem and the significance of it, because he had a big picture hanging in his Dojo. As far as wearing something like that, he thought it was nonsense. Nobody on Okinawa ever wore one. People from Okinawa who visit The United States have a Gi just for The United States. They don't wear that same Gi on Okinawa. You don't see anybody on Okinawa wearing anything like the Mizu Gami.

Dr. A: Why has it become so popular if it's not the tradition?

ML: We made it popular in America, because we felt it was a symbol of Isshin Ryu. We felt proud of ourselves. We wanted everyone to know that we were Isshin Ryu Karate Ka.

Dr. A: Symbolism is important to Americans. Did Grandmaster Shimabuku have a meditation time in his daily activities? What was his spiritual practice? Did he try to teach this or pass anything along to his students or was it totally private?

ML: He had a communication problem on things of this nature. He also felt that everyone's relationship with God was a personal thing, like his relationship. He didn't go around with a big sign on his Gi saying "I'm a Christian." If you talked to him about Christianity, he would tell you that he was a Christian.

Dr. A: As in any Dojo, people have problems. As these problems came up, did he have any way of counseling people? Did he take people under his wing, like you becoming good friends with him? When you went out to enjoy a little Saki, did you have conversations about these things?

ML: We never went out to have a little Saki. We had that at the Dojo. You have to remember, his Dojo started after you stepped out of his front door. This was all an open area. Once he stepped into his house, he was away from the Dojo. He was a great story teller and that was when you would learn more. He would have a cup of Saki and everyone would gather around and he would tell stories. Remember, the orient, Africa, everywhere except America, had a story teller. He was the historian, they didn't have things written. They had the story tellers who handed this information down, from generation to generation.

Dr. A: He would sit around and talk, just like we do. We sit around telling Karate stories and talk about the past. The younger people learn from the older people, what it was like before them.

ML: I never missed any of those sessions, because you learned so much at them. That's when you saw the true Tatsuo Shimabuku.

Dr. A: His spirituality was private, personal, he felt that each person should have their own relationship with God. He didn't do a lot of counseling because he didn't go around and socialize with his students.

ML: This is right. I probably went with him as much as anyone did. I remember a track meet and that was something that filled my heart with joy, seeing the enthusiasm of all the different villages who had a representative entering these track events. In a race with 12 to 14 competitors, even if you came in last, the supporters from your village congratulated you just as if you set a new world record. I thought this was so heart warming. In America, if you don't finish first, nobody is going to have anything to do with you. They don't pat you on the back and congratulate you. These people felt so proud of the guy who represented them. He was kind of a hero, regardless of how he finished. The fact he represented them made them proud of this man. Grandmaster Shimabuku liked to do things a little bit differently at these track meets. Nothing ever started on time in Okinawa, I don't care what it was. If an event was suppose to be at 8:00 in the morning, nobody started to get ready to go until 8:00 a.m. or after. They knew it wasn't going to start until 9:00 a.m. anyway or maybe a little after. I got down to the Dojo early and Grandmaster Shimabuku had just gotten up and was having a cup of tea. Finally, he decided it was time to put on his street clothes and prepare himself properly to go to the track meet. They had benches for people to sit on, but all the benches were full. So, he went down to the first row and ran people off of this bench and laid down so he'd be more comfortable watching the track meet. No one refused to do this. In America, if you go up and tell people in the front row to get up and move because you need a place to lie down, you'd have a lot of problems. The people were so respectful to him, it was something, I guess, they were accustomed to.

Dr. A: Was he well known in Chun Village as a martial artist at that time?

ML: He was well known, that's how I found out about him to start with. I knew there were several well known and competent practitioners like Shimabuku on Okinawa and I started inquiring. The house girl at the camp where I was stationed told me who to go to and tried to explain how to get there. I had no idea, so she took me down there the first time. We went into Agina to get on a bus. She told the bus driver where to stop, it was literally in the middle of nowhere. Then you walk a path through rice paddies. She told me he was a great instructor, but that was the only English description they had. She wanted me to know, for sure, that this was the best instructor on Okinawa.

Dr. A: At that time, however, there were many prominent Karate sensei. Who were some of the other prominent teachers?

ML: His brother Eizo, Master Uechi and several more prominent instructors were much more accesible than Grandmaster Shimabuku.

Dr. A: Who would ever realize this was the heart of Karate? There were a lot of masters, but few who would teach an American.

ML: That's right. When Grandmaster Shimabuku decided to move to Agina, we're the ones, contrary to popular belief, who secured Master Shimabuku's first contract with the United States Marine Corp. $200.00 per month is a fabulous salary. I guess he thanked me 100 times for that because a skilled worker on Okinawa, at that time, was making approximately 8 cents an hour. Here's a man with a contract receiving a check for $200.00 every month.

Dr. A: For teaching Karate, which was unheard of until then.

ML: This is why he moved to Agina, to be closer to the marine base and maintain this relationship.

Dr. A: What was the relationship with his brother, Eizo Shimabuku?

ML: They already terminated it before I arrived on the scene, when he started the Isshin Ryu system.

Dr. A: They both trained with Chotoku Kyan, who was also called Chan Migwa, small eyes.

ML: I've heard that, but I've also heard that Grandmaster Shimabuku was his brother's instructor for many years.

Dr. A: His brother, Eizo Shimabuku, now heads the Shorin Ryu system.

ML: Yes. That's the reason he stayed in the Shorin Ryu. Tatsuo, his brother and teacher, founded the Isshin Ryu system. If Eizo came over to Isshin Ryu, he'd be the number two man. He wanted to stay in the Shorin Ryu System, so he would be the number one man.

Dr. A: However, in Okinawa, there is no number one man in Shorin Ryu anymore, there's six.

ML: It's just like Isshin Ryu. We've got different splinter groups. Okinawa has exactly the same thing.

Dr. A: Even Uechi Ryu has six groups or more in Okinawa. Goju Ryu has at least six. Some are more respected than others. Is this splintering, Master Long, the natural way of Karate, the way it has to be?

ML: No, I don't think so at all. I think it's a lack of respect from people who don't realize what their purpose of being in the systems constitutes and from people who can't follow direct orders. To me, it's very clear. If you're my sensei and we have some type of conflict, automatically, I apologize to my sensei. That is correct, period, there is no argument. You don't break away from your senior saying you don't see things the same way your sensei does. Where did you get this vast amount of knowledge to dispute your sensei? The only thing you have is what you got from him.

Dr. A: There are situations where a student starts out with an instructor who doesn't have the knowledge to be a sensei. Isn't it inevitable that this student is going to leave this teacher?

ML: This is true, but I don't think they should leave in a disrespectful spirit. I think they should talk to the sensei about it. Tell him that he would like more detailed instruction so he progresses and ask his blessing to go to another Dojo.

Dr. A: Let's talk more about the splintering and the Shimabuku situation. You have a small island, a small community. Two brothers are going to be historically famous. Their sons are going to be historically famous. The son–in–law, Angi Uezu, is going to be historically famous in the martial arts. Yet, they don't get along. Right now, I understand that Master Shimabuku's wife lives with Ciso. Kichiro and Eizo, Shimabuku's uncle, don't get along and both had systems over there. Isn't Isshin Ryu about harmony and getting along, The One Heart Method, or The One Heart, One Mind Method?

ML: That's the way Grandmaster Shimabuku envisioned it and that's the way he wanted to see it. As long as there are humans, there are going to be mistakes. It seems they don't care what their sensei wanted, it's what they themselves want. That's the biggest mistake anyone can make. If you can't accept your sensei's guidance, you'll never be a leader. Like we tell everyone in the Marine Corps, you can never give orders until you learn how to take orders.

Dr. A: Yet, what is the protocol if you get a student who is a powerful leader? One of my teachers, in another system, I've known since 1969. He heads an organization and is the chief technical advisor in this country. After I started teaching at their Hombu Dojo and my class grew larger than the entire student enrollment, he told me, "A leader cannot follow a follower. It's destiny that you take your group out of our organization because you're a leader and quite honestly, I'm a follower. You can't follow me. You have to move on."

ML: This is true, but your sensei should see that and be the one who tells you that your value is in your own Dojo.

Dr. A: Eventually, that happened through writing books and producing video tapes. People may be intimidated by the physical abilities of a young person or the intelligence of someone. It makes me suspect, personally, because a student cannot ever go ahead of his sensei.

ML: This is true, but a good instructor is never intimidated by anyone. My son is a good example. He was in charge of the public service commission, truck safety inspections, for East Tennessee, covering a large area and several counties. He had a lieutenant who was a big, overpowering physical specimen. One day, he came in real strong. My son looked up at him, saying, "Lieutenant, sit down and cut out the bull --. My father is the most intimidating man in the world, you're not in his class." That was his way of saying sit down and shut up. I don't care how intimidating you may be, you're a lieutenant. Do what I tell you.

Dr. A: What can we do, as it is in Okinawa, where the father was directly involved with his own son and brothers and everybody splintered off? How can we expect people to keep together in the United States, where we don't have the strong influence of family and heritage like Shimabuku?

ML: That's one thing that should never have occurred on Okinawa. I know for a fact, it was one reason why Grandmaster Shimabuku chose to retire, because of the conflict with Kichiro. It should never have been a problem, but I think Grandmaster Shimabuku should have called his son in, just like any other instructor he had and said, "Look, you're overstepping your bounds. You've got one of two choices, either come back and follow my direction, or leave." But he wasn't willing to do that with Kichiro.

Dr. A: In the martial arts, especially in the United States, there is no way to pull or remove someone's rank or to regulate or de–license them because there are no licensing and regulation laws.

ML: There is no procedure for that. If I promote you and you do something that is really bad, we'll refuse to recognize your rank, but there is no procedure for pulling your rank. I can only pull the recognition, I cannot pull the rank.

Dr. A: And that person could continue anyway. In Japan, they had the Dai Nippon Butoku Kai, which was the licensing and recognition board to which you made application. Karate did not get accepted into the Butoku Kai until 1936. It was just prior to that, when they started giving belt ranks in Okinawa.

ML: In the Isshin Ryu Dojo, Grandmaster Shimabuku gave only one belt rank. You stayed at white belt until you made Shodan. He felt that all these in between belts were for people who didn't set their sights high. No records are kept until you make Shodan, because you're not considered to be a student until that rank. After you move up to Shodan, he felt you were ready for training. You've got the background for it, you've got the knowledge, you have the stamina, you have the desire, so he could train you. He didn't want somebody who had their sights set on green belt and would be satisfied, then leave. He didn't want that situation to exist in his Dojo.

Dr. A: How did this occur in the United States?

ML: Money. I have seen belts I've never heard of. I call it the rainbow system. The instructors and the Dojo sign you up with a contract to a certain belt rank. You have a green belt with a yellow tip, a white belt with green or brown tips. All different colors. Those are a commercial gimmick, they don't exist in the orient. The only belts I ever saw in the orient were white, green, brown, black, red & white and red.

Dr. A: On Okinawa?

ML: Yes, even in Japan. On my way to visit Grandmaster Shimabuku in 1974, we stopped by the Seibukan Academy in Kyoto, Japan and had a nice visit with Master Suzuki, a Goju Ryu Master and the director of the academy. It was unreal, the records they keep. I have a certificate from the Seibukan Academy, issued to me because of Master Suzuki's respect for Grandmaster Shimabuku. We were his students, so he issued a membership certificate and rank certificate from the Seibukan Academy to me. The way they keep records is very simple; they have a big book, they stamp half in the book and half on your certificate.

Dr. A: This is the same method I use for Shito Kan. I keep a journal and each certificate is stamped at the top.

Author's Note: *This is a traditional method of keeping track of students. Ranks are recorded beginning at Shodan. Teaching certificates are also recorded. Above Shodan, belt colors correspond with teacher certifications. Shidoin is solid black, Renshi is Black and red Kyoshi is red and white and Hanshi is solid red. Kyu levels, those below black belt, are typically white, green and brown.*

ML: These numbers are matched, so if you say you have a rank certificate from the Seibukan Academy, the number of your certificate will match the entry in their book of records. It's a double check.

Dr. A: This is the way I was taught to keep log records. Do you keep a record, yourself, of your black belts?

ML: No. I did at one time, but I no longer keep a log of any type.

Dr. A: How many black belts would you say you have?

ML: It would be just a few over 200.

Dr. A: That's not very many for the number of students you've taught.

ML: Most people don't qualify and there are people who will tell you they got their black belt from me, but they did not. They got their black belt from one of my students who is now a teacher. Some of J.C. Burris's students claim they came under me, but this is incorrect. They don't come under me at all, they come under Mr. Burris.

Dr. A: Are most of your black belts active?

ML: No. I have had so many disappointments in black belts. People run around saying they got this from me or trained and done this or that. But they don't have a Dojo. They left the Dojo and wanted to give clinics and seminars. Well, if you don't have a Dojo, you certainly can't give clinics and seminars. Why would I want to bring somebody in for my students to see who doesn't have a Dojo? He doesn't teach anybody, he doesn't train anybody, but wants to come in and share this vast knowledge. I didn't let people like that come into my Dojo and train.

Dr. A: I was fortunate because I was given an opportunity to teach at a young age. By 1978, I already taught 20,000 students. My first ten years I put in literally 12 hours a day, 5 1/2 days a week. I never missed a workout in the first ten years. Today, attendance is a problem in the Dojo. People get rank as a black belt, the first grade and drop out. They lack the seriousness. Over the years I figured out one thing for sure, drop out rate is 100% unless they teach.

ML: I've had so many students tell me they don't want the responsibility. If you don't want that type of responsibility, what are you doing here? What's your goal in life? What do you want to achieve? Unless you are willing to accept responsibility, I don't even want you as a student.

Dr. A: Americans don't understand when they join a club, the sensei today will sign them up on a contract. They're desperate to get a new student. They teach them almost anything they want, some, they almost baby–sit. Once you have the financial agreement of a contract, the instructor is in debt to the student, instead of the student having the responsibility to the teacher. All of a sudden, the teacher starts telling the student to take responsibility and teach. The students coming in under those commercial terms feel they should be taught because they pay for it. Money puts them in the driver's seat and they can be demanding. Under the old Giri system, the debt of obligation, there was never a contract. The individual applied for membership to become a student. Then the student would pay. Originally, money was not a comfortable issue for sensei to deal with, still isn't today. How much does commercialism get in the way? Is that what these students don't understand right up front that if they don't teach, they're going to quit; if they don't take responsibility, they can't fulfill the requirement of a black belt?

ML: Commercialism did away with tradition and history. Commercialism is for the almighty dollar and most commercialism is directed at this student. They claim they will make you a champion, because there is so much competition you have to outdo the guys down the street.

Dr. A: When I first started out, I worked for a company and sold thousands of contracts, we had thousands of students. Yet, I can honestly say, I never walked out on the training floor in that Dojo, never stood in front of a student, ever, for the money. There is no amount of money that can buy my knowledge. That has to come from my heart, my desire to pass on the tradition, my burning desire, inside, to develop another student. I never once did it for the money, no matter how much or how little they paid me to be a member.

ML: You would be shocked if I told you the approximate percentage of members in my Dojo who I asked to leave, because I felt they were in the wrong place, their heart wasn't in it, or they were wasting my time. I wasn't a bully about it. I would just call people in and politely say you're taking up floor space that the other students need. You're not serious. You come in and go through the motions. I don't see any real effort. I don't see you sweat. I don't see any accomplishment whatsoever. So, what I'm going to do today is cancel your contract. You no longer owe me any money, because you are no longer a student here. You don't belong in my Dojo, you belong where they'll let you be more relaxed and set your own pace. You can't do that here.

Dr. A: Where does that start, students with that attitude, the dabbler or unserious attitude?

ML: They don't know how to sweat, they don't know what physical work is. They don't know they're building up stamina. They don't know they're giving themselves a solid mind and they'll be a decision maker, able to see the world from a different perspective. If they come in the Dojo and learn history, tradition and what their place is by assuming the responsibility that goes with it, they will move up the ladder. Unless they're willing to do that with the proper attitude, you can't teach a person. They will pay you money, but they will take up space and take up your time and you'll never see any fruits from it.

Dr. A: Literally, the amount of money charged for martial arts today is very small. If you're a doctor, a lawyer, or a CPA, you could not afford to take a client on for $50.00 a month. So, the fruits of the labor is the debt of obligation this student makes to teach, to multiply himself by sharing what he's learned. Without that tradition in place, where the student is trained, becomes a teacher and passes the art on, sensei could never afford to teach someone for so little money each month.

Author's Note: The Sensei is reliant upon students and future students to maintain the tradition and tenets of their organization.

ML: Another thing I don't think I've discussed with you is what Mr. Burris and the I.I.K.A. did for me. After all the years and effort I put in, all the times I carried them when they had the option of going to an event or not, I was obligated to go to everything and I did. I would work all day, get some of my students and we would drive all night to get to a tournament. They'd compete in that tournament with only a few hours sleep and then, get back in the car and drive home. The student today doesn't understand the hardships people like you and me and so many other people endured. This was the only choice we had. You either did it that way or you didn't do it. So, they decided, since I'm now retired, to have a retirement fund. There are several Dojo that send $25.00 a month to me directly for my retirement. They want me to live a little bit more comfortable and this is what they've been doing. I really appreciate it, but I didn't think it was necessary. However, they felt because I gave so much, they wanted to make my retirement a little bit better.

When the Student is Ready, the Teacher Appears

ML: Ordinarily, you learn Karate, then you open a Dojo. James Morbeto had a lot of money and obviously he wanted to be a Karate Ka. He hired Grandmaster Tatsuo Shimabuku to come over and train him and members of the Dojo. This is what Grandmaster Shimabuku was doing when I came to visit in 1964 in Pittsburgh, with a car load of my black belters. This is the first time we had seen each other since 1957. James Morbeto is the one that bought the Dojo and hired Grandmaster Tatsuo Shimabuku to come from Okinawa to teach at the Dojo for three months. This is a joke that I have told for years. Grandmaster Shimabuku took a lot of delight in telling this joke, that this is the only man that he had ever seen or heard of that did things backwards. He said, "Ordinarily people have a lot of training, then they open a Dojo. Here is a man with no training that buys a Dojo and hires me to come teach him." This is a part of history of the Pittsburgh Dojo.

Dr. A: When I asked William Duessel on the radio show about that he said, "I've heard the story that whenever Grandmaster Shimabuku was asked about Pittsburgh he would say, "Pittsburgh number ten, Pittsburgh number ten." We got off the air and he said, "Oh, God! Did you have to bring that up?"

ML: He knew what you were talking about and he should have explained it. Grandmaster Shimabuku was treated so poorly there, that when I showed up with my black belters it was just, "Mister Long," I sure am glad you are here. The story was that they did not feed him on a regular basis and he was so hungry that he went to a local grocery store and bought a chicken and was eating this chicken raw.

Dr. A: This was James Morbeto?

ML: Yes.

Dr. A: That was a fortuitous meeting, how did they locate Grandmaster Shimabuku?

ML: I have no idea. No one contacted me on how to locate him, but I guess maybe Harry Smith had told him how to locate him.

Dr. A: Harry Smith is who William Duessel was training with at the time.

ML: Yes and Harry Smith and Dick Keith opened a Dojo at the same time in Harrisburg, PA. Dick Keith was a marine master sergeant who was making a career out of the Marine Corps. and he was on recruiting duty in Harrisburg. Harry Smith and Dick Keith trained at the same time with Grandmaster Shimabuku when I did, but they opened a Dojo. Then Dick Keith got transferred back and Harry Smith kept the Dojo. That Dojo has been open all the time. A fellow by the name of George Iberl is at the Dojo whenever Harry Smith is gone. Harry takes unwanted vacations occasionally. It is kind of a long story there but, that was William Duessel's first instructor. That was also George Dillman's first instructor.

Dr. A: Harry Smith?

ML: Yes.

Dr. A: What is Harry Smith today in Isshin Ryu?

ML: Harry Smith, as far as I'm concerned, is not in Isshin Ryu. Just recently, a story was related to me about George Iberl. Several years ago Iberl contacted me, his students wrote me letter, wanting me to recognize Iberl as an 8th. He says that Grandmaster Shimabuku had promoted him to a 8th. He had his certificate and wanted to know if I would authenticate his rank. I said, "I don't know. Send me a copy of Master Shimabuku's certificate and let me see it." He said, "Well, it was too big to send." I said, "What do you mean too big to send?" He started talking some story about it being on a big piece of plywood. I said, "Mr. Iberl, let me explain a few things to you. I have never heard of Grandmaster Shimabuku issuing a piece of plywood as a certificate. He's got certificates, plenty of certificates. That's hooey and I'm not going to buy that story at all." Well, of course from then on Iberl didn't really care for me all that much because what he was asking for was something that I cannot award someone that I have not seen. The last time I had seen Iberl prior to that was not a good experience at all. He did not know how to referee, he did not know how to conduct himself as a chief 7th Dan and I had a very low opinion of Iberl. A Sensei I know was reading that Iberl was saying that he was a Tenth Dan. I stated that Iberl does not have the background, the training or the knowledge. I said, "You could not multiply his knowledge by five and get enough knowledge to say that he's a 10th Dan in Isshin Ryu Karate. He's a 'johnny come lately' that did not work." He said, "Well, he says he just gave up his 10th ." I said, "What do you mean he gave up his 10th Dan?" He said, "Well, he promoted himself to 10th after Harry Smith took an unplanned vacation. Harry is back now, so Iberl lowered himself to a 9th so Harry could be the 10th." We talked about it, joked about it and made comments about it. Later, this Sensei who read about Iberl called me back and said, "Mr. Smith is back on his unplanned vacation again, so Iberl is a 10th again." See, there were some good people that came out of that Dojo but, the leadership itself made a mockery of Karate in that Dojo.

Dr. A: William Duessel in '64 was presented his Shodan there and on his current tape series he discusses the background and history. His tape series is endorsed now by Sensei Kichiro Shimabuku. He performs the eight Kata and then on a second tape, the weapons Kata including a short Sai Kata. There is footage of Grandmaster Tatsuo Shimabuku actually doing and he is a very straightforward man. Sensei Duessel has recovered now from open heart surgery. He is 68 years old now. He knows that starting in '64, he was not one of the original pioneers and he is a little concerned about that. He is now interested in coming out and demonstrating more and he realizes that he has to circulate because Kichiro Shimabuku does not circulate, does not demonstrate much and he feels that it is important as a senior Dan.

Getting back to the last time that I really had anything to do with Mr. William Duessel was when he nominated some people for Hall of Fame awards at the Isshin Ryu Hall of Fame. I asked Duessel why he did not bring his group and come down, this was for all Isshin Ryu Karate Ka. He told me that he was with Kichiro Shimabuku, Kichiro did not let them participate in other organizations events. I said, "In that case, the hell with you. I'm not going to nominate any of your people for the Hall of Fame Award if you are not willing to come and be a part of us, be a part of Isshin Ryu and be there for celebration. Absolutely not."

Dr. A: That's understandable.

ML: To me that was just a prime insult. I invite the man in, with his students. This was for Isshin Ryu Karate Ka. It was not for the IIKA, or the AOKA, or the Order of Isshin Ryu, WIKA, it is for Isshin Ryu.

Dr. A: Some of these people are having a change of heart because they are getting older. They are starting to put the politics and rank aside. They are wishing to really advance the Art. People like William Duessel say they have a change of heart, are they still welcome at the Hall of Fame Tournament?

ML: Absolutely. He is in Isshin Ryu Karate, he has a right to have a change of heart because this time it will be a change of heart that would dictate to help the growth of Isshin Ryu Karate. I would be thrilled to have William Duessel bring his students and come down.

Dr. A: We have gotten to know each other and he is very genuine. I had him on the radio show as a guest two times. His health does not allow him to do much, but he is recovering rapidly. He spoke that he might be interested in circulating other circles a little bit more.

ML: All these other people are welcome too. Lewis Lizotte is welcome. If they will just come down and be a credit to Isshin Ryu.

Dr. A: Where is Lewis Lizotte today, as far as your understanding?

ML: My understanding was that Lewis Lizotte had a lot of problems. I hope that's not true, but I'm afraid that it is, because I don't wish anything bad on anyone.

Dr. A: Who and what is he in Isshin Ryu today?

ML: It all depends on who you're talking to. He promoted himself to a tenth Dan. I wrote him a letter and I explained to him, I said, "Lewis, the last thing we need in Isshin Ryu is a tenth Dan. You are not even in the same generation as Mr. Nagle and I." He came back and said, "Willie Adams has a picture of you and me training together on Okinawa." I said, "Lewis, you're crazier than hell. You were Don Nagle's student, you were not Tatsuo Shimabuku's student. Willie Adams does not have a picture of me on Okinawa with anybody. You were not there, Willie Adams was not there. You went later."

Dr. A: So, he was Don Nagle's student. How does a person promote themselves to tenth degree black belt?

ML: What he had in mind, he was having a banquet at a tournament. He patterned his banquet after the Isshin Ryu Hall of Fame Banquet, which I told him that he could not do. I said, "This is my format. You can not use this format." He had the same awards except he did not call it the Hall of Fame, so therefore, I had no real legal recourse. He invited Don Nagle and I there and he was going to declare himself a tenth Dan. He wanted his picture made with us which would authenticate it. When Don Nagle and I found out what the man's intentions were, we said, "No, you mark this off, fellow, if you want to have a fiasco, Don Nagle and Harold Long will not be there."

Dr. A: Is he the current president of the AOKA?

ML: Yes.

Dr. A: Willie Adams is the vice chairman?

ML: Yes, the same Willie Adams who owes me over $800.00 that I have sued for and not been able to get a legal process on. Willie Adams, if he ever makes himself visible and I know where he is at a certain time, I will have Willie Adams put in jail.

Dr. A: What does he owe you the money for?

ML: For Hall of Fame tickets that he did not sell and he turned in later. We had to pay for those meals, so Willie Adams owes the money. We had another man under the same circumstances, Sam Santilli, Sam understood that he owed the money, we had to pay for those meals, so Sam reimbursed me for what he owed, Willie Adams hid.

Dr. A: I have noticed in the last couple of years, Willie Adams, Sam Santilli and Lewis Lizotte, have not been at the Hall of Fame Tournament.

ML: No, they have not. This is because Lewis Lizotte acted like he was offended because I did not come to his fiasco. I do not care if I offend every one of those people. The fact is everyone of them are junior to me. If they are thinking that I am going to give my approval to something that they do not deserve, the answer is absolutely not. I am not looking for favoritism with these people. I am the tenth Dan. Lewis Lizotte in his lifetime will never be a tenth Dan. He can promote himself to a twentieth Dan, but that will not improve his knowledge one iota.

Dr. A: Is their rank coming through the AOKA organization?

ML: I do not know where it comes from. He just says that he is going to be promoted to a tenth Dan. In fact I can show you a couple of letters I wrote to him and told him that he was not going to be a tenth Dan. The last thing we need in this system is another tenth Dan. What I am trying to impress on him, is that his teacher is a tenth Dan. Under no circumstances do you go to the same rank as your teacher. Under no circumstances does he have the background, he was not even in the same generation. I think that Lewis has a tremendous ego problem.

Dr. A: Does the AOKA, the American Okinawan Karate Association have the power and authority to promote him to a tenth Dan?

ML: I don't think so because they don't have anyone on their board that trained directly under Grandmaster Tatsuo Shimabuku.

Dr. A: How about Willie Adams, who is claiming to be a ninth or tenth Dan now?

ML: Well, he got his from the AOKA. He did not get it from any person in authority, other than just the organization.

Dr. A: There was no tenth Dan to promote him to a ninth Dan on the board.

ML: No, this is correct.

Dr. A: The OAKA (Okinawan American Karate Association) was dissolved and unrecognized or disbarred or unlicensed by Grandmaster Tatsuo Shimabuku and the name was changed to AOKA, correct?

ML: This was 1967 when the big change over was made. Armstrong took what was the AOKA or the OAKA and changed it around to the AOKA.

Dr. A: This was not with the permission of Grandmaster Tatsuo Shimabuku.

ML: No it was not. Steve Armstrong wrote Grandmaster Tatsuo Shimabuku in January of 1967 the most insulting letter and it was about me. He said it was not Harold Long that brought you over to this country, it was me. That was all the way through the letter. Grandmaster Shimabuku was just stunned. Tomiko Chukini called me up and said, "You will not believe a letter that Steve Armstrong asked me to write to Grandmaster Shimabuku. I told him no."

Dr. A: This was just prior to him having some brain tumors. Maybe his thinking was being affected at that time.

ML: I'm sure it was. I think Steve's mind was being affected much prior to the brain tumor being discovered. I have always told people that it just did not sound like Steve Armstrong. I said, "I can't imagine Steve Armstrong or anyone else writing Grandmaster Shimabuku a letter like that." Then it was not very much longer it was discovered that he had a brain tumor. In fact I believe that he has had three brain operations throughout the years to have tumors removed. I will go back and give him credit, I feel that he was not in the proper frame of mind when he wrote that thing.

Dr. A: What is the World Karate Union Hall of Fame and who runs that?

ML: The World Karate Union Hall of Fame is really just getting started. They are good people and they are doing what they feel is right. They already have a branch in Australia and are opening a branch in Europe. I am not that familiar with their history. Gary Alexander and Al Smith are both on their board and both of them have a real solid background in Karate.

Dr. A: Gary Alexander was an Isshin Ryu man.

ML: Yes, he was. He calls himself Isshin Ryu Plus. I have no idea what Isshin Ryu Plus is. He also says he is a tenth Dan, but he was a student of Don Nagle.

Dr. A: You were in Okinawa training in 1955 and 1956?

ML: Yes.

Dr. A: Was Don Nagle there at the same time?

ML: Yes he was.

Dr. A: Did you see each other there?

ML: Sure. We knew each other well. It was Harold Mitchum and Don Nagle who had never met.

Dr. A: What made you want to start the International Isshin Ryu Association?

ML: I felt that The American Okinawan Karate Association would not attract anyone. Since the geographical locations were so different, we had to have another organization that was not going to commercialize the Isshin Ryu system. Steve Armstrong wanted to sell equipment and supplies. He wanted to put Isshin Ryu on everything, even an Isshin Ryu toothbrush. My vision was to teach Isshin Ryu Karate, so I felt I didn't belong in the A.O.K.A. I wasn't going to support the purpose of the A.O.K.A., so I asked Grandmaster Shimabuku for permission to start another organization. That was my purpose of going to talk with him in 1974.

Dr. A: Steve Armstrong came after you and Don Nagle.

ML: Yes.

Dr. A: He was not the next full senior person was he?

ML: He and Mitchum and Advincula trained together.

Dr. A: Then Steve Armstrong started the A.O.K.A.

ML: Originally, it was The Okinawan American Karate Association. Steve took it over and changed it to The American Okinawan Karate Association.

Dr. A: To make it more palatable to Americans?

ML: I think that's what it was. At one time, Steve was telling everyone we were having difficulty getting rank certificates from Okinawa. We discovered that when we sent overseas mail orders, Grandmaster Shimabuku had no idea what it was. He didn't realize that a money order was legitimate currency that he could take to the bank. So, he put all those checks in a drawer, never realizing it was money we sent as fees for certificates which, of course, we never got. In the meantime, Steve Armstrong convinced everyone he had a direct pipeline to Okinawa. He wanted you to send your money to him, not to Okinawa and he assured you that you would get your certificate. What he didn't tell us was that he had a whole locker box full of certificates with Master Shimabuku's name on them. He took one that Grandmaster Shimabuku had signed and duplicated Master Shimabuku's signature and seals. So, he was selling rank certificates that Grandmaster Shimabuku had never heard of.

Dr. A: Is that why they decided to call certificates awarded before a certain date, invalid? Or did that have nothing to do with it?

ML: Grandmaster Shimabuku never told me that my certificate wasn't valid. He had my address and we corresponded. If my certificate was not valid, why did Grandmaster Shimabuku promote me to a seventh Dan in 1960? Why did he promote me to an eighth Dan in 1966?

Dr. A: When you left Okinawa you were a sixth Dan?

ML: Yes.

Dr. A: Was that a common rank that he gave out to people who stayed 19 months with him?

ML: He felt you had to have enough rank to be heard, but you have to look at the total number of hours we trained. That was not a common rank he gave to everyone, only the people he felt were going to be true to their word and teach and promote Isshin Ryu Karate.

Dr. A: What happened after people found out Steve Armstrong had a locker full of certificates he was selling? Is there anyone today with high rank from Steve Armstrong who is relying on one of the certificates he wrote?

ML: I don't think so. What Steve did was sell these certificates to lower ranking people. They thought if they had a rank certificate, there was a record kept in Okinawa. Later, they found out there was no record in Okinawa because nothing was ever sent. I know about the locker box full of certificates because I saw them. Grandmaster Shimabuku was so irate. He said he wanted to promote Don Nagle, Steve Armstrong and I to eighth Dan and would send us a certificate after he returned to Okinawa. That's when Steve revealed the certificates. He opened up his locker box and it was full of certificates with Master Shimabuku's signature and seal on them. How would you feel if you found one of your students selling rank certificates with your name and seal on them? Steve was so sure he was going to be appointed Master Shimabuku's representative in the United States. He didn't know I had already been appointed to that position. That was his purpose of bringing Grandmaster Shimabuku over here, to sell him on the idea of appointing him to be the U.S.A. representative. When Grandmaster Shimabuku failed to do that and went back to Okinawa, Steve wrote a letter of resignation to Grandmaster Shimabuku. This was in January of 1967. In response, Grandmaster Shimabuku wrote a letter dismissing him.

Dr. A: So, he resigned in '67 and was dismissed in '67. Did Steve Armstrong keep the A.O.K.A.?.

ML: Yes.

Dr. A: Then it was no longer an Okinawan sanctioned organization.

ML: Right, it was Steve Armstrong's organization basically.

Dr. A: But everyone assumed he was the appointed successor in the United States because he didn't tell them otherwise.

ML: He led people to believe several different things. He told people he also had a letter just like mine, but never showed it to anyone. He told people that Grandmaster Shimabuku signed a Judan certificate for him which he was to keep in a safety deposit box and, after ten years, he would be a Judan. This is not true. No one person can promote you to a Judan rank, that takes an organization. The organization has to bestow it, because you cannot promote anyone to a rank equal to your own. There were several inaccurate things, but, to me, the rank shouldn't have been important. You should put your training foremost and rank takes care of itself.

Dr. A: At the time you trained, Shimabuku Sensei already had Okinawan students who had been with him for years.

ML: They left the Shorin Ryu system and followed him when he formed the Isshin Ryu System. But, he also lost several students when he formed the Isshin Ryu System. In the mid 50's, when Grandmaster Shimabuku had more students than he could handle, he sent the overflow to Master Uechi, who was a friend of his.

Author's Note: Prior to creating the Isshin Ryu system Grandmaster Tatsuo Shimabuku taught what was called Chan Migwa Te. This was named after the nickname of Chotoku Kyan, Migwa meaning "small eyes."

Dr. A: When I spoke with Arsenio Advincula he stated that all senior students left Sensei Kichiro Shimabuku and would not stay with him prior to his father's, Grandmaster Tatsuo Shimabuku, death. He claims that he knows definitely that Kichiro did not have the system turned over to him nor did his father give him the Menkyo Kaiden or a 10th Dan ranking. Kichiro took control of the organization and almost pushed his father out before his death. How much truth is there to that?

ML: I don't know how Kichiro achieved a Judan. When I was on Okinawa in 1974, never, at any time, did Grandmaster Tatsuo Shimabuku forbid me to start an organization. Nor did he mention, or suggest, that I incorporate or work with Kichiro.

Dr. A: How did the Okinawan nationals feel when he gave higher ranks to Americans who only trained for a year and a half or two years?

ML: He didn't care because, at that time, he was not in favor with the other instructors on Okinawa anyway. You see, he had the audacity to change tradition, from the power block to the deflection block and the corkscrew punch to the vertical punch.

Dr. A: He modified the kata considerably.

ML: Yes he did. He took the kata from the Shorin Ryu system and from the Goju Ryu system. [He] changed those and modified them to reflect his training and knowledge.

Author's Note: The Isshin Ryu Kata Keizu or lineage is as follows:

Shorin Ryu Derivation: Chinto, Kushanku (both from Chotoku Kyan via Yasutsune Itosu and Sokon Matsumora of Shuri, Okinawa), Naihanchi (from Choki Motobu, possibly from Tomari, Okinawa through Kosaku Matsumora), Seisan (also found in Naha systems).

Tomari Derivation: Wansu (Shorin Ryu version from Chotoku Kyan learned from Kosaku Matsumora).

Goju Ryu Derivation: Seiuchin, Sanchin (both from Chojun Miyagi via Kanryo Higaonna of Naha, Okinawa.

Tatsuo Shimabuku then created his own master Kata; Sunsu. These are the eight Kata that are found in Isshin Ryu. No other Kata are recognized by any legitimate Isshin Ryu Masters as Isshin Ryu Kata. Each of the Masters mentioned above have created their own Kata. It is traditional that after a certain point of mastery that this should occur. Shito Kan Karate Do Kata Keizu is as follows:

Shuri Te: The Pinan Kata Series (Nidan, Sandan, Shodan, Yondan, Godan) from Yasutsune Itosu who created them from Kushanku Kata. These were originally developed as beginner's forms in the early 1900's. These Kata are in the Shito Kan system through Kanken Toyama of Shudo Kan and Eizo Onishi of Koei Kan.

Shorin Ryu: The Naihanchin Series (Shodan, Nidan, Sandan) from Kanken Toyama via Eizo Onishi.

Naha Te: Sanchin Kata in the pre World War II version of Kanryo Higaonna via Juhatsu Kiyoda of Toon Ryu and Eizo Onishi.

Eight Isshin Ryu Kata in their original form as Grandmaster Tatsuo Shimabuku passed them on to Master Harold Long; Seisan, Seiuchin, Wansu, Sanchin, Naihanchi, Chinto, Kushanku, and Sunsu.

Eight Shito Kan Kata: Tachi Kata, Ukemi and Nokote Kata, Yonju Shichi, Zensho, Bushi No Kata, Sankaishu Kokyu Kata, Renshi Bo Kata, Kyoshi No Kata, Hanshi No Kata. These Kata were all created by Dr. Aiello.

Dr. A: Then came up with his own system, of course. He didn't care what those students felt, he was going to appoint who he wanted, when he wanted.

ML: Yes.

Dr. A: Was he formal with his testing? Before you left, did he take you through a big formal test?

ML: He didn't take you through a test at all. He said that you were tested everyday when you came into the Dojo.

Dr. A: So, how did the people in Isshin Ryu arrive at the formal testing they have?

ML: I don't know. I never had formal testing in my life, nor do my students take part in a formal test. I know what my students know everyday they come into the Dojo. I look for weak points and, if you were under consideration for promotion, I'd probably have as many as ten black belters look at you doing different things trying to find your weaknesses or flaws. The good things were obvious, what we were looking for was what you needed real work on.

Dr. A: Grandmaster Shimabuku just presented you with your certificate before you returned to the United States.

ML: Yes.

Dr. A: Did he tell you not to use that rank when you got back?

ML: No, he did not.

Dr. A: We hear the story that he told people to wait ten years and then they would be that rank. He never did that with you?

ML: No. Naturally, he didn't tell me that because he wouldn't have promoted me to a seventh Dan in 1960.

Author's Note: We return here to talking about James Morbeto and Grandmaster Shimabuku's disappointment in this trip as opposed to his subsequent visit with Master Long.

Dr. A: That is the Pittsburgh story. It is not talked about but he did call it number ten and almost did not come back to the country because of it.

ML: This is true because I think that he felt that maybe everybody was going to treat him like that and he certainly did not want that. He wanted to stay home where at least he could eat.

Dr. A: He cut his trip short. It was suppose to be six months, it was cut down to three months or less. He did award some black belts at that time.

ML: When he came to visit my Dojo in 1966, after he went to Pittsburgh, other than greeting me, the first thing he did was start apologizing for the Mizu Gami they had painted on the wall. He was so embarrassed by the dragon, he said the dragon looked like a chicken. I believe I have the pictures of that pathetic looking Mizu Gami. When I went out to visit him at Steve Armstrong's Dojo and I was present and I knew the situation when those films were made. I was also present in Pittsburgh when those films were made.

To make a long story short, when Grandmaster Shimabuku came to visit me, in Knoxville, he wanted to go visit Don Nagle. He came to visit me first. To me this was a major event. I could not ask for a higher honor. My teacher was coming to visit me. He was met at the plane. He had no idea of what was going on when the flight attendant asked everyone else to remain on the plane because they had a dignitary. They rolled out the red carpet and the mayor presented him with a key to the city. We had a fifty–car police escorted motorcade from the airport to my Dojo where we had it all set up for a reception in his honor. He just could not imagine this was for him. Steve Armstrong had the audacity to write me a letter and tell me that he thought that was too big for Grandmaster Shimabuku. I asked Steve, "Who in the hell appointed you to be the chief of protocol in this system?" What Steve was also feeling and I wouldn't tell this unless I had Harry Acklin, who will verify the whole thing because there was only three people who went to see Grandmaster Shimabuku out there because Steve Armstrong asked each of us to pay him $100.00 each to be there for a week. Bob Osmond from L.A. was there, also Harry Acklin from Cleveland, Ohio and myself from Tennessee. Nobody else would go because they did not have that kind of money. Steve Armstrong told Grandmaster Shimabuku that he would give him half of all the money that he took in. The fact is, he told Grandmaster Shimabuku that nobody paid.

Tomiko Chukini was the one telling me this because she was Master Shimabuku's interpreter while he was out there. She would always call and tell me what was going on or write me letters. When Grandmaster Shimabuku came to my Dojo I charged everyone that came into my Dojo, my students and everybody. I did not keep any of this money, that was for Grandmaster Shimabuku because he was at my Dojo for a week. I did not let him stay in a hotel, I wanted him at my home. Every morning when he got up, my wife would find out what he wanted for breakfast and whatever we wanted that is what we fixed. My Dojo opened up at noon in those days and stayed open until 9:00 PM. At noontime, he and I would go to lunch and he would eat a very light lunch. He wanted soup for lunch. In the evening we would usually go to this Chinese restaurant that he really liked. He could have all the Oriental food he wanted. He told me he did not want any rice, he said he ate rice ever since he was a little kid and he really did not like rice, but he loved noodles. It didn't matter if it was spaghetti, egg noodles, macaroni, if it was noodles, that was just the ultimate food. I took him to meet a man by the name of Nelson Nee, a Chinese Martial Artist who also owned this restaurant. He was the Dean of foreign students at the University of Tennessee. I took Grandmaster Shimabuku there every evening for dinner and I always let a different group go with us to have the meal because I wanted everybody to be exposed to him outside of the Dojo. After dinner I would take him home. He would go in and take his clothes off. My wife had to practically physically take his long johns off because she wanted to wash his clothes. Obviously, no one else had offered to wash his clothes for him. She wanted to wash his clothes and make sure his bath was ready and all of these things. I finally explained to him that in America the wife always took care of the man, washed his clothes, same as in the Orient. He very reluctantly let her have his clothes to wash. Obviously, he had been neglected somewhere else too and he really did not know how to react to this. Bless his heart, every night before he would go to bed he would tell these stories and I would interpret it to the family on what he was trying to get across to them. Every night we would sit there and drink a cup of whiskey. I bought him Tennessee Black Label, the best sipping whiskey. He would sit there and sip his whiskey and tell his stories. Each night before he went to bed, he would go around and say good night to each member of my family. My doctor examined Grandmaster Shimabuku one day because he was not feeling well. My doctor, who is also my best friend and one of my Shodans, said that he had the heart of a thirty–year–old man. He said he was amazed at how well developed Grandmaster Shimabuku was.

Dr. A: What did he eventually die from?

ML: Stroke.

The Lost Kata and the Weapons of Isshin Ryu

Dr. A: Some Isshin Ryu people came by the radio station and we let them sit in on a show. After the show they were talking about how they are being taught pressure points and reflex techniques. Everything they were telling me a doctor learns in their first year of medical school. It is called kinesiology and body mechanics. These are well known in the medical world. The average doctor learns that and dismisses it. They do not realize this knowledge that they are so excited about and they think it is some hidden mystery is basic Chiropractic technique and knowledge. They are trying to study it off of scrolls that some ancient Master wrote down when the local medical school has text books, tapes, research files on the subject. They go to a seminar and this teacher will come out who has little knowledge and passes this on as some great part of the Martial Arts.

Author's Note: Beyond World War II in Japan the art of "Bone Setting" or what we would call Chiropractic in the West became a popular form of healing and was in great demand. Because of this, even those who had only rudimentary skills became viewed as masters. This lead to the licensure of Bone Setters in an attempt to keep those who were fraudulent from practicing. In order to attain a license one had to have a teaching certificate in Karate, Judo or Jujutsu. Today, Japan is the home of one of the largest Chiropractic colleges and the Chiropractic healing profession as such is more popular than ever.

Martial Arts and natural healing practices have gone hand in hand (pardon the pun) since the beginning of each of their recorded histories. Understanding the human form, biomechanics, anatomy and physiology and neurology are quintessential Chiropractic subjects of study, as they are for Martial Arts. The study of Arts such as Karate, Judo or Jujutsu are ideal ways for those studying Chiropractic to understand applied biomechanics and physiology. Combining the study of these particular forms of Budo with the unique and unparalleled healing profession of Chiropractic will lead one to an unprecedented understanding and depth of comprehension beyond that which could be reached by solo study of either Art. Chiropractic Specific was formally discovered in 1895 by D.D. Palmer and was developed into the world wide healing Art that it is today by B.J. Palmer, his son. B.J. Palmer travelled the world and wrote 24 books (the Green Books) on the Art, science and philosophy of Chiropractic. In addition, he travelled a great deal in the Orient and studied the Eastern healing Arts. In one of his books he writes of the "Torque Recoil Adjusting Table" which is based upon Jujutsu principles. This indicates that he had knowledge of at least the Art of Jujutsu and that he may have been the first American to study Martial Arts.

ML: I have taught pressure points and nerve centers all of my time in Karate. To me, it is not a big deal. This is something that goes hand in hand with the normal training. But, as far as me ever holding a clinic or a seminar, I see no reason to because fighting techniques and hold breaking techniques is where I emphasize nerve centers and pressure points. The fact is, if that is all you know, you will always go down in defeat because you have to put your hands on someone to find the pressure point. If someone grabbed my arm, he is not going to have time to feel around because I am going to deck him. Therefore, the information he passes, what little there is, is completely useless. I have seen a letter that someone has been going to some Isshin Ryu Dojo teaching them the lost Isshin Ryu Kata. How in the world does this fool think he has a lost Isshin Ryu Kata? Grandmaster Shimabuku was Isshin Ryu. He did not have a Kata that he did not teach. Only a fool would believe something like that. This is the blind leading the blind.

Dr. A: Is this Gojushiho Kata?

ML: Yes, but that was not an Isshin Ryu Kata.

Dr. A: Uechi Ryu now has a lost Uechi Ryu Kata. These Kata are well known all across the world today but they were never part of these systems. When Grandmaster Shimabuku died, the system of Isshin Ryu was set.

ML: Yes.

Dr. A: Isshin R}u, for the record, consists of eight empty hand Kata.

ML: Yes. Seisan, Seiuchin, Wansu, Naihanchi, Sanchin, Chinto, Kushanku and Sunsu.

Dr. A: There is no hidden, lost or secret Kata?

ML: No. For the record, there is no lost Kata. This is what Grandmaster Shimabuku considered to be the complete system of Isshin Ryu Karate.

I have heard a lot of different comments about the weapons that he trained with. He trained Bo, Sai and Tonfa. There were no Nunchaku or Kama. He got his training in the weapons from a weapons instructor. Grandmaster Shimabuku was probably the first person to incorporate the Bo, Sai and Tonfa into a system of Karate.

Dr. A: He trained weapons with Shinken Taira and Moden Yabiku?

ML: Yes. Grandmaster Shimabuku felt this was a part of history and tradition and it should be kept alive. He wanted an Isshin Ryu Black Belter to know these things and how they came about. As a Karate Ka, you went to a weapons instructor. When he went to a Bo instructor, the only thing that this guy did was teach the Bo. The Sai instructor, he taught the Sai. The Tonfa instructor, he taught the Tonfa. Therefore, there was even a specialty back in those days.

Dr. A: Kobudo is even more of a specialty today. They are trying to restore it.

ML: They make a show out of it. I go to a tournament and it makes me sick in my stomach. They do not know the weapon. They do not know what the weapon was designed for and they do not know how to use it. They whirl a weapon around, take a bow and the crowd goes wild. Here is a whole group of fools in the stand applauding a bigger fool. There is no Martial Arts involved, it is showmanship.

Dr. A: Yet, it is still growing that way.

ML: Sure it is.

Dr. A: They do not have a basis and foundation for the weapons. They are not using authentic weapons. They are using imitations. Yet there are fifth, sixth, seventh, eighth and ninth Dan standing around letting it go on that way, instead of judging that is based upon traditional standards.

ML: Yes.

Dr. A: Why don't they do something about it?

ML: They have not accepted any responsibility. They do not want to make an issue, yet that is what their belt rank calls for. If there is an issue involved, then you be involved. I cannot stand by and be a judge and give somebody a seven when they deserve a two. There was a tournament in New York called a Tribute to a Master. That was to raise money for Master Shimabuku's headstone at his grave site on Okinawa. I told the judges of the black belt Kata, if it is not the way Grandmaster Shimabuku did the Kata, you judge downward. Showmanship has no place in the Isshin Ryu system. We will not tolerate showmanship. Kata is judged on its merit.

Dr. A: You do not use the weapons for ranking in Isshin Ryu, yet today we are seeing people taking modified weapons Kata and they are using them for ranking in Isshin Ryu. What is the benefit for them? Why are they not recognizing that Kobudo is a separate Art, teaching it on the side and sharing that part of the Art to pass it on?

ML: I do not understand that myself because I never used it as part of the ranking and I have told all of my black belts that this is not Karate, this is a Kobudo system that has an ancient history. I have never used that as part of a promotion system. In fact, I started training only black belts but this was something that they did not get in a regular class, I had special classes for it. I did not teach that as a regular requirement. I only taught it to the people that wanted to learn.

Dr. A: I have trained in weapons for twenty–five years under some very prominent people. I would never consider that Karate at all. My students start with weapons when they are black belts. I do not think people can commit enough time today to their training to divide it between the weapons. Until they show that they are going to be around for years and they have a good base of Karate, until they get those eight Kata down so that they can perform those forward, backward, in and out and know some basic bunkai, I do not see the point in giving them more things that are going to distract them because they become like toys then.

ML: This is true. My attitude now is, do not teach anyone any weaponry until after they get to be a Sensei themselves. Then only for history and tradition. Do not forget the definition of Karate; Kara: Empty, Te: Hand. Once you put something in your hand, a weapon, then it is no longer Karate.

The Techniques of Isshin Ryu

Dr. A: Did [Grandmaster Shimabuku] film the charts the way you teach the charts today?
ML: He didn't film the charts at all.

ML: During the filming Grandmaster Shimabuku was sick. He tried to convey this to Steve Armstrong. I told Steve a couple of times, let's do this filming another time because Grandmaster Shimabuku is sick. Steve said, "Well, I've got this man with a camera and the film and everything." Grandmaster Shimabuku saw immediately and his attitude was all right, get your film ready. You want to see a Kata? Here is a Kata. He did it as quickly as he could, got through it and went back home to go to bed.

Dr. A: It ended up that is what you have today.

ML: Absolutely. I have told everybody, even when Grandmaster Shimabuku was not at his best, he was better than everybody else.

Dr. A: So, he did not film the charts. Was there any reason why he did not film the charts? He just assumed that everybody knew the charts.

ML: I'm sure he did.

Dr. A: There is even controversy about the charts. Not that much but enough. It would have been nice to have him doing the charts. He did not do Bo Sai Kumite on those films, he did some Bo and Sai bunkai.

ML: No Bo Sai Kumite.

Dr. A: Originally his Bo Sai Kumite was different from what we have today.

ML: Not from what I teach, it is not. Grandmaster Tatsuo Shimabuku taught my black belters the Bo Sai Kumite himself while he was there in 1966. I had taught them, but he did not know I had trained them. He took them off into a side room that I had and he taught them himself just to make sure they had it right.

Dr. A: When Grandmaster Shimabuku taught the charts, just for the historical records, you would start at the Dojo and he would teach you some loosening up exercises?

ML: No. He would take you through the charts and he would expect you to remember them in just a few days' time. You would come in and automatically know that the first part of your workout would be to go through the charts. Then you get whatever Kata that you were due to get at that time.

Dr. A: Did he start everyone with the same Kata?

ML: Oh yes. He started everyone with Seisan Kata.

Dr. A: He did not jump around like some of the Masters did? In something like Uechi Ryu, they would start everyone with Sanchin Kata, but then some others would be given one other Kata only.

ML: The only difference between the sequence that Grandmaster Shimabuku taught and the sequence that I taught, he had Sanchin Kata last. That would come after Sunsu Kata. I teach the Sanchin Kata after Naihanchin. Seisan, Seiuchin, Naihanchin, Sanchin, Wansu, Chinto, Kushanku, Sunsu. My opinion is the people need to have this knowledge, this information so that they can start to practice. That gets your movements, your teaching and your mind coordinating.

Dr. A: He expected you to pick up the charts in the first couple weeks, at least. Where would he take you from there? Would he work with you with a single technique and then into multiple repetitions across the floor for an hour?

ML: No. He would work with you individually on these techniques. He did not want you to have an opponent when you were working on these techniques.

Dr. A: Did he have mirrors to work with?

ML: No, we worked outside. You would work on a technique and if you were not doing it exactly right, he would come back and show you why you needed to do it exactly right. For example, you step out and cross the arms over on the block, the X block, he would explain to you that it is not something that you would just run through. He would explain the importance of every technique. "This block is good," he would say, "but this block is better." It was just amazing and I was awed by the continuity of the defense into an offense.

Dr. A: At that point, did he incorporate Makiwara training for his students?

ML: As soon as you could handle it. The Makiwara training he had was in different levels. He had a platform with a Makiwara board that tapered up, then it split up. It made a real noise when you hit it. Originally he put a rice mat on there for you to hit. When you punch that rice mat, it had to go out and all the way back and make the second impact. He was so specific, that you had to make two impacts. One impact and stay there and let it come back and hit you, I guess that was to make sure that you had the proper form and the proper tension. I never did fully understand that part.

Dr. A: Probably to create double the impact, focus, then the dynamic tension of strength and penetration. The way the Makiwara are now, we have two boards, because you hit one against the other, it goes out and comes back and the force comes back into your body and you absorb that force through. If the stance is not correct, you hold the force in your body. If the Seisan stance is correct, the force actually transfers back to the floor and you do not absorb it. It is like grounding your body out, checking your stance at the same time.

ML: Grandmaster Tatsuo Shimabuku explained the part about your body absorbing the shock, it comes through the fist, through the arms, through the shoulders and down the body. Another thing that he did, after you got accustomed to this type of punching on the Makiwara board, the lower half of the Makiwara board was for your kicks. He did not want you to leave your foot out, he wanted you to make an impact and then swing right back. Then you got to the point where he took the rice mat off. Boom, it came back and hit you. Grandmaster Shimabuku said when you were learning fighting techniques, you learn there is no such thing as pain if you're fighting. If you get a broken bone, it's better than being dead.

Dr. A: Everyone did Makiwara?

ML: Yes. After we moved to Agina, he had concrete for us to work out on. He had a cinder block wall put up so people would not be bothered with spectators. He had monkey pod or iron wood, as he referred to it. 4 x 4's sunk down and concrete was poured in around it. He used a very thin rice mat, there is no give to it whatsoever. He said this way you toughening your arms, your shoulders, your body.

Dr. A: He practiced that often?

ML: Oh yes. The only difference that he would do about half the time was a punch. He did not stand in the same position that you and I stand in, he would always make this little move in, all the time.

Dr. A: Shuffle step in a little bit.

ML: Shuffle step, absolutely.

Author's Note: Makiwara, the Okinawan striking post, is a very important training tool for all traditional Karate Ka. Appropriately named "The Board of Wisdom" in the first book written about Makiwara in English, "Honing of the Warrior Spirit," the Makiwara is used to develope the great Kime (focus) of a Master. This is the only way to develop the Ikken Hissattsu (one blow, one kill) to any degree.

It is not uncommon today for a person to call themselves a Karate Master without ever having hit a Makiwara board. This is simply a farce. All of the greatest Karate Masters in history taught that, to become great, one must use Makiwara training daily. Lack of this element of training is just one of the reasons that Karate "Masters" of today lack the focus and effectiveness of the ancient Masters. Leaving out this training or attempting to substitute it with other forms of training such as heavy bag work will only lead to a practitioner of lesser quality and skill. Without the Makiwara board the training is not truly Okinawan Martial Arts.

Keeping Records and Standards

Dr. A: I hear quite often, "The trends have changed, society has changed, you have to keep up with that." However, we do not have to keep up with anything. We need to keep our standards up and not cave in to these trends. Our job is to create Martial Artists not to pay attention to social changes.

ML: People concerned about social trends do not grasp the essence of Karate.

Dr. A: There are less practitioners on Okinawa doing Isshin Ryu today?

ML: Why should they do Isshin Ryu when there really is not anybody there to teach them?

Dr. A: Where do you think all the seniors that were there before Grandmaster Shimabuku passed away, all the Okinawan Nationals, where did all his senior Okinawan students go?

ML: They left.

Dr. A: Why didn't they go with Angi Uezu?

ML: They were all senior to Angi Uezu.

Dr. A: Did you know of anything that Grandmaster Tatsuo Shimabuku put in writing? Did he have a ledger of all his students?

ML: Grandmaster Shimabuku, as far as I know, never put anything in writing. He did have a log book, but I do not know when he started this. I do not know how accurate it was, or how well kept. Mr. Advincula told me at one time, that he had all these records, but he has never been able to produce them. I would have to look at the handwriting. I would recognize Master Shimabuku's handwriting. At one time, Kichiro was signing his father's name to rank certificates. I told him, "You are not your father. I do not want your name in place of your father's name on my student's certificates."

Dr. A: Did you keep a log or a record at one time of all your black belts?

ML: I sure did.

Dr. A: Up until what year?

ML: Up until last year.

Dr. A: You have records for people that state that they were black belts under you.

ML: I sure do.

Dr. A: It does not seem like you can forget who your black belts are over the years.

ML: You do not forget. I have had people say, "You don't remember me." I will say, "Why should I remember you?" I get offended when these people come up an do not address me properly. I know immediately they have never trained with me or they would know the proper way to address me. I do not answer to "you" or "hey, you" or "hey, buddy," or anything like that. That is not language that is applicable to me. Anyone that comes up to you and says, "I know you probably don't remember me," then you have no reason to remember him, he is not a significant individual.

Dr. A: Grandmaster seems to be a new title being used frequently.

ML: I do not feel comfortable with that title because that was my Sensei's title. To me that would be setting myself up on the same level with my teacher. No one ever achieves the same level as their teacher. You can have the same rank, but it does not mean you are at the same level because he was before you and obviously he is senior.

Dr. A: The tradition is always to hold your Sensei at a higher level.

ML: Absolutely.

Author's Note: In society today, there is a pronounce lack of etiquette. This has spilled over into the world of Martial Arts, which has been one of the bastions of good manners and behavior. Proper etiquette never goes out of style, even when the rest of society has given up on its use. It is always correct to refer to a Doctor as such, Dr. So–and–So, in their place of work as well as in social contact. The same is true of the Martial Artists who have attained titles. It is assumed that they will be referred to by their proper titles during class or in the training center, however, they should expect the same respect and recognition out of class as well. "The Dojo is where the Sensei is" should be remembered just as it is taught that once one becomes a black belt and a Sensei then he is a black belt and a Sensei 24 hours a day, not just when wearing the belt. Professors, Pastors and Priests all expect this type of recognition and respect, so should Martial Artists demand the same for their accomplishments and efforts.

Dr. A: Without Grandmaster Tatsuo Shimabuku, you would not be in Isshin Ryu, there would be no Isshin Ryu. In the United States had there been no Harold Long or Don Nagle, there would be no Isshin Ryu. The people that came after were secondary. You laid the foundation. The pioneers in this country like Dr. Peter Urban, Sensei George Mattson and yourself, have the weight of the world resting on your shoulders. The senior Dan do not realize the weight of the Isshin Ryu Martial Arts world is going to come down on our shoulders soon.

ML: This is true.

Dr. A: They will be responsible for what is going to go on with it. They have to know the right thing to do with this. The magnitude of that is awesome and they do not even seem to be acknowledging that.

ML: The irony of the situation is this. There are so many people that I have always referred to as the "do nothing crowd." Those people will celebrate my death. You think that people say things that are harsh behind my back now, they will go public with it then.

Dr. A: People have stopped trying to say anything about you around me. They are very careful because I have called them out on it recently. They know better because they have no legitimate grounds. They were not in Chun Village. I'm concerned about the individuals that state they are your friend, but their actions do not show it except when they are right in front of you. Angi Uezu, who has his own organization, where many of his students may be taking an opposing position to you, yet Master Uezu is not. When we all met again at Metro Airport during your last trip here, it was "Gentleman Harold Long," hugging, renewing an old friendship and he recognized you as his senior. It was very obvious that he did not consider himself senior to you. Showing you how well he was doing, like a child would show their father almost, proud to show you that even though he had a stroke, that he could still function. If we did not have a picture of that you know it would not exist historically.

ML: That is correct.

Dr. A: People would deny that occurred, but you two got along just fine. People within his group might be critical of our group, which is ridiculous politics, there is no foundation for it.

ML: If Kichiro Shimabuku and I got together right now I assure you that he would not act as a senior Dan. I would sit down and be courteous to him. He has made a contribution to Karate. It does not make any difference whether I like him personally or not. That has nothing to do with professionalism. He is the son of my Sensei, although not the favorite son. Grandmaster Shimabuku used to say, "Kichiro does not understand Karate." Ciso, the youngest son, who very few people ever heard about, he was truly his father's son because he was a very intelligent young man. He was the one at the Dojo, helping his father. He was the one that should have been selected to carry on his father's tradition. That would have probably solved fifty percent of the problems that are in the Isshin Ryu System today.

Dr. A: Do you think in the future, with the next generation of seniors on the way up, we will be able to sit down in a group together and be like the Isshin Ryu Council was suppose to be. Agree to disagree, but show a unity.

ML: I would like to see it occur in the future. People are going to have to be more visible. Move outside of their own little group.

Dr. A: I think that we are going to see some organizations go by the wayside. They will have token representation, and unless they have legitimate credentials and make a contribution to the Arts, they will have no authority. Even if you have the ability but, you do not have the credentials that handicaps you terribly. It shows that something has not gone correctly in the process.

ML: I have two focal points, one was on my teacher and the other one was on my students.

Dr. A: You left yourself out.

ML: I did not focus on myself because, the way I look at it, I was doing what I was obligated to do and what I had been charged to do. I have told my students time and time again, "Do not ever forget your heritage." If it had not been for my teacher, Grandmaster Shimabuku, none of us would have ever existed in Isshin Ryu. I have spent my life teaching exactly the way my teacher charged me to do. My Sensei was the focal point, I was just a means of disseminating the information to different people.

Dr. A: Part of our ranking is having the knowledge, having the ability to conduct the classes, set up a curriculum, to supervise groups of black belts, to help run the organization, take care of a Dojo. If something were to happen to me, my senior students know what they are suppose to do to continue on with this organization. These are not just Karate Ka, they are high–powered future Sensei, there is no doubt. They know their role. They know their destiny is to do something with this, not just to play with it. They have all dedicated their lives, pretty much, to this. They take it as seriously as I do on a day–to–day basis. It shows. They carry large respect in our organization by Sandan level. They have a depth of knowledge and a good solid base of materials. It has taken some of the workload off of me with classes and testing and different things of that type.

ML: I gain strength from the young enthusiastic Karate Ka. My enthusiasm comes into being and it is a contagious thing. I thrive on it and I want to meet everyone and I know that I cannot do it any other way.

Dr. A: We put the push on to support you at the Hall of Fame Tournament. You came up here and supported us. I told our black belts as long you are down there and you need the support, we will turn out down there.

ML: This year you will not see me selling equipment, you will see me standing at the front door to make sure everyone is greeted properly and welcomed properly at the Isshin Ryu Hall of Fame.

Dr. A: Will you have a Gi on?

ML: Sure, I will.

Dr. A: My students were worried because they did not see you with a Gi on, you were selling equipment. They like to see you in a Gi and Obi (belt).

Author's Note: Since Master Long's retirement from running the Isshin Ryu Hall of Fame Tournament and Awards Banquet he has endeavored to stay out of the way of those who currently run the event. Due to popular request Master Long has agreed to return to the Hall of Fame wearing formal Isshin Ryu attire (a Gi and Obi) this coming year.

On the Airwaves

Editors Note: The Dr. Aiello Show, "Warrior Talk" has been fortunate enough to have had Master Long as a guest many times. He has supported the show and spread the word far and wide in an effort to encourage other Martial Artists to become involved in this great innovation in the Martial Arts. "Warrior Talk" has been nationally syndicated since early 1997 and can be heard across the United States and Canada on talk radio stations via satellite.

ML: You see as time goes on and your radio show grows into a national syndicated show, you're going to get into so many markets all over the North American continent and you are going to be in the same position in the Martial Arts as it is right now. People can not say too much about you because with one fiery comment on your show, you can destroy anybody you want to destroy.

Dr. A: Do you think so?

ML: You wouldn't, but you could if the occasion called for it.

Dr. A: If they get too pushy I can get pretty tough, but I try not to hurt anyone on the air.

ML: Absolutely.

Dr. A: I try to be fair, but at the same time I am not going to let something get out of hand.

ML: See, you're not defensive either. You know what you are doing is right. You do not have to apologize to anybody, you do not have to defend your show because the people that you have on your show and what you are presenting to the public, this is what the public needs to know. As long as the public knows this and recognizes it, all these other people with their little groups over here, then you have effectively killed the information or the propaganda that they put out.

Dr. A: We have a lot of cross reference points, that helps. We just bring more people on to verify history, tradition, background, facts and it is entertainment for people at the same time. Imagine just driving down the road, hearing this. I cannot fathom hearing it because I could hardly fathom even just having a book to read on this subject at one time. Now I have a couple hundred books on this and we are talking with Masters of all styles. We are constantly on the air and it stuns me how sometimes we talk to people and their lack of knowledge about what they do. Or bizarre, incorrect knowledge. Information that if you just use some common sense you would know it is not even worth bothering your mind with.

ML: This is true.

Dr. A: It is staggering in some ways.

ML: These people that have the high rank that do not deserve them, or are not doing anything. You are effectively killing them by having them on the show because they come across as being mad. "I have this rank, but I really don't have the knowledge that goes with it." See, you can be the best doctor, the best surgeon in the world, outside of China that is, but if no one knows about you then all this knowledge and expertise is worthless. You have to let people know about it. Look at the efforts of the Better Business Bureau. This is an organization whose purpose is to let you know whether the store or this company is legitimate or not, what their background is and how many complaints they have had about it. You are giving the Martial Arts the same safe guard that the Better Business Bureau is giving all the cities throughout the country.

Dr. A: We have collected a national web, we still need to build in some of it, a blanket of Martial Artist all over the country who are legitimate, respectable people who come on and speak intelligently about their Arts. We hope to escalate all the Arts. We want to get more students into all of the Dojo by creating an interest in Martial Arts in the eyes of the lay public.

Author's Note: On the show, "Warrior Talk" we hope that the lay people in the audience will be able to make educated, intelligent decisions about where to train and who to train under. One of our main goals is to afford our audience with the wisdom of the Masters so that they can differentiate the good from the bad in the Martial Arts.

Editor's Note: Many people think that they can learn about Karate or Martial Arts the way they buy clothes or test drive a car. "I'll try it awhile and if I don't like it I'll send it back." Traditional Martial Arts, whatever the style may be, do not operate on that basis. This is why education and correct information are so critical for the potential student. Knowing what to look for in a Sensei or in a training center is essential. Using proper protocol is a must if one wishes to become involved with a Master of the Martial Arts for all Masters demand that even those who are inquiring use the correct channels. Master Long speaks about his policy, which mirrors that of Masters of the past.

ML: My policy about letting other Isshin Ryu students come to my Dojo, I would not accept a student from another Isshin Ryu Dojo, locally, unless their Sensei called me and told me that it was all right and that they had left with their blessing. As far as letting a student come from another Dojo and sign up, my answer was no.

Dr. A: Do you think the other Dojo did the same thing?

ML: Probably not.

Dr. A: That was more common in the past than it is today where people do not know each other that well. They do not hold the respect within the same styles, or different styles. There has been a real, general lack of recognition for anyone outside of their system, or anyone that they do not know.

ML: This is true.

Dr. A: In Aikido, it is splintered, but they all call what they do Aikido. They all say it's Tomiki Aikido, or Nakamura Aikido meaning their last name and their Aikido system, that they trained under Ueshiba Sensei. They all recognize that it is Aikido and they all build the Art. They all have their own slant on the Art, so therefore they keep a public image of conformity, even though they cannot stand each other. Then there are the factions; some focus more on the physical part, some on his Kotodama chanting, some more on the Omoto Kyo religion, some on Gozo Shioda, a very hard Jujutsu like Aikido and others where you almost don't touch each other. There is even Aikido where they compete at sports tournaments, which is totally against what Ueshiba Sensei stood for. Yet they are all under the banner Aikido. Aikido is promoted, in general, very well because they know they need people coming into Aikido if they are going to survive. Karate, if they are doing Shito Ryu or Shoto Kan or Shorin Ryu or whatever, they feel it is almost like not doing the same thing. There are no brothers or sisters or cousins or uncles within what they are doing in some parts of the country, unlike Aikido, Judo, Tae Kwon Do, etc.

Author's Note: *Kotodama is a form of chanting sounds used by Morehi Ueshiba founder of Aikido. It is also used in other systems of Jujutsu. Kotodama means "true word" in the Buddhist religion. It was from this theory and practice of sound and vibration that the Kiai (spirit uniting yell) evolved.*

ML: You have to prepare yourself and research knowledge of everyone that is going to be on your show. You have to be able to discuss these things with them and talk about things. You can not do that if you do not have the proper information to study without even being there.

Dr. A: We get background information on everybody. If they do not have it or if we do not know who they are already, that they are historically somebody, they send us a biography. A book, a tape or something that we can verify who they are and what they do. We have had some guests on without solid verification, it really did not present well. There are no guarantees someone will be good even if they are a legitimate individual. They may not talk well, or they may not have the personality, but if they are credible, the information they dispense is accurate and informative.

ML: This is true.

Dr. A: Sometimes it is hard because sometimes we slip a little bit...

ML: Right.

Dr. A: You really opened the eyes of a lot of people this weekend. Just your presence, talking with them, being at the test, coming by the Dojo.

ML: This is a joy to me. I thrive on things like this. You can not isolate yourself from people.

Dr. A: What really disturbs me is that you are sitting here available to people, after 43 years of grooming people up, you know how hard it is to teach people. It is heartbreaking, you put a lot of effort and time and energy into it and then they just quit. They just bomb out for the silliest reasons, "I cracked my toe, I'm done."

ML: I think the best reason that I can think of is that they have told so many different things and have put themselves in so many different positions that they do not want the truth to be known. They do not want me coming in and talking to their students, or training their students.

Dr. A: At what point are we going to draw the line? When are the head Dan no longer going to accept this stuff being done in their presence? Our organization attends the Hall of Fame Tournament once a year. We participate in historical support of you because you founded that tournament. Also to support J.C. Burris and Toby Cooling because they need support, trying to accomplish what they have politically and with their tournament. Yet, the higher ranks standing around watching and ten feet away is somebody doing something totally obnoxious and it is ignored. When is this going to stop? When are the people that have accepted a seventh, eighth or ninth Dan, going to turn and say, "What are you doing? Why are you doing it? Who is your teacher?" Then talk to the teacher about what their student is doing. When is this going to happen?

ML: When I quit doing it, that is when it ceased to exist. I used to call instructors in and I would ask them, "What in the world are you teaching? I saw your students out there. That is not Isshin Ryu Karate. What the hell is it that you are teaching them? What do you know? What did you forget? If you are trying to think that you are greater than Grandmaster Shimabuku, then I suggest, right now, that you take that belt off, that Gi off and get out. If you ever bring students, that appear before me again at that level, I will personally run all of you off." I did not set out to win a popularity contest. I have heard people talk about "Tournament Kata." There is no such thing as a "Tournament Kata." You either do the Kata properly or do not do it at all. Traditional Kata is the only Kata that exists. Tournaments are something that we took up in the western world. They made money, brought people together and it served a purpose. Now, it does not serve a good purpose.

Dr. A: What has to happen in the future? What will it take to correct it?

ML: We seem to do the sensational things. The television programs and the movies with the Martial Arts, these are a fantasy thing. It is sensationalism. The audience really likes to see but those things do not exist. Some people try to take this fantasy to the Dojo. You cannot do this in a legitimate Dojo.

Dr. A: It seems to me there has to be a rising up within Isshin Ryu of the true leaders. They need to bond together through friendship, support and set standards that are higher for other people to see and follow.

ML: There is no need to have standards, if you are not going to have an enforcement of them. I would suggest to do away with tournaments. Train people at the Dojo the way they should be trained. Have regional clinics and seminars by senior Dan, who follow the true, traditional Isshin Ryu. To have a strict standard for promotion. To come right back to the basics which Grandmaster Shimabuku felt were necessary to have this system and for it to be able to grow and prosper.

Dr. A: How many teachers do you have that are willing to do what you just said?

ML: Probably no more than four.

Author's Note: The world of Martial Arts is torn down the middle on the subject of tournaments. The most stringent of the orthodox traditionalist Martial Arts groups disdain competitions. Those who practice traditional Martial Art Ryu Ha feel tournaments lack the realism and create a carnival like atmosphere which is not conducive to the true spirit of Budo.

Tournaments have both elements of good and bad for the Martial Arts. Within the last seven or eight years there has been a resurgence of the traditional tournament and the international Martial sport community is struggling for control. The lines of demarcation are even more blurred by things like the Olympics, an arena that attracts even some hard core anti–tournament. There is a great deal of resentment towards the redefining of Budo into sport–Budo. The senior Dan of traditional systems feel that this is another attempt at commercialization and waters down the Art further.

The Ideal Dojo

Dr. A: How does the Shito Kan Dojo fit in within that format?

ML: You have all the fine points. You fit in the scheme of things because you are teaching traditional Karate. You are teaching good, strong, solid Karate. You have the enthusiasm in your Dojo. You have what I consider to be an ideal Dojo. This is a Martial Arts training hall and I get so enthusiastic when I see a Dojo like this and see the training and everyone is sweating. A Dojo is a place of learning.

Dr. A: At one time we had Dojo in all parts of the country. I had representatives in California, Wisconsin, New Jersey, Florida, Canada and Mexico. When I went through school to get my Doctorate in Chiropractic and my Ph.D., I worked with all the black belts, but they had to guide the organization. They got way off track. I came back and found the same things in my own organization. Phony weapons for showmanship, Kata had gone by the wayside, fighting had become number one. The fighting had declined, it was not street effective, it was tournament fighting. When you and I met I set this new organization up, I reorganized and cleaned house. I unlicensed all of those people and told them to go their own way. To change the name of what they were doing, teach whatever they want but they were not going to teach Shito Kan and they were not going to be part of the Isshin Ryu Organization that I was with.

ML: Our relationship is not only professional but it is a personal relationship too. You finally found someone that believes in the traditional way of doing things. You do not have a commercial Dojo. Commercial Dojo go out and put on a big show at a tournament and they are judged by how many students they take and how many trophies they win. That is not a part of Karate at all. That is showmanship that feeds egos. I have never had that problem, because I have never had an ego. My attitude has been that I really do not care what people think of me, as long as I am fulfilling my obligation to my Sensei.

Dr. A: Should senior Dan have their own Dojo?

ML: If they do not have Dojo, they should not have the rank because they are not fulfilling their obligation. Just their existence is certainly not a blessing to anyone.

Dr. A: To be a Sensei you have to train regularity, you have to stay competent. It is a continuing process.

ML: The day that you stop training you are no longer a Sensei. The Gi and the belt should come off and stay off.

Dr. A: The organization that we have put together now, has been proving now that you can teach traditional Karate, that you can keep it basic and pure. You can have tough, high standards for rank. You can require educational material, physical material and you require payment from each student. Everybody starts at the bottom and works. You do not have to go out to tournaments every weekend and get trophies. You do not have to sell belt ranks. You can be successful at the same time. Our organization grows, we add a new Dojo every year, we had our fourth Dojo in the Detroit area open this year.

ML: You've proven, beyond a doubt, that your method is correct. Your method is the traditional method, as it was done on Okinawa. There was not any sensationalism on Okinawa. There were not any tournaments, there were Shiai for competition and there were no trophies, no awards, you did not win any titles. You went to demonstrate your skills to all the other Dojo that were involved there.

Dr. A: At a festival.

ML: Yes. What you were doing was saying, "This is the way my Sensei trained me. He wants me to be a skillful person. This is the level of skill that I have."

Dr. A: It comes down to financial motivation. They are trying to make a living, they feel they cannot by using the old fashioned methods.

ML: That is part of it, the other part is that these Sensei are not really accepting the responsibility they have been charged with. Let's do away with this competition and trophies. Do it the way it was done in the Orient. There is no winner or loser. They have already won because they have gone out and displayed their degree of skill for everyone to see. Everybody should get the same recognition.

Dr. A: How do we put it back on track?

ML: The first step is teaching the traditional Martial Arts. Have a demonstration of skills.

Dr. A: Is this going to start at the Hall of Fame this year?

ML: I would like to just do away with the Hall of Fame Tournament and just have the Hall of Fame Banquet. Have clinics and seminars. Let's do some teaching while we have all these people here.

Dr. A: That is where we come back to, they need to train under somebody who guides them. I spend the time with you to make sure things are going correctly, the way Grandmaster Shimabuku did. The rewards come for doing it the right way.

ML: I have told all of my senior Dan, "the greatest reward is self–satisfaction. Knowing that you did things properly. Knowing that you are a part of building the Isshin Ryu system." To me, that is the greatest reward.

Dr. A: And watching your students grow up and transmit the same message.

ML: That is a reward, absolutely. That is the reason I nominated you for an award with the World Karate Union Hall of Fame. I nominated about five more people for awards because I felt that it is time that you are recognized for accomplishment. A group of Karate Ka who want to recognize people that have accomplished things. People we can point to with pride. This is their recognition. I do not nominate people for these awards, then I am not doing what I should do. The truth itself is, how do you stack up with all the other Karate Ka that I have worked with? People of all systems of Karate are considered for these awards. I have nominated you for it because I have confidence in you and the level that you have achieved. The recognition is rightfully yours.

Dr. A: Thank you very much for the nomination. That is very, very nice and I will follow through with that. My number one reward is the knowledge that I get from you. I want to make sure that I have all the knowledge, all the information and that I have it straight, so I know that I am doing it the right way for myself and my students. I want to know, in my heart, that my message is correct, true and clear, for my own satisfaction. I can sleep at night knowing that I am doing it the correct way, the way it was intended to be passed on from Grandmaster Shimabuku to you to me. That is all I care about, regardless of what other people think of me, I cannot worry to much about that. I just have to make sure that I'm doing the best job I can do.

ML: You have the same thirst for knowledge that I had when I trained under Grandmaster Shimabuku. I did not miss anything. I wanted to be in on everything that he did and I wanted to make sure that I had the knowledge because you cannot train without a full understanding of what you are doing. Master Shimabuku's relationship with me was strictly teacher, student. He felt so sure that I would teach the way I promised I would after I got back to the United States, he gave me a little bit more knowledge than most of the people there received.

Dr. A: Have you ever seen a group like ours before?

ML: No, I have not. I have had some close associations in the Dojo. I used to pride myself on the closeness we had in the Dojo. Mine has never reached the level that you have in your Dojo.

Dr. A: It is not just friendship, there is a professional relationship going on.

ML: There is no friendship in the Dojo, the friendship is outside the Dojo because you have to have the professionalism. Once you go in the Dojo and bow in that is another culture, another science, another world.

Dr. A: It is inevitable that the leaders of Isshin Ryu, whether it is this generation, or the next, there is going to be some type of umbrella cooperative agreement among some of the heads at least. It may be the World Head of Family Sokeship Council may force it.

ML: What I have thought about doing, time and time again, was going to Okinawa. Writing a letter to Angi Uezu, Kichiro and Ciso Shimabuku and expecting an answer in return. We are going to come to some type of agreement where all of us point to Grandmaster Tatsuo Shimabuku. We are all going to admit that in our own way we are continuing his work and we are all going to cooperate in the future. I would insist that we sit down and talk about this.

Dr. A: That needs to be done because they each have their own perspective on how things should be taught. Politics and egos just don't seem to allow it.

ML: Dr. Aiello, you and I should be the problem solvers. If I made a trip to Okinawa like that I would like you to make the trip with me.

Dr. A: Thank you very much. We may think of that in the future.

ML: I would not mind writing a letter myself and just explain to them that I would like to bring Dr. Aiello with me. I would like to come over and reach some type of a happy medium so that we can all serve the cause of Isshin Ryu Karate as Grandmaster Tatsuo Shimabuku wanted it done. Forget about position, forget about ourselves, because I would sacrifice myself in a minute to improve Isshin Ryu Karate.

Dr. A: If we went to Okinawa, I do not know how far our meeting would go, so many years have gone past.

ML: I would be very diplomatic. Grandmaster Tatsuo Shimabuku knew that unless he got Isshin Ryu off of the island of Okinawa, that it would never be known. Kichiro Shimabuku did not bring it off the island. Angi Uezu did not bring it off the island. Don Nagle and I brought it off the island. It is amazing to me how there can be that much jealousy involved and how everyone wants to be the captain of the ship. It is not important who is captain of the ship, it is where the ship is going and what purpose it is serving. I would be willing to sacrifice, to get things back on an even course. Get everyone working together and show some unity, some intelligence and direction. Kichiro could have been having all the glory he ever thought about having if he had tried to work with us and not undermine us. You cannot change facts. You can fabricate anything you want, but how can you be untruthful and dishonest and expect someone to respect you?

ML: The only way to get it is by bowing in and working.

Dr. A: People say to me all the time, "Dr. Aiello, how do you do all this? You run your clinic, you have the Dojo, oversee all the Dojo, you write books, you do a radio show and you have personal hobbies." People do not understand, number one, you have to have good support people around you. People that can back you up and run everything. Our senior Sensei handle a lot of that already. The other thing is, you have to learn to compartmentalize your mind. When you are dealing with a particular subject, you are totally into that one hundred percent. We call this present time consciousness.

ML: This is true. There is an old saying that I have heard for years and years, "If you want things done right, give it to a busy man." Busy people are successful people. If they are going to sit around with absolutely nothing to do, you do not want to give them anything to do. Obviously he does not have a lot of capabilities, or he would already be doing something.

Dr. A: People will say they are out of work, they cannot find work. Work is something you create, you may not be able to find a job, but there is always work. If you start working, a job will come along. There is always someway to become creative. This is especially true in the Martial Arts.

ML: I have never been unemployed a day in my life, even now that I have retired I am employed.

Dr. A: I will bet you are doing more work now than when you were working.

ML: I have more time to do it. I can be more selective now.

Dr. A: Your retirement, I think, has been one of the very best things, because it is enabling you to work on your own material. Beyond work for an association. To work on doing the Tatsuo Shimabuku–Harold Long work that you have laid the foundation for. Now your focus comes right on it, no commercialism, no politics. It is really wonderful to see it. There are so many people that retire and stop doing things.

ML: I do not have the capabilities of quitting or stopping. It is just not my makeup. I have to have things to do and I have always accepted responsibility. Therefore, I feel as if I am obligated to help those who actually want help and need help. You would be surprised at how many people that need help but do not admit it. They justify being wrong rather than to correct themselves and do it right.

Dr. A: One of the problems, with some of the intermediate ranked individuals between 5th and 7th Dan, like you are speaking of, is that over the years, they have veered off track in their own direction. If they had been with an organization with a credible, recognized 10th Dan they could seek a little guidance and advice. You can get so off track and into what you are doing and think that you are doing some great, creative, genius work. Sometimes it is too unrelated to the Art you are doing, you forget the students may not even have the basics. That is why aligning with an organization is important and associating with someone above you, if possible. As long as you have your senior there, it should be done that way. My great wish is that these people that I have come to know over the years, would just organize into a group and work within a group to make the changes that are necessary, rather than function on their own and be isolated.

Author's Note: These people need to do the right thing and put Isshin Ryu ahead of their egos. They need to place themselves under the auspices of either yourself, Don Nagle or Kichiro Shimabuku, all 10th Dan. All Isshin Ryu would benefit from this, but these people would have to recognize authority and seniority.

ML: They are misleading their students. What they are doing is not fair to them.

Dr. A: The students are unaware. They become more like gurus than Sensei. They are not functioning within the hierarchy of Karate, therefore they are not functioning as a Sensei.

ML: They are seeing themselves in a different light from what everyone else is seeing them. I think some of these people think they are going to be the savior of their system of Karate. Actually they are a detriment to it because they do not have any input. They do not work with anyone and they want to isolate their students. I think in this situation they are completely wrong. They get to the point where they will not workout. They consider a bow as people paying homage to them. They lose the concept of Budo.

Dr. A: There is a fine line between art, practical application, philosophy, science and mysticism. The day comes for all of us when we have to be the senior. That is a sad day when there is no one above you, no mentor. You have to stand up and take the lead. The fine line that I see is where they get so into their own work, they do not relate to outside sources. They want people to think they have a divine source of knowledge that others do not have, then they become mystics. They are not a Sensei at that point. A Sensei works with the techniques that their Sensei taught them. A Sensei works, studies and explores the methods so they can expand out the parameters, like with Bunkai and create their own Bunkai. A lot of the work that is being passed off as Karate is acupuncture work being recycled through Karate. They are getting cursory knowledge of acupuncture and then trying to pass this off as advanced Karate or Martial Arts knowledge, when in reality it is not. A lot of acupuncture is not scientifically based. If they are basing their materials on this type of foundation it is going to be discredited at some point in time. That is going to be unfortunate because they are spending a lot of time working on it.

ML: What concerns me more than anything else is they are making a tremendous living from these clinics and seminars in different areas of the country. Many people show up, spend their money to get knowledge that is not going to help their self defense ability one iota.

The Awesome Responsibility of Hanshi

Editor's Note: Dr. Aiello and Master Long speak of the eventful weekend in Detroit, Michigan in March of 1997 when Master Long surprisingly presented Dr. Aiello with a Hanshi Certificate. This is the first Hanshi certification granted by Master Harold Long and one of very few Hanshi, Master Instructor certificates given by a patriarch to a student.

Author's Note: Professor Jigoro Kano established the Kyu/Dan ranking system for Judo, his newly formed Martial Art and sport derived from a modification of Jujutsu techniques into a form of Budo. Professor Kano's system of classification utilized 10 Kyu, levels below black belt or Mudansha and 10 Dan, levels above black belt or Yudansha for first through third degree black belt and Kodansha for fourth through tenth degree black belt. The Dai Nippon Butoku Kai formed in 1895 by the Emperor of Japan, began granting teachers certificates and titles. They initially used Kyoshi as the first teaching level and Hanshi as the highest. Later Renshi, to be granted before Kyoshi, was added. Renshi is a Sensei, a teacher or low master. Kyoshi is a master teacher. Hanshi is an advanced master teacher or professor level certification.

During the mid–nineteen thirties a synchronization process between Professor Kano's ranking system and the Butoku Kai's teacher certifications began to take place. Today, there is not complete consensus on the levels of rank and the teaching certifications, however, there is some standardization to follow.

Shodan, first degree black belt has no teaching certification or privileges. Nidan and Sandan, second and third degree black belt coincide with Shidoin, certified instructor license. These instructors may teach the system but must be supervised by senior instructors.

Yondan, Godan and Rokudan are forth, fifth and sixth degree black belts and are eligible for Renshi certification. These individuals have full Sensei status at the low master level. To give some perspective, Master Gichin Funakoshi was a Renshi and a fifth Dan. Renshi may teach and test students up to Shodan level. The minimum age for this level is 30 to 40 years of age and in Shito Kan as in many other traditional systems, a red and black belt is worn.

Kyoshi is seventh and eight degree black belt and considered a full master instructor. This is as high as 99% of all practitioners go in the Martial Arts. Kyoshi carries an age requirement of 40 years. Most Kyoshi wear a red and white Obi. Some Ryu allow the red and white Obi to be worn at Rokudan. Kyoshi are qualified to test up to fourth degree black belt without an examining board and with pre–authorized recommendation. Godan testing may be administered by Kyoshi, however, there must be an examining board of Yudansha, four or more certified Shidoin or higher including at least one Renshi level.

Hanshi is ninth or tenth degree black belt. This is full professorial level, advance Master level. Hanshi can only be granted by the patriarch of the Ryu Ha, a 10th Dan or equivalent and recognized by a credible organization or association. Age requirement is approximately 50 years old as a minimum. Exceptions do occur, usually due to death of the Soke, his ill health or advancing age. Hanshi certificates are very rare and usually are reserved for those who are expected to carry on the system or style of the Soke. Hanshi wear a solid red Obi with the permission of the living Grandmaster.

Editor's Note: Dr. Aiello received 9th Dan in Shito Kan Karate Do and also Master Harold Long's personal red Obi on September 21st 1997. This signifies that Dr. Aiello has received the Menkyo Kaiden, personal recommendation to carry on the lineage of Master Harold Long in Isshin Ryu.

Dr. A: This weekend you have presented me with a Hanshi Teacher's Certificate. That's the highest teaching certificate under you that I can achieve?

ML: Yes. This is true.

Dr. A: I am probably the only sixth degree black belt to be granted a Hanshi in the country.

ML: I'm sure you are. Your rank did not reflect your knowledge, you were stagnated as a Godan. You spent more time in Godan than most people have in Karate period. With your background, your years of experience and your accomplishments, then you have earned this. It is not something I give you, I do not give anything, I just recognize that you have earned this.

Dr. A: How many Hanshi certificates have you given out?

ML: One.

Dr. A: One Hanshi certificate?

ML: Yes.

Dr. A: I am very proud of that. I have made a commitment to you to live up to every responsibility. It is a heavy responsibility and I do not take it lightly.

ML: You have to have authority. It was the same with Grandmaster Tatsuo Shimabuku when he was trying to get his system of Karate off the island. Basically we are trying to get things done in America. Don Nagle and I started several years ago but we have had so many people that have failed us. When you and I got together and I saw how much we had in common, saw that our total objective was the same. Someone to carry on this work. When I awarded you Rokudan rank last year, I felt that was the least I could do because your experience dictates more than a Rokudan. The same as your teaching experience, your background and all the contacts that you have throughout the Martial Arts world, throughout the country, well then you should be a Hanshi.

Dr. A: You have given out one Hanshi certificate.

Editor's Note: Dr. Aiello was recognized by the World Head of Family Sokeship Council as a Soke and 9th equivalent several years before this current Hanshi certification. The WHFSC recognition was based upon personal endorsements by Master Long and also Dr. Peter Urban, 10th Dan in Goju Ryu Karate Do. Dr. Aiello, upon receipt of this Hanshi certificate from Master Long, offered to modify his teaching curriculum to teach strictly the Isshin Ryu. After close scrutiny by Master Long of the Shito Kan Karate program and the Warrior Training Centers, Dr. Aiello asked if Master Long deemed it necessary to change for the fulfillment of Giri to the Art of Isshin Ryu. This scrutiny included sitting on the examining board of students to the level of Yondan and Renshi. Master Long recapitulated that he felt that there was greater value in the combination of Isshin Ryu with Shito Kan than anything that would be left if the Shito Kan was removed. Dr. Aiello accepted the Hanshi certification from Master Long and thus has assumed the responsibilities required of a direct student of the current second generation patriarch of Isshin Ryu.

Dr. Aiello is the President of the Kokusai Shito Kan Renmei and functions in this capacity as the Kancho representing the Art of Shito Kan and Isshin Ryu under the Shito Kan name. Dr. Aiello and the Shito Kan Renmei are recognized world wide.

ML: Yes. I have given twelve instructor's certificates but you are the only one that has received the highest certificate.

Dr. A: Domo Arigato, thank you very much. I asked you if I should take the Japanese Kata out of my system and just do the Isshin Ryu Kata. Your statement was, "Not to do that, it would be giving away too much."

ML: I said, "It would be giving up too much for so little in return." You are one of the few people that can handle two systems. You can teach two systems extremely well. You would actually be giving up more than you would receive. Your total accomplishment in the Martial Arts, not just in Isshin Ryu. That has an impact and that broadens the spectrum. That brings in more people. I feel that you should keep doing what you are doing right now, don't change it.

Dr. A: How many dual Isshin Ryu Hanshi will there be?

ML: One. Let me be honest with you and cut some corners. You are a doer. All the positive accomplishments that you are making. You are doing more than anybody else in Isshin Ryu at the present time. I do not know of anybody doing anything other than holding tournaments or having a clinic or seminar. I do not know of a soul out here beating the bushes trying to educate the public of what we have and what we hope to accomplish. They will send out a newsletter, but to the wrong people. We send the newsletters to the people that already know the news. You have the radio program. You have not restricted yourself to Isshin Ryu. You would never be a success if you did. It is all Martial Arts, all qualified Dan on this show and that is going to be the success. It can also be the center of Isshin Ryu because now, as far as I am concerned, you are the official spokesman for Isshin Ryu.

Dr. A: We plan to have every major Martial Arts Master in the country on the radio show someday and give them the time to speak. However, I cannot sit by and let them revise history. They must give the story completely, straight and honest.

ML: This is true.

Dr. A: Hanshi is a very high level. They are going to say how can you be a sixth degree black belt, a Hanshi.

ML: Remember at the same time, I told them that I was basing this on your years of experience in the Martial Arts, what you have achieved, what you have accomplished and what you are trying to do now, what your objectives are in the future. You have earned that certificate.

Dr. A: It has given me an awesome responsibility. As long as you are around, I am not concerned about the weight of the responsibility. You are still the Hanshi–Sei (head of system and above all other Hanshi in that system). You are still here doing it and I think you've got a lot more to go. I think you have a lot more work to do, as of these tapes.

Dr. A: Well, we're not letting you off the hook in a year.

ML: The protocol, as you well know, is the senior is not to stay in contact with all his juniors. It is up to them to stay in contact with the seniors. Grandmaster Shimabuku told me, in no uncertain terms, that it was not his responsibility to stay in contact with me. It was my responsibility to stay in contact with him. I still believe that is the right procedure.

Dr. A: I want your advice, not only until you're gone, after you're gone I'm calling.

ML: Yes, you have my permission to call on me at any time.

Author's Final Note: Master Harold Long has agreed to come out of retirement and reestablish his own personal lineage of Isshin Ryu, as an advisor to Sensei and associations, he will be able to give his time and efforts where they are needed most. He has recently (Fall, 1997) written and mailed out a newsletter to many Isshin Ryu Sensei outlining his intentions. He has had many requests for advice and guidance. Those who ask for his help become his direct students. This reestablishes a correct hierarchy in the Grandmaster Tatsuo Shimabuku/Master Harold Long lineage.

Bibliography

Aiello, Dr. J.L. 1994 *Warrior Legacy.* Berkley, MI
Warrior Broadcasting Network

Alexander, George & Penland, Ken 1993 *The Bubishi:
Martial Art Spirit.* Lake Worth, FL: Yamazato
Publications

Armstrong, Steve 1973 *Seisan Kata of Isshin Ryu
Karate.* Los Angeles, CA: O'Hara Publications

Binswanger, Harry 1986 *The Ayn Rand Lexicon:
Objectivism A to Z.* NY, NY: The Penguin Group

Britton, Dorothy 1980 *A Haiku Journey. Basho's
Narrow Road to a Far Province.*
International, Tokyo: Kodansha

Chandler, Joel 1996 *Isshin Ryu Karate. History and Kata.*
USA: Tatsuo-Kan Publishing

Capra, Fritjof 1984 *The Tao of Physics.* Toronto, NY,
London: Bantam Books

Deshimaru, Taisen 1982 *The Zen Way to the Martial Arts.*
London, England: Penguin Books

Dollar, Alan 1996 *Secrets of Uechi Ryu Karate.* Antioch,
CA: Cherokee Publishing

Euseeff, David D. & Murphey, Millege 1995 *Isshin Ryu:
The History and Evolution of the "One Heart
Way".* Ellicott, MD: David Euseeff

Funakoshi, Gichin 1973 *Karate-Do Kyohan. The Master
Text.* Translated by Tsutomu Oshima. Tokyo,
New York, San Francisco: Kodansha

Funakoshi, Gichin 1988 *Karate-Do Nyumon. The Master
Introductory Text.* Translated by John Teramoto.
Tokyo, NY, London: Kodansha International

Haines, Bruce 1968 *Karate's History and Traditions.*
Rutland, VT: Charles E. Tuttle Co., Inc.

Hassell, Randall G. 1994 *Conversations with the Master:
Masatoshi Nakayama.* St. Louis, MO: Focus
Publishing

Higaonna, Morio 1996 *The History of Karate:
Okinawan Goju Ryu.* USA: Dragon Books

Kano, Jigoro 1986 *Kodokan Judo.* Tokyo, New
York, London: Kodansha International Kansuke,

Yamamoto 1994 *Heiho Okugisho, The Secret of High
Strategy.* Translated by Toshishiro Obata W.M.
Hawley

Long, Harold & McGhee, Tim 1997 *Isshin-Ryu Karate.
The Ultimate Fighting Art.* Mascot, TN: Isshin
Ryu Productions

Mattson, George E. 1974 *Uechi Ryu Karate Do. Classical
Chinese Okinawan Self Defense.* Peabody
Publication Co.

Motobu, Choki 1995 *Okinawan Kempo.* Hamilton
Ontario, Canada: Masters Publication

Musashi, Miyamoto 1994 *Book of Five Rings: Definitive
Interpretation by Steve F. Kaufman.* Rutland, VT,
Tokyo, Japan: Charles E. Tuttle Co.

Nagamine, Shoshin 1996 *The Essence of Okinawan
Karate Do.* Rutland, VT: Charles E. Tuttle Co.

Nitobe, Inazo 1969 *Bushido: The Soul of Japan.* Rutland,
VT & Tokyo, Japan: Charles E. Tuttle Co.

Rand, Ayn 1971 *Atlas Shrugged.* NY, NY: The Penguin
Group

Sadler, A.L. 1988 *The Code of the Samurai. A
Translation of Daidogi Yuzans Budo Sho Shin
Shu.* Rutland, VT: Charles E. Tuttle Co.

Sugawara, Makoto 1988 *Lives of Master Swordsmen.*
Tokyo: East Publications, Inc.

Tsunetomo, Yamamoto 1993 *The Book of the Samurai.*
Translated by William Scott Wilson. Tokyo, NY,
London: Kodansha International

Tzu, Sun 1996 *The Art of War: Definitive Interpretation
by Steve F. Kaufman.* Rutland, VT, Tokyo, Japan:
Charles E. Tuttle Co.

Ueshiba, Kisshomaru 1995 *Aikido* Tokyo, Japan:
Hozansha Publications Co., Ltd.

Ueshiba, Morehei 1991 *Budo: The Teachings of the
Founder of Aikido.* Tokyo, NY, London:
Kodansha International

Uezu, Angi & Jennings, Joseph 1982 *Encyclopedia
of Isshin Ryu Karate.* San Clemente, CA:
Panther Productions

Urban, Dr. Peter 1967 *The Karate Dojo: Traditions
and Tales of a Martial Art.* Rutland, VT &
Tokyo, Japan: Charles E. Tuttle Co.

Warner, Gordon & Draeger, Donn 1982 *Japanese
Swordsmanship: Technique & Practice.* NY &
Tokyo: Weatherhill

Yamaguchi, Gogen 1993 *Karate: Goju Ryu by the Cat,
tenth Dan Gogen Yamaguchi.* Tokyo, Japan:
International Karate Do Goju Kai

Yang, Dr. Jing-Ming 1994 *The Essence of Shaolin White
Crane. Martial Power and Qigong.* Jamaica
Plain, Mass.: YMAA Publication Center

Yutang, Lin 1940 *The Importance of Living.* New York:
The John Day Co.

Publications by the WBN

Honing of the Warrior Spirit-By Dr. J. L. Aiello
Perspectives of a Karate Sensei-By Dr. L. L. Aiello
The Warrior Training Manual-By Dr. J. L. Aiello
Vision of Destiny-By Dr. J. L. Aiello
Warrior Legacy-By Dr. J. L. Aiello
Warrior Within-By Dr. J. L. Aiello
Zensho: American Zen Philosophy and Intermediate Warrior Training Manual-By Dr.J.L.Aiello

Warrior Talk, the Chronicle of the nationally syndicated talk radio program
Legends of the Masters, Cassette tapes of selected radio programs in an attractive book holder
Warrior Adventure Series, video tape training series for beginner through advanced students

Ballet of Birds-By Anna F. Gahr
Granny's Magical Rock Menagerie-By Anna F. Gahr
Short Stories of God's Blessings-By Anna F. Gahr

WBN - Warrior Broadcasting Network, Inc.

Acknowledgments

I would like to thank all of those people who helped out with the production of this book and also in the continued support of the Martial Arts. It is to them that the real Giri, Debt of Obligation, is owed by every student and teacher of any art, for it is they who insure that there will be a Martial Art to practice today and in the future.

Editing:

Dina Baganz, Sensei
Sally Eaton, Sensei
Frances Pavlovics, Sensei
Lynn Ross, Sensei

Typesetting & Layout:

Dina Baganz, Sensei
Deborah Carpenter, Sensei
Lynn Ross, Sensei
Alice Zeiger, Sensei

Transcription:

Catherine Raver, Sensei

Photography:

William Dwyer

Cover & Renditions of Masters:

Martin Brill

Special Thanks

Professor Ed Brown - President, Pioneers, Legends & Masters Hall of Fame

Hanshi J.C. Burris - President, IIKA, International Isshin Ryu Karate Association
> Promoter of Master Harold Long Isshin Ryu Hall of Fame Tournament

Master, Toby Cooling - President, UIC, United Isshin Ryu Council & Order of Isshin Ryu

Sensei Walter Dailey - Editor in Chief, Bugeisha Magazine

Sifu Michael DeMarco - Editor in Chief, Journal of Asian Martial Arts

Michael James - Editor in Chief, Rainbow Publications

Master Sang H. Kim - Author, Founder, Turtle Press

Kaicho Takaishi Kinjo - Founder, Ryu Kyu Kobukai

Sensei George Mattson - Uechi Ryu pioneer, USA

Saikoh Shihan Mikio Nishiuchi - Saikoh Shihan, President Okinawan Kobudo Association, USA

Soke Frank Sanchez - Founder & President, World Head of Family Sokeship Council

Kyoshi John Therien & Shihan Kevin Blok, Board members of the World Kobudo Federation

Dr. Peter Urban - Goju Ryu pioneer, USA

Anthony Mirakian from Watertown, MA. Master Mirakian is the United States pioneer of Meibukan Okinawan Goju Ryu. He is the senior student of Meitoku Yagi, who is President of the Meibukan School of Goju Ryu. Meitoku Yagi Sensei is considered by Goju practitioners to be the Menkyo Kaiden of Chojun Miyagi. Master Mirakian has been very kind in sharing so many hours of his Martial Arts knowledge.

William Duessel from Indian Town, FL. Master Duessel generously provided written materials, video tapes and his vast knowledge via interview. He is currently the senior student of Kichiro Shimabuku who is the Okinawan Grandmaster of Tatsuo Shimabuku's Isshin Ryu Karate System. Kichiro Shimabuku is President of the IWKA, Isshin Ryu World Karate Association. William Duessel received his Shodan directly from Master Tatsuo Shimabuku in 1964.

Deepest gratitude to Grandmaster Harold Long for dedicating 44 years of his life to his Karate teacher, Grandmaster Tatsuo Shimabuku and his beloved art, Isshin Ryu Karate Do. Grandmaster Long gives freely of his time, energy and spirit toward the enhancement of Budo. He has never in the years that I have known him, asked for anything in return. Grandmaster Long's only request of me personally is that I stay true to the path of Budo in daily life and transmit the message of his teacher, Grandmaster Tatsuo Shimabuku, unchanged as it was passed to him. I sincerely thank Grandmaster Long for this opportunity and for his wholehearted support of Shito Kan Karate Do. His kind and understanding way reflects the true spirit of Isshin Ryu and Budo, the One Heart, One Mind method and the Way of the Warrior.

Biography
Dr. J. L. Aiello, Hanshi

Dr. Jerry L. Aiello has been teaching and training in the Martial Arts and Karate for 30 years. He began training in Tang Soo Do in 1967 and trained in Koei Kan, Isshin Ryu and American Karate, achieving rank in these styles. In 1974 Dr. Aiello developed the system of Shito Kan Karate Do and five Kata or forms. In March of 1997 he received the first Hanshi, Master level certification given in Isshin Ryu through Master Harold Long, 10th Dan in Isshin Ryu. On September 21st of 1997 Master Harold Long presented Dr. Aiello with the high honor of Menkyo Kaiden by giving to him his personal Obi (belt). The Menkyo Kaiden means "all passed down" and means the transmission or passing on of the personal lineage. In this case, Master Long has given his heritage of Isshin Ryu from Grandmaster Tatsuo Shimabuku to Dr. Aiello with the expectation of its continued vitality.

Dr. Aiello is recognized by the World Head of Family Sokeship Council and the World Kobudo Federation as founder of the Shito Kan Karate system and holds the title of Kancho and rank of 9th degree black belt. He was inducted into the Sokeship Counsel on the recommendation of Master Harold Long, 10th Dan in Isshin Ryu Karate and Dr. Peter Urban, 10th Dan in Goju Ryu Karate. Dr. Aiello was inducted into the World Kobudo Federation by Kyoshi John Therein, 8th Dan in Jujutsu and Shihan Kevin Blok, 7th Dan in Aikido. He is certified by Saikoh Shihan Mikio Nishiuchi of the International Okinawan Kobudo Renmei as a Shidoin instructor, in Kobudo, ancient Okinawan weapons. Dr. Aiello serves as the Midwest Director of the International Okinawan Kobudo Association. Among his other teaching certifications he includes Shidoin, personally given by Eizo Onishi, founder of Japanese Koei Kan Karate with the recommendation of Shihan Brian Frost.

Dr. Aiello has written 8 books about Karate and the Martial Arts philosophy and is also Producer and Director of the *Warrior Adventure Series*, nine instructional video tapes done in partnership with Paramount/ Fox Inc. He has owned and operated eight Dojo in the past and has taught more than 25,000 students in the arts of Karate and Kobudo throughout the United States. Has taught and travelled the world to expand his wisdom about the Martial Arts, including South America, Greece, Italy, the Bahamas, Canada, Japan and China.

The International Shito Kan Association, which he founded and heads, has Dojo in the Midwest. Dr. Aiello's most recent endeavor was to create and for the past three years be the host of the first Martial Arts talk radio program in the United States and possibly the world, *The Dr. Aiello Show, Warrior Talk*. This innovation in talk radio is dedicated to bringing the values of physical health, achievement and personal excellence that are found in Martial Arts training to the massive radio audience across the country.

Information

The Warrior Broadcasting Network has published many books, newsletters, video tapes and is also the sponsor of the only nationally syndicated talk radio program dedicated solely to the Martial Arts.

If you are interested in obtaining books or tapes, back issues of newsletters or taped broadcasts of radio program *Warrior Talk* contact the Aiello Group and the Warrior Broadcasting Network at the following address or call the numbers listed below.

Aiello Group
Warrior Broadcasting Network
P.O. Box 1412
Berkley, Mi 48072

Toll Free Number:
888-408-6200
Office Telephone Number:
(248) 542-4314
Fax Number:
(248) 542-5414